WHAT COULD I DO?

WHAT COULD I DO?

PETER HICKS

Inter-Varsity Press

INTER-VARSITY PRESS
38 De Montfort Street, Leicester LE1 7GP, England
Email: ivp@uccf.org.uk
World Wide Web: www.ivpbooks.com

First published 2003

British Library Cataloguing in Publication Data
A catalogue record for this book is available from the British Library.

ISBN 0–85111–299–4

Set in Garamond
Typeset in Great Britain by Avocet Typeset, Brill, Aylesbury, Bucks
Printed and bound in Great Britain by Creative Print and Design
(Wales), Ebbw Vale

Inter-Varsity Press is the book-publishing division of the Universities and Colleges Christian Fellowship (formerly the Inter-Varsity Fellowship), a student movement linking Christian Unions in universities and colleges throughout Great Britain, and a member movement of the International Fellowship of Evangelical Students. For more information about local and national activities write to UCCF, 38 De Montfort Street, Leicester LE1 7GP, Email: ivp@uccf.org.uk, or visit the UCCF website at http://www.uccf.org.uk.

CONTENTS

....

PART 2

....

APPENDIXES

PLEASE START HERE

It's not for me to tell you what to do. For one thing, I'm only a learner myself; no way have I got all the answers. More importantly, there's only one person who has the right to tell you what to do, and that's God.

This book tries to suggest what you could do when faced with the various situations and decisions that come our way as we live our Christian lives. Since it's God's guidance that we're after, a lot of the focus is on Jesus and there are plenty of quotations from the Bible.

The contexts in which the various parts of the Bible were written were in many ways different from ours today. Some of the issues that were relevant in Bible days are irrelevant now; many of today's issues were unheard of then. So, as a rule, it's not wise simply to lift a Bible verse out of its context and apply it as God's answer to our specific situation. That doesn't mean that the Bible has nothing to say. In fact, it has an incredible amount to say; as I've worked through the various issues covered in this book I've been thrilled at its relevance and amazing wisdom. But what it does mean is that we generally have to go a bit deeper; we need to dig out its foundational principles and underlying theological truths, and to get our basic relationship with God on a firm footing. From there we can work out the details of our practical Christian living in today's world.

You can start reading the book at any point. In Part 2, the sections on the various topics are more or less complete in themselves. But there's value in reading Part 1 before anything in Part 2. It's only short, and it gives a general introduction to the whole theme of living out our Christianity in the twenty-first century.

Inevitably, a book like this can't cover everything. There's no section on what you could do if you were to win the National Lottery, or if your tent lets in water. But an issue that doesn't have its own section in Part 2 may still be covered somewhere, so it's always worth checking in the index.

What Could I Do? is a companion volume to *What Could I Say?*, which was written as a handbook for helpers. Some topics appear in both books, and in those cases it may be useful to refer to *What Could I Say?* for further background information. Some of the practical suggestions made in *What Could I Say?* have been added here as appendixes.

You're reading this book because you want your Christian beliefs to shape each part of your life. What's the point of being a child of God if it doesn't make a difference to the way you live? At the end of the Sermon on the Mount Jesus talked about two men. One heard his teaching and didn't get round to putting it into practice. His life, said Jesus, collapsed. The other heard it and did put it into practice. Life threw everything it could at him – storms and floods, problems and hassles, temptations and pressures, the lot. And he made it through, strong and firm, built on a good foundation.

He's the one to follow.

PART 1
DESERT ISLANDS
AND SUNSETS

There's an acute shortage of desert islands. All the best ones have been snapped up. And those that are left are rather pricey.

So most of us have to manage without one. We don't have the option of running away from life. We've got to stay where we are: in our family, our street, our place of work – in a very messy world.

How do you live in a messy world? With difficulty. The issues we face seem so muddled; they are never straightforward. As my wife says when I have a go at a bit of DIY that she thinks should take minutes and that I'm still struggling with three hours later, 'Things are never as easy as they look.'

The messiness isn't just in the world. There's a good deal of it in us too. Of course, we ought to be able to see everything clearly, to weigh up issues wisely, to come to balanced decisions, and to go ahead and put them neatly into practice. But so often it isn't like that. We get confused. We're pulled in two directions, or even in half a dozen. And even when we've made the decision we struggle with putting it into action.

Then there's the moral element. Of course, we should choose what is right and good rather than what is wrong and bad. But what is good and right? How do we sort things out when something is good when looked at in one way and bad when looked at in another? Or when one good moral principle says we should do one thing and another good moral principle says we should do the opposite?

God isn't at all worried that we as Christians have to struggle with a messy world. He has strictly limited the number of desert islands. He has not given us some easy way out of the messiness. He allows us to be put in confusing situations, to be faced with conflicting moral principles and to struggle with mixed motives and all the weaknesses of our human nature. We may find it difficult to understand why, but in fact he has some very good reasons.

For a start, he wants us to stay living in this messy world because we're its only hope. If all the Christians were on desert islands, how would the rest of the world find God's answer to its messiness? He thinks it's only reasonable that, if we're going to live alongside people and help them to cope with living in a messy world, we ought to have to cope with its messiness too. That's what happened when Jesus came. He didn't live on a desert island.

Secondly, God can make beautiful things out of messy situations. It's rather like sunsets. If the sky's perfectly clear, all clean and straightforward, the sun will just set. But plaster the sky with a whole mass of puffs of cloud, all mixed up – high cloud, low cloud, thick cloud, thin cloud, dark cloud, light cloud, with bits of blue sky in between – and you'll get the most beautiful sunset.

GREAT IDEA

So, take a messy world, and put a load of Christians in it. People who live like Jesus did. Who struggle with temptation. Who get disappointed. Who know what it is to be frustrated and upset. Who find life tough. Who find opposition and rejection. Who may even get crucified.

And what then? Leave them to get on with it? No way. They wouldn't last a week. Stand by them, and show them how to cope? That's better. Promise that you'll be with them always. Give them your Holy Spirit with all his wisdom and power and goodness. Live in them, so that the life they're living is actually your life. Then they can do what Jesus would do, not just because they choose to do it, but because he's there, in them, doing it through them.

And give them lots of help. Lots of examples in the life of the Lord Jesus. Stories of how he coped. How he faced messy situations. How he made moral decisions. How he lived. How he loved.

And then gave them lots of other teaching. Paul and Peter and John wrestling with issues in a messy world. Lots of great foundational theological principles. Tons of practical advice. All the experience of those first Christians packed into their writings, for us to learn from. Don't necessarily answer all the questions that come up in the twenty-first century. But give them enough to see how to face those questions and find ways of dealing with them that are right for our time.

And then give them each other. To stand by each other. To help and encourage and support each other. To pray together, to seek God's heart and mind. To learn good things from each other. To learn from the past, the story of God's people through the centuries, both the good things and the mistakes and failures. To make up a great team, the people of God in a hurting world. The salt of the earth. Lights shining in the darkness. Living and working and serving together. Bringing in the kingdom.

Sounds a great idea.

NOT AN EASY OPTION

Making a mess is easy. I have no problem making a real mess of my room, or of getting mud everywhere when I'm cleaning out the pond. In fact, I can make a mess of almost anything in a pretty short time. I can smash up a car. I can break up a relationship. I can chop down a tree. And quite a few messes seem to make themselves with the minimum of help from outside. The garden untended turns into a wilderness. A marriage untended withers and dies. A world without salt goes bad.

What's much harder is sorting out a mess: rebuilding the smashed car, recreating trust and love in a relationship, growing another tree, recreating the garden, or changing the world.

As we've seen, God has put us in a messy world. And the task he has given us is to do something about its messiness, to sort things out, to put right what's gone wrong, to find a way through the maze, to make decisions that are good, to be hope and healing, to be Christlike people, salt and light, to live Jesus, to give up on desert islands and get stuck into that messy world. We shouldn't be dragged down or defeated by its messiness. Instead, we should stand against the evil that has invaded God's incredible creation, break its hold, and push back the frontiers of the kingdom of darkness.

Our task is to show a different way: to be different; to be holy, as he is holy; to live and declare truth, because he is truth; to continue what Jesus started, so that God's kingdom comes through us.

In fact, Jesus put it well:

My prayer is not that you take them out of the world but that you protect them from the evil one. They are not of the world, even as I am not of it. Sanctify them by the truth; your word is truth. As you sent me into the world, I have sent them into the world. For them I sanctify myself, that they too may be truly sanctified (John 17:15–19).

Not an easy option. It wasn't easy for him; it would have been much easier to do nothing about the mess. But as God sent Jesus, he sends us.

WE'RE NOT SIMPLE

In the fifth century BC, Leucippus developed the theory that the basic building-blocks of everything were atoms, which he described as tiny, invisible, unchanging, indivisible, fundamental particles of matter. Two and a half millennia later we still accept the existence of atoms, but we've discovered that they are far more complex than Leucippus believed. So far from being unchanging and fundamental, they're made up of amazingly varied patterns of particles which are anything but fixed and final. Atoms aren't simple; they're incredibly complex.

It's the same with us. Some thinkers have been tempted to believe that it's possible to get down to the basic elements that go to make up human persons and analyse them. Some have isolated human reason, or our emotions, wills or experiences, and have seen them as foundational building-blocks of our personhood and behaviour.

No doubt such analyses have some value, but all too often they are far too simplistic. 'I am what I think', 'I am what I experience' or 'I am what happened to me in my childhood' (not to mention 'I am what I eat') may sound neat and clever; but, of course, such statements present only one facet of what makes me the person I am. We're all far more complex than any psychological theory or explanatory analysis can ever begin to describe.

Maybe my thought patterns do shape me. But my experiences shape my thoughts. And different experiences shape different thoughts. The way I react to any given experience depends on a whole host of other factors. Indeed, I might react quite differently to the same experience on different occasions, probably without having any idea why. There's no way we can analyse and understand all the factors that go to make up our reactions and decisions, our thoughts and our feelings. Complexity is the name of the game.

THE WORLD'S NOT SIMPLE, EITHER

It's not just in the area of human personhood that complexity is the name of the game. It's that way in life, too.

I'm faced with a decision, say, whether or not to accept the offer of a job. At first it may seem very simple: do I want the job or do I not want the job? But even that's not as simple as it sounds. Rarely is our motivation total. The good pay makes me want to accept the job; but the long hours make me want to find something else. Other complications arise. Ought I to take the job? Yes, I should, according to the principle that says I should earn good money to pay off the mortgage and support my family. But the job is with a multinational that has a bad record of exploiting people in poorer countries; so I'm confronted with a different principle, which says I shouldn't have anything to do with such an organization. But then I can think of a third principle, which puts my decision into a different perspective again: if all Christians boycott this multinational organization, how will it ever change? Surely I ought to get stuck in and try to influence its policies for good? How do I decide between these three principles? And, of course, we haven't finished yet. Even if I want to do the job, and I decide it's morally OK to do it, I still need to stop and think of the effects or outcomes it may have: how it may affect me, my family or other people, and how others might react.

So it's not just me that's complex. It's everything else too. After all, what would you expect? Of course we're complex, and of course the world's complex. Everything's complex because God is big. And everything he has made expresses his greatness and richness, and the wonder and mystery of his great creative purposes.

What else would we want? Some toy universe where everything works by clockwork, where everything's straightforward and cut and dried? Maybe that's how some would like to try to view the world. But it's not how things are. The real world is big, rich and complex, set before us by a big, rich, complex God.

The best thing of all is that, faced with all the complexities of this incredible world, we've got the Creator and Lord of it all to see us through.

STUCK AND UNSTUCK

Confronted with the complexity of life and of the issues we have to face, Christians react in different ways. Some give up trying to think issues through. Instead of sorting them out and making responsible decisions, they just do what they do. Or they get someone else to tell them what to do. Maybe they know a more mature Christian whom they choose to follow. They submit to a church leader, or they buy a book that tells them what to do.

All these approaches have a lot to be said for them; after all, the Bible tells us to learn from others and to submit to our leaders. But not at the cost of giving up thinking. Doing something just because somebody else does it or tells us to do it could mean that we're opting out of taking the responsibility for our decisions and actions. That's not God's way. At the very least, we ought always to check out the lead we're following, in the context of our own study of the Bible and our own relationship with God.

Other Christians face the complexity of the issues, and rightly set themselves to think things through. Often this works fine, but sometimes they find themselves getting swamped with all the complexities, and find it desperately hard to know what to do. Since they know that it's important to get things right, they get stuck. They don't know which way to go, and they're afraid of going the wrong way, so they don't go anywhere. This can't be right, either. God hasn't called us to be stuck.

Come to think of it, God hasn't called us to be afraid, either. Well, not so afraid that we get stuck. Fear has its place; it isn't always a bad thing. But God doesn't want us to live with it permanently. Nor does he want it to paralyse our Christian living. He wants us to trust and go forward, not to be afraid and stay still.

There's an interesting passage in chapter 16 of Acts. Paul, Silas and Timothy were on a missionary tour. The whole world lay before them, thousands of places where the gospel hadn't yet been preached. So where were they to go next? They were in Phrygia; they could go on to Asia, Mysia or Bithynia, not to mention other places further afield. How did they decide where God wanted them?

The answer is: they didn't. Not to start with, anyhow. But they didn't stay stuck where they were. No doubt they prayed. Then they packed their bags and set out for Asia. But they were wrong. God didn't want them there, so he stopped them. The Bible doesn't tell us exactly how; it just says that they were 'kept by the Holy Spirit from preaching the word in the province of Asia' (Acts 16:6). So they turned round and headed for Bithynia, in the opposite direction. Wrong again. 'They tried to enter Bithynia, but the Spirit of Jesus would not allow them to' (verse 7). But that didn't worry them. They changed direction again and went to Troas. Getting warm. There God called them to Macedonia, and so the gospel came to Europe.

Of course, God could have given them the call to Macedonia several days earlier, and so have avoided all the uncertainty. But he didn't. He let them get it wrong a time or two first. We don't know why. They don't seem to have been particularly thick or disobedient. They were keen to do what he wanted, to hear and follow his leading. They trusted him to open up the way. In fact, they trusted him so much that they were confident that he would not let them get it totally wrong. Meanwhile, they kept moving.

'EXPECT GREAT THINGS; ATTEMPT GREAT THINGS'

Scholars delight to debate over the precise words of William Carey's call to his fellow Baptists in 1792, when, in a sermon on Isaiah 54:2–3, he challenged them to do something about the needs of a world that didn't know the gospel of Christ. But there's no doubt about two points. The first was his conviction that we are each called to go forward with vision and faith. And the second was that, as we do so, God will do great things.

A year or two ago, in the little church I pastor in my spare time, we decided we'd make it all right for people to do crazy things. If someone came up with an idea, however way out it might seem, we'd be prepared to try it, provided we felt there was a reasonable likelihood that God was in it, and we could see our way to giving it a go. But we added one other condition. If it didn't work, we'd drop it; and we wouldn't view dropping it as some sort of failure. To do nothing would be the failure. To try something with the belief that this may be God's way forward, and then to find it isn't, is progress, not failure. In fact, we thought four out of five things we tried might not work out; but if we tried five and one of them worked, that would be fantastic success.

There are at least two reasons why this is a good policy. The first is that it's a great way of spawning new ideas and going forward in exciting new ways. It doesn't permit a cosy, secure and dull 'We'll do it this way because we've always done it this way' attitude. It opens the door to plenty of interest and adventure as people try new things and develop new skills. It provides lots of opportunity for God to lead us forward.

The second good point about this policy is that, handled rightly, you're in a win-win situation. If you try something and it works – great! But trying something, and then finding it doesn't work, can be equally great. It's an excellent way of learning. Of course, we can let it destroy our self-confidence or lead to the 'We tried that in the 1960s and it didn't work then, so we'll never try it again' attitude. But it doesn't have to be like that. We can give each other permission to make a number of attempts before finding the right answer. We can accept that none of us is all-wise or hears God accurately first time. We can learn to take disappointment in our stride. We can get plenty of practice at turning setbacks into springboards, learning from mistakes, showing grace and helping others when plans and hopes don't work out.

Of course, lots of people poured cold water on William Carey. No doubt he often felt life would be far easier if he settled for the dull and routine. But he went for the big thing, the crazy thing. And God didn't let him down.

TRY TRUST

What are you afraid of? That things will go wrong and get in a mess? Maybe they will. But that's nothing new. The whole world has gone wrong and is in a mess. One more mess won't make the sky fall in. And we know we've got a God who's big enough to bring all sorts of good things out of messes.

Are you afraid you'll get it wrong? Sometimes you will. But why is that a problem? If God let Paul, Silas and Timothy get their destination wrong but still did great things through them, why should you worry? Take it as a compliment; God is dealing with you in the same way he dealt with Paul.

Are you afraid that God will let you down? Don't be. He has never let anyone down, and he's not going to start with you.

We've said that fear isn't always bad. But God doesn't want it to control our lives or to stop us going forward. He wants to replace it with trust and peace. Here are four steps to take in order to deal with those fears.

The first is to put God in charge of everything. That sounds straightforward. After all, he is God, so it's fairly obvious that he's the only one who can be in charge of everything. But, being what we are, we don't always find it simple to let him be God. In fact, we sometimes find it positively hard to let him take charge. So the first step may demand some courage. I hope the material in the next few sections will help.

The second step follows closely on the first. In fact, we can take it only after we've taken the first. It's to put the responsibility for sorting things out fairly and squarely on God's shoulders. We need to be like little children. We need to be able to say, 'I don't know the way, but you do. If I go in the wrong direction, you've got to head me off. If I get things wrong, you've got to sort them out. I accept that you're God, and in charge of everything. Now I specifically hand over the responsibility for this situation to you. I'm going to do what I think you want me to do, but yours is the responsibility to make sure that in the end everything works out right.'

The third step is to keep trusting God's ability to cope with any situation. It's putting Matthew 6:25–34 into operation and keeping it in operation. We specifically choose to trust our heavenly Father. We reject worry, fear and panic as a way of life. This may take some doing (more on this later), but it's one of the greatest acts we can ever do; it's the secret of peace and joy, and of a strong relationship of confidence and love between us and our God.

The fourth step is to get on with living. Be the person God is calling you to be. Don't wait until all the problems are solved and all the questions answered. Live out that relationship of trust in God. As Paul puts it in Colossians 2:6, go around in Christ (New International Version: 'continue to live in him'). Some people go around in a daze, some in a bad temper, and others in fear. But it's our calling to go around in Christ. And that's a place where you never have to be afraid.

WORKING TO RULE

There's something attractive about having a clear set of instructions to follow in any given situation. Given *A*, then *B*. Given *C*, then *D*. Everything is cut and dried. It's all very straightforward. There's no need to think matters through or to wrestle with moral issues; no need to meet with God and seek his mind.

From time to time Christians have slipped into the habit of establishing fixed codes of conduct and defining exactly what a Christian may or may not do. Though such an approach has many superficial advantages, ultimately it's always a disaster. That's because it always ends in legalism, doing something because it's what the rules say we should do, and losing sight of why we do it. Legalism was the big mistake of the Jewish leaders of the first century, which Jesus denounced so vigorously.

> They tie up heavy loads and put them on men's shoulders, but they themselves are not willing to lift a finger to move them ... Woe to you, blind guides. You say, 'If anyone swears

by the temple it means nothing; but if anyone swears by the gold of the temple he is bound by his oath.' You blind fools! Which is greater: the gold, or the temple that makes the gold sacred? ... Woe to you, teachers of the law and Pharisees, you hypocrites! You give a tenth of your spices – mint, dill and cummin. But you have neglected the more important matters of the law – justice, mercy and faithfulness' (Matt. 23:4, 16–17, 23).

In any case, we've already seen that a legalistic approach is far too simplistic for real life. There may be no problem if we're confronted with a case of simply *A* or *C*; *B* or *D* may well follow perfectly satisfactorily. But in real life it's all too often *A* plus *C* plus a bit of *E* and elements of *FGHJK*, complicated by *LMN*, and so on. Simplistic legalism just doesn't work.

There are even bigger problems with the legalistic approach. It makes us less than human. We do what we're told to do, without taking personal responsibility for our decision and its results. Even worse, it doesn't require any contact with God. We make our decisions and live our lives by looking up the correct procedures in the rule book, instead of by talking the issues through with the Lord.

Working to rule won't work. It's not the way of Jesus. He didn't turn to the rule book; instead, he turned to his Father.

WHAT COMES NATURALLY

It was a piece of cake. Or, rather, six pieces of cake set before six hungry people. Each person had to choose one piece.

Mandy went for the biggest. Her principle was, 'Never mind the others; look after me.'

Mave took a small piece. She thought it looked stale.

Maggie also took a small piece. She believed that cake makes you fat.

Maddy took any old piece. She wasn't going to eat it anyway, because it might contain nuts.

Mary took the piece that was nearest to her. Her mummy had taught her to take the piece that was nearest to her.

Maud engineered it so that she took the last piece that was left. She worked on the principle, 'Put everyone else first and yourself last.'

Whenever we're faced with a choice we're influenced by what we believe and the attitudes we've adopted. Sometimes we're aware of these beliefs. Often we're not. But they're there all the same, unconsciously influencing how we choose.

It isn't that they control our choices. Mandy could decide to have a small piece of cake, and Maggie could choose a big piece. But they're usually pretty influential. They're often a fall-back position; they determine what we do if we don't make the effort to think things through and do something else.

For most of us, these beliefs and attitudes are a mixed lot. They come from all over the place. Some of them we've worked out for ourselves. Others we picked up along the way, from home, school, the media or the experiences of life. Some of them are true and helpful, but some are rubbishy. Some are partly true and partly false. Even as Christians, most of us are still substantially influenced by beliefs we picked up before we became Christians, and by attitudes and concepts that have been instilled into us by the media or other non-Christian influences around us.

The outcome of our ingrained beliefs and attitudes, then, can be for good or for bad. And usually we're not even aware that they're influencing our choices.

There are two courses of action we can take to avoid making bad choices as a result of the influence of inadequate beliefs that we may have picked up.

The first is to keep checking which underlying beliefs or attitudes are affecting our specific choices. Instead of doing just what comes 'naturally', we should stop and ask ourselves, 'What's making me do this?' We go to blare our horn at a bad driver. But why? Because we think that'll make him or her a better driver? We should be so lucky! Because it's right to express our anger? Is it? To let the other driver know we disapprove? What's the point of that?

There's another, more profound, way of cutting down on those bad choices. That's by replacing the inadequate beliefs and attitudes by others that are true, beautiful and good. Instead of getting upset at bad drivers, we feel the love and the grace of Jesus for them. Instead of believing something or adopting an attitude because that's the way we were brought up, or what everyone else does, we make the mind of Christ and the whole counsel of God the core of all our thinking, so that living it out just comes naturally.

START WITH GOD

That's it, then. We want our thinking to be reshaped so that it becomes much more in tune with the mind of Christ and the heart of God, instead of letting our choices be influenced by beliefs and attitudes that we've picked up from all over the place. If I had to sum up in two words the key to doing this, I think I'd suggest 'God first'.

'In the beginning God created.' That's where the Bible starts. Yet it's one of the hardest things for most people to take on board. Something in all of us rebels against it. We don't want to be someone else's creation. We want to be our own creation and our own creators. We want to be in charge of our lives and of our world. We want to decide what is and what isn't, what's right and what's wrong, what's good and what's bad. We don't want to admit that somebody else got there before us, that God is the Creator, that we have to accept what he has done, and that God is first.

When someone asked Jesus what the most important thing in life is, Jesus replied, 'Loving God' (Mark 12:28–30). This means putting God first, in the place where he matters more than anything else, and where what he says goes. God must be first in my living, my being and my doing. Number one out of the Ten Commandments was, in effect, 'Put God first' (see Exod. 20:3). Maybe the essence of all human sin and evil is the refusal to put God first. 'Me first' is the quickest road to disaster and damnation (Matt. 10:38–39).

This entails putting 'God first' in my choosing. 'Not what I want, but what God wants' (cf. Luke 22:42). It's an incredibly simple principle. But somehow we manage to be experts at forgetting it. Maybe that's the clearest expression of our fallenness: not that we commit 'big' sins, but that we want to run our lives and make our decisions our own way, without interference from God. We won't put God first.

Somewhere hidden inside all of us is a voice that tells us we know better than God. We'll make a better job of our lives if we're in control. Let God take charge, says the voice, and in no time we'll be in a mess. 'God first' will destroy us. Put ourselves in charge, and everything will be fine. We know best.

You can't get much further from the truth than that. The fact is that 'God first' will in no way destroy us. Rather, it offers us the only real hope of truly making us, and of fulfilling the incredible potential God has put in each one of us. He is the Creator; he alone knows right from wrong, what's good and what's bad for each of us. It's saying, 'Me first', when the truth is 'God first', that will destroy us.

John knew Jesus well. He grew very close to him. He knew what made him tick. And, in several places in his Gospel, John summed up Jesus' secret. Jesus, for all his wisdom and divinity, didn't make his own decisions. He didn't follow his own ideas. He didn't put himself first. Instead, he put God, his Father, first. His food was to do what the Father wanted. He did only what he saw his Father doing. His only interest was to please the one who had sent him, and to do his will (John 4:34; 5:19; 5:30; 6:38).

There's an example to follow.

GOD FIRST

'God first' is a good principle for the whole of life. But it's also a good approach to methodology.

When faced with a difficult decision, it's always tempting to start with the problem, the issues, what's at stake, how hard it is to decide, and how awful it will be if we get it wrong. But maybe that's not the best place to begin. I suggest it's much better to start with God. That's the context that will make sense of what we've got to decide. That's where we'll get the help we need. That's what really matters.

'Here I am, God. I've got to make a choice over which course of study I'm going to follow. It's a big choice, and it could have huge effects. It could change the whole direction of my life. And I've no idea which way to choose.

'OK, then. Instead of starting with the problem, I'll start with you.

'You are creator and Lord, sovereign, wise, all-knowing, almighty, working all things together for good for those who love you. That's worth thinking about for a few minutes. It puts me and my problem into context.

'You are gracious, merciful, compassionate and understanding. You're a Father who will never give his children a bad gift. You have promised never to fail me or leave me in the lurch. You are someone I can trust utterly in every situation, even when faced with this decision. You know where I'm at. And you've got what it takes to get me through it. That's great.

'You are good and truthful and holy, pure and beautiful, with no shady bits and no messing about. You have very good eyesight – eyes that see right into me, that burn with fire, and that see where I've got things wrong and where I need to be sorted out. OK, Lord, look right into me and see my motives, my beliefs, my attitudes. Altogether they're a messy lot. I need your holiness to sort them out – your Holy Spirit, the Spirit of holiness.

'You are the God who speaks. That's great; it means you'll tell me what to do. But maybe, before I hear you saying what I've got to do, I need to listen to what else you've said – directions you've given in the Bible or things you've said to me by your Spirit on other occasions. I don't suppose I've any right to expect you to say something new to me if I'm ignoring what you've already told me. It's no good saying, 'Guide me over this course' if I'm disobeying you over some other issue. So I guess I need to spend time listening.

'You are the God of righteousness, the one who has a burning passion that everything in the world should be beautiful, pure and true. You want justice and freedom for the oppressed; goodness springing up from the earth; righteousness flowing down from the mountains; people filled with love, peace, compassion, truth and loveliness. You want the whole earth to be filled with your glory, your kingdom to come, and your will to be done. That's a vision worth having. And that's the backdrop against which I choose my course.

'You are my God, my Lord, my Saviour, the one who loved me and gave himself for me. You are the God who didn't spare your only Son, but gave him for me, and who guarantees to give me everything else I need. You are my Redeemer, the one who has turned disaster into glory, darkness into light, and failure into hope. You are my Lord, the one I belong to, the one I've promised to follow and obey, the one to whom I've given every part of me, and the one for whom I live. Yours is the kingdom, the power and the glory.'

God first. Of course, that's it. My relationship with him is the crucial factor in all decision-making. If I'm out of tune with him, there's a fair chance I'll make a mess of the decision. If my relationship with him is right, if he's in my heart and I'm in his, the problem of the decision is placed in its right focus. He can cope with it. He'll make sure it's OK. That's guaranteed.

PUTTING GOD ON THE SPOT

No way should we ever deliberately push God into a corner. But there will be plenty of times when circumstances beyond our control create a situation where God does seem to be pushed into a corner, and where we can't see the way he's going to get himself out. A great mountain range stands in the way, too high for us to climb, and with no way through. How are you going to cope with that, God?

There's no shortage of biblical examples of such situations. The Son of God hanging dead on a cross is the chief one. But there are plenty of others: thousands of hungry people and a handful of bread and fish; a decomposing Lazarus and a hostile crowd; Peter or Paul locked up in prison; a world to win and a handful of very human people to win it; the whole might of the Roman Empire determined to stamp out the tiny Christian church. How will you cope with that, Lord?

He doesn't always do so in the way we'd think. He doesn't always rip out the mountain range and fling it into the Pacific straight away. Sometimes he works the slow, hard way, calling us to struggle and climb until we get to the top. Sometimes he works the Hebrews 11:35–39 way, and we never actually see what he's up to; our part of the story ends before the summit. James, Stephen, Peter and Paul were all killed by their enemies.

But God has a remarkable way of getting us out of holes. In fact, to adapt 1 Corinthians 10:13, God knows everything about every hole we could ever find ourselves in, and he guarantees that he will always produce a way out that in the long run will be the very best.

On refusing the angels

'Stupid lot!' I thought, when I was a kid. 'All those people who were offered three wishes by their fairy godmother. Without exception they squandered them, and made a total mess of things. Now, if it happened to me I wouldn't need three wishes. I'd need only one, and I'd be set up for life.'

And what would I have asked for if I'd been given just one wish? Easy: that whenever I wanted a wish I could have what I wished for – an infinite number, a whole lifetime of every wish being fulfilled. What a prospect!

As it was, no fairy godmother ever appeared, so I was never able to put my plan into operation. And that's just as well. If the people in the stories made such a mess of things with just three wishes, think of my potential for disaster with an infinite number! Now I know that it was a rich mercy that I didn't always get what I wanted. My ardent prayers for the school to burn down, or for my homework to be done miraculously, remained unanswered. However attractive the quick answer and the easy way out were, most of the time I had to follow the tough option, take the long road and face life as it really was, rather than escape into the fantasy of fairy stories.

But we all still find the quick fix and the easy answer so much more attractive. And many people seem to imagine that if God loves us he must necessarily give us the quick fix or an easy way out. But any thoughtful person will realize that that could never be right. Nor could our understanding of prayer mean that God has to give us everything we ask for. Thank goodness he doesn't!

There are times when we do have the choice. There's no need for a fairy godmother. The easy answer is totally within our power. The way is open. We can choose the soft option, the quick fix. It's there in front of us. Sometimes it may be OK for us to do so. To refuse the job. To avoid the pain. To ignore the situation. Nothing wrong in that; we can't do everything. But sometimes, to be nearest to the heart of Jesus, we shall choose the hard road, the tough way; not because we're masochists, or afraid to accept the easy option from his hand, but because we follow the one whose whole life was marked by choosing what was tough, whether it was the incarnation, saying no to the devil during the temptations in the wilderness, or the cross itself.

'I've only got to ask my Father,' said Jesus in Gethsemane, 'and he'll put 60,000 angels at my disposal' (see Matt. 26:53). That would have been more than enough to solve all his problems at one go. But he refused the angels.

THANKS FOR THE GIFT, LORD; I DON'T WANT IT

You don't develop courage unless you're threatened by danger. You can't show forgiveness unless someone has wronged you. So if

God wants us to become more courageous, he'll allow us to go through dangerous experiences. To develop our forgiving spirit, he'll let us be wronged. To enable us to grow in love, he'll put lots of unlovely people in our way. To stretch our faith he'll allow us to go through difficult times.

But we could react the wrong way. We could let the dangerous experience make us more fearful. We could let being wronged make us angry and resentful instead of forgiving. We could choose to practise our hate on the unlovely people. When he puts us through a tough time in order to increase our trust in him, we could react by choosing to give up believing in him at all.

Why does God allow us the freedom to react negatively to what he's doing in our lives, as well as to react positively? That question belongs to the huge issue of human freedom. Why did God give human beings freedom in the first place? Why did he give us brains and then leave it to us to choose whether to use them to invent weapons of mass destruction or to find a cure for cancer? Why did he give us bodies and leave it to us to choose to use them for his glory or for our own selfish indulgence? Why did he give us a world to live in and then leave it to us to choose whether to pollute and destroy it or to make it heaven on earth?

I think I know the answer to that question. Or, perhaps, I think I know what the answer might be. It's that freedom is an essential and fantastic part of being truly human. Cabbages may be content; computers may be clever; but when God made human beings in his image he put something really terrific in us that reflects a key part of his own nature: the ability to make real choices, to be creative, to take responsibility, to be free. Without freedom we could be cabbages or computers. Only with freedom are we truly human, made in the image of God.

And, of course, you can't have freedom without the ability to choose between real alternatives. If I do something because I'm made to do it, like a programmed computer, I'm not freely choosing to do it. If God had said, 'Be good', 'Love your neighbour', or 'Obey my commands', and then constructed us so that we could not disobey, our goodness, love or obedience would at best be shadowy. Love that is forced isn't real love. Obedience where there's no chance to disobey is hardly obedience. If I have to struggle with anger and resentment when I've been wronged, and then eventually manage to forgive the person, that seems to be a much truer form of forgiveness than if I'm programmed to forgive. If I struggle with fear or doubt, but then come through courageous or trusting, these are much more genuine forms of courage and faith than if I have no choice but to be brave or to trust.

The risk of making a wrong choice is an inevitable part of having freedom, and being free is an inevitable part of being human. We're not cabbages or computers. God has made us human beings, in his own image, with the gift of freedom.

Anything he sends our way we can refuse. That applies to gifts that are obviously good, such as salvation and the presence of the Holy Spirit, and to other things, which we tend to call 'bad', such as problem situations and times of testing. The choice is always ours.

BUT WHAT ABOUT ...?

There are plenty of situations for which the Bible gives clear principles by which we should make a decision. If someone wrongs us, we should choose to forgive. If our neighbour is in need, we should help. If someone tries to seduce us, we should say no.

In a messy world, however, we inevitably come across situations where clear biblical principles clash, and one has to be set aside in favour of another, more important, one. Our 'neighbour' is living rough on the streets and is undoubtedly in need; but to obey Luke 6:30 and give him some money would only further his drug habit, and so break the principle of showing true love to him. Some Christians, often in times of war or persecution, have been faced with agonizing decisions, and have rightly chosen, say, to tell lies in order to protect others, or to offer sexual services to a camp guard in order to secure the safety of another prisoner. The story of Rahab and the spies, recorded in Joshua 2 and spoken of with approval in Hebrews 11:31, is often cited as a biblical example of this. We can all imagine situations in which it would be right to go against almost any of the specific Christian commands and principles that are clearly taught in the Bible, when they are over-ridden by something more important.

There are two points we can make here. The first is that any specific principle must be interpreted and applied in the context of the whole revealed truth and will of God. No one part should ever be allowed to become so dominant that it overrules all the rest. That, as we've seen, was the mistake made by the Jewish teachers of the law and the Pharisees, when certain elements of the law became sacrosanct at the expense of others. They neglected 'justice and mercy and faithfulness' in order to obey the command to tithe down to the last detail (Matt. 23:23). Foundational principles that reflected the heart of God had been pushed to one side in order to obey a specific command. Jesus stated that it was possible to keep both their strict rules on tithing and the other principles. But sometimes we have to make a choice. Sometimes one command or principle has to yield before another, more foundational, one.

We could put it this way. God has graciously given us commands and principles by which to direct our living and make our decisions. Since they're God's commands and principles, they're beautiful, true, good and important. But we must never let them become more important than God himself. We're back to 'God first'.

The second point we need to make here is that these exceptional situations truly are exceptional. We can never say, 'If it's occasionally right to tell a lie to save a person's life, it's always OK to tell a lie for any reason we choose,' or, 'If I shouldn't give money to the homeless guy in the street, I don't need to give money to anybody.' Making an occasional exception doesn't annul the principle. For most of the time the principles of truthfulness and generosity will remain inviolable.

PLEASE, NO WEDGES

Granddad is in his nineties. He's very frail; his mental capacities are fading; his quality of life is poor. He's continually frustrated at his own weakness and limitations, and longs to be set free from his body so that he can be at home with the Lord. 'Don't keep me alive artificially,' he begs us. 'I want to depart and to be with Christ, which is far better.'

And now he's got pneumonia. 'We'll have to get him into hospital,' says the doctor. 'They've got the equipment there that'll save him.'

'Please, let me stay at home,' begs Granddad.

How do we choose what to do? Should we stick to the principle of preserving life wherever possible? Or should our love for Granddad and our respect for him as a person take precedence? If he stays at home and dies, would we not be responsible for killing him? Yet is it the way of love to insist that he goes into hospital and drags out two or three more weary years of existence on earth?

We've seen that this kind of situation, in which two or more foundational principles seem to pull us in opposing directions, is to be looked on as exceptional. We should never allow it to be normative, to establish a new principle or to set a precedent. We always need to be wary of people who start talking about 'the thin end of the wedge' in these sorts of circumstances. 'Allow one old person to die when he or she could have been kept alive artificially,' they say, 'and you'll have legalized euthanasia for everyone in no time at all.' The 'thin end of the wedge' argument is unreliable, as you can see from statements such as 'One sip of wine and you'll be a drunken alcoholic in no time,' or 'If I admit I've made a mistake, no-one will ever trust me again.'

Rather than setting a precedent, then, each of these special situations is to be looked on as unique, special, with features and aspects that make each one different from every other. That should take some of the pressure off the choice. We're not trying to establish a universal principle; we're simply trying to find out what's right in this unique situation.

There's something else that helps to take the pressure off. God is perfectly aware that the choice is a difficult one. And he's willing to carry the responsibility for it – if we let him.

He may do this in a number of ways. He may take the matter out of our hands. The doctor may insist that Granddad go in to hospital, and phone the ambulance. Or Granddad may suddenly change his mind. Or the hospital may have no spare beds.

Alternatively, God may accept our choice. We've worked it all out. We've talked it through with him. We've done all we need to do. We've made our decision. Graciously and lovingly he takes it on board and fits it into his great purposes. And he blesses us and gives us his peace.

ONLY ONE WAY TO THE TOP OF THE MOUNTAIN?

Philosophers love puzzles and paradoxes. One of their puzzles concerns God's freedom. God, they say, since he is perfect, must always do the perfect thing. In any given situation there can only be one perfect thing; anything else will be less than perfect. So in any situation God has no choice; there is only ever one thing that he can do. Therefore, says the puzzle, God has no freedom.

There are several answers to this. Some people make a distinction between God's moral choices and his general choices, agreeing that God can do only what is morally perfect, but pointing out that he has total freedom in all other areas. He could, for instance, have chosen to create our solar system with ten planets or fifty or a thousand, or designed planet Earth with green or blue vegetation.

Others answer the puzzle by going a stage further. They suggest that distinguishing between God's moral and non-moral choices is not particularly helpful, since all God's choices have moral implications. They challenge the idea that there's only one 'perfect' and therefore right option in any moral situation. Given the complexity of moral issues and the infinite wisdom and resources of God, there may well be several possible choices, all of which would bring about very good results, all of the greatest value.

Most of us would want to approach the puzzle from the other end. We know that God is free, we'd say. This must mean that he has freedom of choice. So we can conclude that there are open options in all areas of choosing.

What about us? Is there only ever one right choice in a given situation? Is there only one way to the top of the mountain? Just one 'right' house that I should buy? Just one job that I should take?

If that were so, it would put tremendous pressure on decision-making. If there's only one right house or job for me, and I go for the wrong one, I've made a dreadful mistake; I've made a wrong choice; I've sinned; for the next few years I'll be living outside God's will. And matters get even worse when you include all our decisions. It's not just that only one house is the right one. What if only one breakfast cereal were the right one? I could start the day in disobedience to God by having bran flakes instead of muesli. I could sin by walking to work rather than cycling.

Mercifully, it's not so. Even if there are still philosophical puzzles over God's choices, we can be absolutely sure that he doesn't put that kind of pressure on us. Instead, in any given situation there's a range of possible courses of action. Some will be bad, and others good. He calls us to choose one of the good ones; his wisdom and resources are such that he has no problem fitting our choice into his perfect purposes.

Confronted with a mountain, there are several routes to the top. Confronted with a fistful of estate agents' leaflets, there are several houses where God could bless and use me for his glory. Confronted with dishonesty or injustice in the workplace, there are various steps I could take that would show his truth, love and goodness. Confronted with poverty and hunger in the world, there are several ways I could choose to share my riches.

What matters, of course, is that I use my house, whichever one I buy, for his glory; that I fulfil my contract and do my job well, whether it's with this firm or that firm, and whether I walk or cycle to get there; whether I care for justice and for the poor and hungry; whether, in fact, I'm using my freedom and choice to express the heart of God.

HOW ABOUT A TALKING ASS?

So the choice is ours. But he promises to help us make it, to guide us and to save us from making a total mess of it.

How does he guide us? In all sorts of ways. The God who never repeats the design of a snowflake or of a blade of grass doesn't have to limit himself in the way he guides.

He certainly didn't limit himself in Bible days. There are stories of his using dreams, a pillar of fire, a talking ass, a burning bush, words of prophecy, an angelic choir, a still small voice, the drawing of lots, individuals, circumstances, visions, and many other means. He's got any number of ways of guiding us, and we can be sure that he'll pick the ones that best suit us and our situation. It may be something spectacular, like a vision or a voice from heaven. It may be the prompting of the Spirit as we study the Bible or pray, or a sense of peace and oneness with him as we move forward in a particular direction. It may be that he blocks off this route and then that, until we're following the one he knows is best. How he does so is up to him. It's not for us to demand he guide us in a particular way, even if that's the way he led us last time, or the way he guided a friend of ours.

But there's a sense in which all these ways of guiding are only extras, a supplement to the real thing. God's foundational way of guiding us is by living in us. 'We have the mind of Christ,' said Paul (1 Cor. 2:16); it's not me that's living, but 'Christ lives in me' (Gal. 2:20). It's back to that deep relationship: the people of God filled with the Spirit of God and living the life of God. Once that's in place, talking asses aren't really necessary.

THE PRIORITY AND THE PROMISE

So it's back to the Sermon on the Mount. The whole of Matthew 6, the central chapter of the Sermon, is taken up with one theme: what matters is our relationship with God.

The chapter starts with teaching about giving to others, prayer and fasting. In each case, says Jesus, the key factor is not the outward action, but our relationship with our Father, 'who sees what is done in secret' (Matt. 6:4, 6, 18). The middle section of the chapter states in three ways that we all are faced with the foundational choice: to put God first in our lives, or to push him out and replace him with something else. We are called to focus on treasures in heaven, to have bodies full of light, and to acknowledge God as our master.

Then comes the final section of the chapter, on the issues of daily life that cause us concern, with its climax in verse 33: 'seek first his kingdom and his righteousness, and all these things will be given to you as well'.

It could hardly be clearer: put God in his central place, and everything else will follow. Situations may seem impossibly complex; choices may seem desperately hard; issues may be too big for us to make a balanced decision. But our heavenly Father knows all about every one of them, says Jesus. Maybe those who don't have a heavenly Father are justified in worrying about these things. But with us it's different. If we put him first, he takes the ultimate responsibility for everything else. And that's a promise.

SOME BIBLE PASSAGES
RELEVANT TO MAKING
DECISIONS

The LORD himself goes before you and will be with you; he will never leave you nor forsake you (Deut. 31:8).

I will instruct you and teach you in the way you should go;
    I will counsel you and watch over you (Ps. 32:8).

Trust in the LORD with all your heart
    and lean not on your own understanding;
in all your ways acknowledge him,
    and he will make your paths straight (Prov. 3:5–6).

Therefore I tell you, do not worry, about your life, what you will eat or drink; or about your body, what you will wear. Is not life more important than food, and the body more important than clothes? Look at the birds of the air; they do not sow or reap or store away in barns, and yet your heavenly Father feeds them. Are you not much more valuable than they? ... So do not worry, saying, 'What shall we eat?' or 'What shall we drink?' or 'What shall we wear?' For the pagans run after all these things, and your heavenly Father knows that you need them. But seek first his kingdom and his righteousness, and all these things will be given to you as well (Matt. 6:25–26, 31–33).

But when he, the Spirit of truth, comes, he will guide you into all truth ... He will bring glory to me by taking from what is mine and making it known to you (John 16:13–14).

We have an obligation – but it is not to the sinful nature, to live according to it ... those who are led by the Spirit of God are sons of God. For you did not receive a spirit that makes you a slave again to fear, but you received the Spirit of sonship ... the Spirit helps us in our weakness. We do not know what we ought to pray for, but the Spirit himself intercedes for us with groans that words cannot express. And he who searches our hearts knows the mind of the Spirit, because the Spirit intercedes for the saints in accordance with God's will.

And we know that in all things God works for the good of those who love him, who have been called according to his purpose ...

What, then, shall we say in response to this? If God is for us, who can be against us? He who did not spare his own Son, but gave him up for us all – how will he not also, along with him, graciously give us all things? (Rom. 8:12, 14–15, 26–28, 31–32. See the whole chapter).

> 'Who has known the mind of the Lord
> that he may instruct him?'

But we have the mind of Christ (1 Cor. 2:16).

[We ask] God to fill you with the knowledge of his will through all spiritual wisdom and understanding. And we pray this in order that you may live a life worthy of the Lord and may please him in every way: bearing fruit in every good work, growing in the knowledge of God (Col. 1:9–10).

MAÑANA

Spanish may not be your strong point, but *mañana* is a word most of us know lots about. 'Don't do it today if you can possibly put it off till tomorrow.'

Of course, there are occasions when we need time to reflect. We need to give ourselves the space to get a situation in perspective, to pray or to seek the counsel of others. But there's got to come a time when *mañana* is wrong. A decision has to be made.

Something's got to be done. Putting it off any longer is not just cowardice or laziness; it's folly, and may even be disobedience to the call of God. Not *mañana*, but 'Now is the time' (2 Cor. 6:2).

When Luke described Jesus setting out for Jerusalem on that final journey to the cross, he used a phrase that literally means, 'he fixed his face' (Luke 9:51). In fact, the sense of Jesus' commitment and resolution was so strong that Mark tells us his disciples and those with him were 'astonished' and 'afraid' (Mark 10:32). Here was a man who had made up his mind, and was resolutely going forward in the way he knew was right.

Forget *mañana*. It'll waste years of your life. It'll make you weak and increasingly unable to take a decision or to get down to action. It'll take away your effectiveness, and your ability to give a clear lead to others.

Try another foreign word, this time from ancient Greece. It's the word Paul uses in 2 Corinthians 6:2: *kairos*. It's a great word. Though the New International Version translates it 'time', it means much more than that. It means the right time, the critical moment, the key point. It's the word Mark uses in 1:15, when Jesus says, 'The time has come ... The kingdom of God is near.' This is the time, the *kairos*, the right time, the key moment. And it's now, says Paul. Not *mañana*.

STEPPING OUT

You've got a big decision to make. You want to get it right, but maybe you're still not too sure how to set about it. Here are ten steps that may help.

1. Accept that there is no fixed pattern of Christian decision-making. God guides in all sorts of ways; in the Bible he uses a pillar of fire, a talking ass, a choir of angels, a storm, a still small voice, the drawing of lots, individuals, a church meeting, and many other things. Accept, further, that very often he gives *us* the privilege of doing the actual decision-making. He superintends the process, but he treats us as mature and wise adults, not as robots. In effect he tells us, 'You're a child of God; you have the mind of Christ; I've given you my Holy Spirit. Now I'm going to trust you to make the decision; and you, in your turn, must trust me that I'll not let you make a mess of it.'

2. Recognize that, as a Christian, your life does not belong to you. What you want is God's way forward, not yours. Though God undoubtedly takes account of your preferences, your attitude must be that of Jesus in Gethsemane: 'Not my will, but yours be done' (Luke 22:42).

3. Tell God very clearly that you are willing to do whatever he wants you to do, both with regard to the specific issue and in any other area. Write this down so that you are very clear what you are saying to God and what implications could follow. It is no good saying to God, 'Please guide me over whether I should go for job *A* or job *B*, but, whatever you do, don't start talking about me becoming a missionary.' There is only one thing you can truly ask God: 'Lord, I'm puzzling over job *A* or job *B*. I'd like you to show me if one of them is right; but, if you want to show me something completely different, please do so. I'm ready for anything.'

4. Check your motives. Since we are very good at deceiving ourselves, specifically ask the Holy Spirit to help you see things clearly. 'Why do I want a different job? Am I really motivated by the higher salary or the status?' It may be that God wants you to have more money or increased status, but if these are your major motives you need to admit that to God and ask him to sort you out. The issue for God may well not be whether or not you have more money, but whether or not your relationship with him is strong enough to avoid the spiritual damage the 'love of money' could do to you (1 Tim. 6:9–10).

5. Get close to God. It's always easier to hear someone speaking if we are near them. Spend a day with him. Fast and pray. Don't spend the day repeating 'Guide me, guide me, guide me'; you need to say that only once (Matt. 6:7–8), so you'll have lots of time for more important things. Spend the time in worship, in letting the Spirit search and renew your heart, in loving Jesus, in realizing afresh the power and glory of who God is, what Christ

has done and what the Bible teaches, and so on. Whether or not God says anything on the specific issue (and there's a fair chance he won't), he'll be thrilled to spend that time with you; for him you are much more important than the decision.

6. Check that there is no part of your life where you are acting contrary to what you know is the will of God. Recall the things he has said to you in the past, the great commands of Jesus, the major principles of Christian living. It's not a question of 'Unless I've got everything perfectly correct he won't show me the right way now' – if we had to get every detail right every time, we'd never get anywhere. Rather, this is giving God the opportunity to point out something to us that is important to him, something he wants us to get right for our sakes, something that in his purposes needs to be in place before he can lead us forward on the next step.

7. Take the opportunity to make a general inventory of your life, who you are, the way you've come and where you are going. You are a unique creation of God; you only have one life to live; you want to enter heaven with the words 'Well done, good and faithful servant' (Matt. 25:21) ringing in your ears. How are you shaping? How do you want to shape? How does this time of decision tie in with it all?

8. Do all the investigation you can on the specific issue. Gather information. Make lists of pros and cons. Read through relevant Bible passages. Consult wise and discerning friends – several of them, not just the ones you know will push you in the direction you secretly want to go. Depending on your theology, collect prophecies (again, beware of putting too much weight on just one) and words of knowledge, write out Bible verses that 'jump out at you', even draw lots. Put the results of all this investigation together. If everything points in the same direction, or nearly so, take very careful note. It doesn't necessarily settle the issue, but it looks like being a strong pointer.

9. When you are getting near to making the decision, put the onus on God to stop you if, despite all the above points, you are getting it wrong and are deciding to do something he really doesn't want you to do. Ask him to intervene in such a way that you will get the message clearly. Then relax. He'll have no problem intervening if he needs to.

10. Decide. Do what you think is right. It's as easy as that. If you get hit by a thunderbolt, think again. But if not, go ahead. If you still have doubts, give them over to God. As a last resort, remember that our God is so clever and so loving that if, even after all these steps, we still make the 'wrong' decision, he can sort it out; it is just one more of those 'all things' that he will work together for good (Rom. 8:28). So stop worrying. Accept his peace. Praise him and love him for his grace and guidance.

Part 2
Alcohol, tobacco, caffeine and other drugs

Alcohol is the only drug mentioned in the Scriptures. Wine is commended for its benefits, and strong warnings are given against its dangers. Some in the first-century Christian community chose to abstain and Paul taught that we are free to drink it or abstain, except where our exercise of that freedom would harm someone weaker in the faith (see Rom. 14:1 – 15:2). Jesus commanded that every time we drink it we should remember him.

The biblical principles on alcohol can be extended to other drugs. If they have benefits and their use will not harm us or others, we are free to use them. This would apply to drinking coffee and to using drugs medicinally. If their effects harm us or others, we should not use them. For most Christians this would prohibit the use of tobacco, but some would argue that for them the benefits outweigh the potential harm, and so, provided no-one else is adversely affected, they are free to smoke. In view of the huge proportion of crimes of violence and of road accidents that directly result from the abuse of alcohol, many Christians choose to exercise their freedom to abstain from alcohol. In the same way, as cannabis becomes more socially acceptable, Christians need to think through the positive and negative issues involved in its use.

Addiction is very different from the occasional enjoyment or use of alcohol and the like. Since it involves losing control of some aspect of our minds or of our bodies, it would seem unacceptable for Christians, since our bodies are the temple of the Holy Spirit; we are not our own (1 Cor. 6:19). Paul explicitly states that we are not to be mastered by anything except Christ (Rom. 6:12–14; 1 Cor. 6:12). It is possible, of course, to be addicted also to certain foods, solvents, gambling, pornography and lust.

Some Christians depend on certain drugs or medicinal substances in order to stay alive, or to enable their body to function correctly. These would include insulin, painkillers and drugs required to control high blood pressure or heart malfunction. The high dependency involved in the use of such substances should not be seen as a form of unacceptable addiction, but rather as a God-given means of controlling an illness.

Some relevant Bible teaching

> He makes grass to grow for the cattle
>   and plants for men to cultivate –
>   bringing food from the earth:
> wine that gladdens the heart of man,
>   oil to make his face shine,
>   and bread that sustains his heart (Ps. 104:14–15).

> Wine is a mocker and beer a brawler;
>   whoever is led astray by them is not wise (Prov. 20:1).

[Jesus] visited Cana in Galilee, where he had turned the water into wine (John 4:46).

... our old self was crucified with him so that the body of sin might be done away with, that we should no longer be slaves to sin ... Therefore do not let sin reign in your mortal body so that you obey its evil desires. Do not offer the parts of your body to sin, as instruments of wickedness, but rather offer yourselves to God, as those who have been brought from death to life; and offer the parts of your body to him as instruments of righteousness. For sin shall not be your master (Rom. 6:6, 12–14).

... let us put aside the deeds of darkness and put on the armour of light. Let us behave decently, as in the daytime, not in orgies and drunkenness ... Rather, clothe yourselves with the Lord Jesus Christ, and do not think about how to gratify the desires of the sinful nature (Rom. 13:12–14).

... let us stop passing judgment on one another. Instead, make up your mind not to put any stumbling-block or obstacle in your brother's way ... It is better not to eat meat or drink wine or to do anything else that will cause your brother to fall (Rom. 14:13, 21).

... I will not be mastered by anything ... Do you not know that your bodies are members of Christ himself? ... Do you not know that your body is a temple of the Holy Spirit, who is in you, whom you have received from God? You are not your own; you were bought at a price. Therefore honour God with your body (1 Cor. 6:12, 15, 19–20).

... he took the cup, saying, 'This cup is the new covenant in my blood; do this, whenever you drink it, in remembrance of me.' For whenever you eat this bread and drink this cup, you proclaim the Lord's death, until he comes' (1 Cor. 11:25–26).

... live by the Spirit, and you will not gratify the desires of the sinful nature ... The acts of the sinful nature are ... drunkenness, orgies, and the like ... But the fruit of the Spirit is ... self-control ... Since we live by the Spirit, let us keep in step with the Spirit (Gal. 5:16, 19, 21, 22, 25).

Be very careful, then, how you live ... Do not get drunk on wine, which leads to debauchery. Instead, be filled with the Spirit (Eph. 5:15, 18).

Stop drinking only water, and use a little wine because of your stomach and your frequent illnesses (1 Tim. 5:23).

What could I do?

Accept your freedom – and the responsibility that goes with it. Don't simply do what those around you do, whether they indulge or abstain. Here's an aspect of life in which God invites you to make a responsible choice.

Check the 'weaker Christian' situation. Will your decision affect anyone adversely? What is the Christlike thing to do, if so?

Ensure that you're not getting hooked. 'I will not be mastered by anything' (1 Cor. 6:12). One way of doing this is to abstain for a specific period: for example, no tea or coffee for a week; no chocolate or alcohol during the time of Lent; a month without having a cigarette.

Set in place certain precautions. Almost invariably, those who've drunk more than they ought feel fine, and quite capable, say, of driving safely. Those who are becoming addicted to some substance or practice always feel they've got the habit safely under control. Accept that you are not the best person to judge in these matters; agree to submit to the judgment of someone who knows you well and is qualified to make a more objective assessment. Perhaps your spouse is the best person to keep an eye on your drinking, and your doctor on your smoking or your use of drugs for sleeping or pain relief.

Enjoy your freedom. Drink your coffee (decaffeinated or otherwise), and give thanks to God (Rom. 14:6).

ANIMALS

The other day I drowned a rat. It had been caught in a trap, and I didn't know what else to do with it. But I still felt bad when I plunged the trap under the water.

Is God an animal lover? Of course. He made all living creatures and his love constantly reaches out to them all. Not one of them is ever forgotten (Luke 12:6). He loves rats, wasps and bacteria as well as baby lambs and guinea pigs. Does that mean he could never do anything to harm them? Not at all. In his purposes in a fallen world, all animal life, like human life, is subject to pain, ageing and death. Our bodies destroy harmful bacteria. Swallows feed on flies. Owls eat mice. The Bible sanctions the use of both vegetation and animals for food. Jesus rode on a donkey and ate fish and meat.

Can we then do what we like with animals? No. The Bible clearly teaches that we are responsible and answerable to God for the way we treat any aspect of his creation; we may use plants and animals for food, but selfish exploitation, cruelty and violence are condemned.

Christians are sometimes criticized by those concerned for animal rights because we teach that there is a fundamental difference between human beings and other living creatures. Science, many animal-rights defenders would say, has established that there is no difference between humans and animals, so the rights of humans should not take precedence over the rights of animals. Christians reply that the so-called scientific worldview not only debases humans; it debases animals as well, since both humans and animals are seen as nothing more than the product of a chance, meaningless process that takes away all their intrinsic value. Christianity, on the other hand, teaches that neither animals nor humans are the product of chance. Both are the planned and deliberate creation of God. Even more than that, both are held in being and cared for and loved by God; the one who holds the stars in their places watches over every sparrow.

But that is not to say that there is no intrinsic difference between human beings and other creatures. The Bible tells us that we alone are made 'in the image of God' (Gen. 1:27). All of God's creation is good; every creature is the object of his care and love. But only men and women are made in his image.

The fact that Christians refuse to put humans on the same level as animals does not mean that we wish to deny that animals have rights. Indeed, as responsible stewards of God's creation, we should be at the forefront of the debate on just what those rights are and how they can be safeguarded.

Some Bible teaching on animals

And God said, 'Let the water teem with living creatures, and let birds fly above the earth across the expanse of the sky.' So God created the great creatures of the sea and every living and moving thing with which the water teems, according to their kinds, and every winged bird according to its kind. And God saw that it was good. God blessed them and said, 'Be fruitful and increase in number and fill the water in the seas, and let the birds increase on the earth.' ...

And God said, 'Let the land produce living creatures according to their kinds: livestock, creatures that move along the ground,

and wild animals, each according to its kind.' And it was so ...
And God saw that it was good (Gen. 1:20–22, 24–25).

'Six days do your work, but on the seventh day do not work, so
that your ox and your donkey may rest ... (Exod. 23:12).

If you see your brother's donkey or his ox fallen on the road, do
not ignore it. Help him to get it to its feet ... Do not muzzle an
ox while it is treading out the grain (Deut. 22:4; 25:4).

> Praise the LORD ...
> He provides food for the cattle
>   and for the young ravens when they call (Ps. 147:1, 9).

> Praise the LORD ...
> Praise the LORD from the earth,
>   you great sea creatures and all ocean depths ...
> wild animals and all cattle,
>   small creatures and flying birds ...
> Let them praise the name of the LORD,
>   for his name alone is exalted;
>   his splendour is above the earth and the heavens
>   (Ps. 148:1, 7, 10, 13).

> A righteous man cares for the needs of his animal
>   but the kindest acts of the wicked are cruel (Prov. 12:10).

'Look at the birds of the air; they do not sow or reap or store away
in barns, and yet your heavenly Father feeds them' (Matt. 6:26).

'Are not five sparrows sold for two pennies? Yet not one of them
is forgotten by God' (Luke 12:6).

The creation was subjected to frustration, not by its own choice,
but by the will of the one who subjected it, in hope that the
creation itself will be liberated from its bondage to decay and
brought into the glorious freedom of the children of God (Rom.
8:20–21).

What could I do?

Develop a God-based approach to animals and other forms of life. Refuse to be shaped by traditions, sentimentality, self-interest or the latest fashion. Instead, seek to build an understanding of animals as part of God's creation, and to view them with the love and concern that God himself shows.

Fight cruelty to animals. Voice your objections to inhumane farming methods, cruel sports and unnecessary experimentation. Be discerning in the products you buy. Support farms that operate responsibly by buying their produce.

Support wildlife conservation. Human greed and exploitation have already done a huge amount of damage to our planet. We have a responsibility to preserve life, especially when it is threatened with extinction.

Keep a balance. The pet industry is big business. The amount spent worldwide on manufactured pet food would be more than enough to provide all needed food and medicine for every one of the three million African children who die of malnutrition or easily preventable diseases each year. Rats are multiplying rapidly thanks to plentiful supplies of discarded food in the richer countries, and they have to be controlled. Fish, already decimated by greedy overfishing, may need to be protected by culling seals.

Work and pray for the coming of God's kingdom. It's not the animal kingdom that matters most, nor the human kingdom. What matters is God's kingdom: 'your kingdom come, your will be done on earth as it is in heaven' (Matt. 6:10). As Christians we are already experiencing something of the reality of this; but it is God's desire that much more yet should be seen; that righteousness, for all creation and not just for human beings, should rain down upon the earth that God has created, and spring up and grow upon it (Is. 45:8). The key to this righteousness is Christ. In a great prophetic passage Isaiah described the coming of his kingdom:

> ... with righteousness he will judge the needy,
>   with justice he will give decisions for the poor of the earth.
> He will strike the earth with the rod of his mouth;

with the breath of his lips he will slay the wicked.
Righteousness will be his belt
and faithfulness the sash round his waist.

The wolf will live with the lamb,
the leopard will lie down with the goat,
the calf and the lion and the yearling together;
and a little child will lead them.
The cow will feed with the bear,
their young will lie down together,
and the lion will eat straw like the ox.
The infant will play near the hole of the cobra,
and the young child put his hand into the viper's nest.
They will neither harm nor destroy
on all my holy mountain,
for the earth will be full of the knowledge of the LORD
as the waters cover the sea (Is. 11:4–9).

BEING DIFFERENT
– BEING YOU

For all our individualism, most of us are hugely shaped by the culture around us. We often have no choice; we have to fit into the world's way of doing things in order to live in the world. And the world's way of doing things isn't necessarily wrong. Neither is it necessarily right. The Bible challenges us to accept that as Christians we are different from those around us. We have a different perspective, and different values, principles and goals. We are called to *be* different, to express a whole new way of being and living and doing, and to be God's special people, his new humanity, the body of Christ.

The New Testament gives at least three reasons why we should be different in many respects from those around us. In the first place, we *are* different, and we need to be true to what we are. Secondly, much of what others are and do falls short of God's standards; their values and practices are frequently opposed to God's truth and purposes. Thirdly, if we fail to be different we'll fail in our calling to show God to the world; we'll cease to be the 'light of the world' (Matt. 5:14); we won't fulfil Peter's vision of declaring 'the praises of him who called you out of darkness into his wonderful light' so that those around us may see the difference being a Christian makes 'and glorify God' (1 Pet. 2:9, 12).

Some relevant New Testament passages

'You are the salt of the earth. But if the salt loses its saltiness, how can it be made salty again? It is no longer good for anything, except to be thrown out and trampled by men.

'You are the light of the world. A city on a hill cannot be hidden. Neither do people light a lamp and put it under a bowl, Instead they put it on its stand, and it gives light to everyone in the house. In the same way, let your light shine before men, that they may see your good deeds and praise your Father in heaven' (Matt. 5:13–16).
'Come, follow me,' Jesus said (Mark 1:17).

'I [Jesus] am not praying for the world, but for those you have given me, for they are yours. All I have is yours, and all you have is mine. And glory has come to me through them …

'My prayer is not that you take them out of the world but that you protect them from the evil one. They are not of the world, even as I am not of it. Sanctify them by the truth; your word is truth. As you sent me into the world, I have sent them into the world' (John 17:9–10, 15–18).

Do not conform any longer to the pattern of this world, but be transformed by the renewing of your mind. Then you will be able to test and approve what God's will is – his good, pleasing and perfect will (Rom. 12:2–3).

Do you not know that your body is a temple of the Holy Spirit, who is in you, whom you have received from God? You are not your own; you were bought at a price. Therefore honour God with your body (1 Cor. 6:19–20).

I have been crucified with Christ and I no longer live, but Christ lives in me (Gal. 2:20).

See to it that no-one takes you captive thorough hollow and deceptive philosophy, which depends on human traditions and the basic principles of this world rather than on Christ ... You died with Christ to the basic principles of this world (Col. 2:8, 20).

Put to death, therefore, whatever belongs to your earthly nature ... You used to walk in these ways, in the life you once lived. But now you must rid yourselves of all such things ... since you have taken off your old self with its practices and have put on the new self, which is being renewed in knowledge in the image of its Creator (Col. 3:5, 7–8, 9–10).

Religion that God our Father accepts as pure and faultless is this: to look after orphans and widows in their distress and to keep oneself from being polluted by the world (Jas. 1:27).

... don't you know that friendship with the world is hatred towards God? Anyone who chooses to be a friend of the world becomes an enemy of God (Jas. 4:4).

... do not conform to the evil desires you had when you lived in ignorance (1 Pet. 1:14).

... you are a chosen people, a royal priesthood, a holy nation, a people belonging to God, that you may declare the praises of him who called you out of darkness into his wonderful light ...
    Dear friends, I urge you, as aliens and strangers in the world, to abstain from sinful desires, which war against your soul. Live such good lives among the pagans that, though they accuse you of doing wrong, they may see your good deeds and glorify God on the day he visits us (1 Pet. 2:9, 11–12).

Do not love the world or anything in the world. If anyone loves the world, the love of the Father is not in him. For everything in the world – the cravings of sinful man, the lust of his eyes and the boasting of what he has and does – comes not from the Father but from the world. The world and its desires pass away, but the man who does the will of God lives for ever (1 John 2:15–17).

What could I do?

Be the real you. You can't be true to your real self and just be the same as everybody else. After all, you're a unique person, an individual creation of God, shaped by all the experiences you've been through, both good and bad. There's no-one in the world the same as you; you have a unique way of seeing things and a unique contribution to make. But, even more than that, you've got something fantastic to offer. You're different from most of the people around you because you're a Christian. You belong to the living God (1 Pet. 2:9). Christ lives in you (Gal. 2:20). Your body is the temple of the Holy Spirit (1 Cor. 6:19). You're the light of the world (Matt. 5:14).

Sort out anything you find in yourself that's not the real you. There are two main areas to focus on. The first is things left over from before you became a Christian. Ask the Holy Spirit to show you the parts of your life you've not yet handed over to the lordship of Jesus, and ask for his strength to keep working at getting rid of them. But the other area is where you've simply followed the trend of the people around, to think like them, accept their values and attitudes, and do the things they do. You won't generally be able to get rid of deeply ingrained ways of thinking or acting overnight, but, by God's grace, as you keep working at it, you'll be able to replace them with patterns of thought and behaviour that truly express the life of Christ in you (Col. 2:8; 3:5–10).

Let your light shine. Throw away the 'bowls' of fear or diffidence or following the crowd. Be as unmistakably clear as a city on the top of a hill (Matt. 5:14–16). Be unashamedly different.

Keep in close touch with Jesus. After all, he's the real light of the world. And, says Paul, he's the real you (Gal. 2:20). He's your life (Col. 3:4). So you need lots of him.

Shape the world; don't be shaped by it. Be a world-changer. Set the trends. Suggest the policies. If you can't do it on a world scale, do it on whatever scale you can: at the local Residents' Association meetings, on the Board of School Governors, in the workplace, in the bus queue or the shop. Show them God's way and God's values.

Encourage other Christians to be world-shapers. All too often we get slack. The church of Jesus Christ ceases to be seen as a body of revolutionaries, putting forward a radical alternative to the ways of the world. We slip into a dull conformity that neither attracts nor challenges anybody. The writer to the Hebrews calls us to 'spur one another on towards love and good deeds' (Heb. 10:24). The word the writer uses describes getting an animal to move forward by sticking a goad into it; it gives us our English word 'paroxysm'. Do all you can (graciously, of course) to wake your fellow Christians up to their responsibilities and opportunities here and to get them moving.

THE BIBLE: LEARNING FROM THE BIBLE

The Bible has had quite a battering from the sceptics through the past couple of hundred years. Countless thinkers, some of them very intelligent, have set themselves to demonstrate once and for all that it cannot be what it claims to be, a Holy-Spirit-inspired book that tells us God's truth. But, almost incredibly, the Bible has survived every attack, and remains the world's best-read and best-loved book, with power to change lives and answer every human need, and, supremely, to bring women and men face to face with the living God.

As Christians we know we should study the Bible and learn from it. Many of us have the responsibility of teaching it to others; all of us know we should be letting its teaching shape our lives so that those around us see the reality of God in us. But understanding the Bible and applying its truth to ourselves or to other situations isn't always easy. Maybe the attacks on the Bible have dented our confidence in it, even though every single argument raised against it has been satisfactorily answered by reputable Bible scholars. We've all come across people who have misunderstood and misapplied the Bible, sometimes in a very dogmatic fashion, and this tends to make us cautious: how do we know that we've got it right?

The Bible is God's gift to us, a gift he expects us to accept and use. It's much more than a record of humankind's search after God. It's God's living Word; as Paul put it, when referring to the gospel, it's 'the power of God for the salvation of everyone who believes' (Rom. 1:16). We read it not just to be informed and enlightened; we read it to be changed.

What Bible passages tell us about the Bible

> How can a young man keep his way pure?
>   By living according to your word ...
> Open my eyes that I may see
>   wonderful things in your law ...
> I run in the path of your commands
>   for you have set my heart free ...
> Oh, how I love your law!
>   I meditate on it all day long ...
> Your word is a lamp to my feet
>   and a light for my path ...
> Your promises have been thoroughly tested,
>   and your servant loves them ...
> All your words are true;
>   all your righteous laws are eternal
>   (Ps. 119:9, 18, 32, 97, 105, 140, 160).

'... everyone who hears these words of mine and puts them into practice is like a wise man who built his house on the rock. The rain came down, the streams rose, and the winds blew and beat against that house; yet it did not fall, because it had its foundation on the rock. But everyone who hears these words of mine and does not put them into practice is like a foolish man who built his house on sand. The rain came down, the streams rose, and the winds blew and beat against that house, and it fell with a great crash' (Matt. 7:24–27).

'... the Scripture cannot be broken' (John 10:35).

... everything that was written in the past was written to teach us, so that through endurance and the encouragement of the Scriptures we might have hope (Rom. 15:4).

Do your best to present yourself to God as one approved, a workman who does not need to be ashamed and who correctly handles the word of truth (2 Tim. 2:15).

... continue in what you have learned and have become convinced of, because you know those from whom you learned it, and how from infancy you have known the holy Scriptures, which are able to make you wise for salvation through faith in Christ Jesus. All Scripture is God-breathed and is useful for teaching, rebuking, correcting and training in righteousness, so that the man of God may be thoroughly equipped for every good work. In the presence of God and of Christ Jesus, who will judge the living and the dead, and in view of his appearing and his kingdom, I give you this charge: Preach the Word; be prepared in season and out of season; correct, rebuke and encourage – with great patience and careful instruction (2 Tim. 3:14 – 4:2).

In the past God spoke to our forefathers through the prophets at many times and in various ways, but in these last days he has spoken to us by his Son (Heb. 1:1–2).

Above all, you must understand that no prophecy of Scripture came about by the prophet's own interpretation. For prophecy never had its origin in the will of man, but men spoke from God as they were carried along by the Holy Spirit (2 Pet. 1:20–21).

... our dear brother Paul also wrote to you with the wisdom that God gave him ... His letters contain some things that are hard to understand, which ignorant and unstable people distort, as they do the other Scriptures, to their own destruction (2 Pet. 3:15–17).

What could I do to learn from the Bible?

Settle in your mind that the Bible is what it claims to be. Either it is, as it claims, God's book, a message from the living God to anyone who will read it; or it's false, its claims are untrue, and it can safely be ignored. If it is a message from God, it's the most important book we can ever lay our hands on. To study God's message, to take it on board, to let it change our lives, and to declare it to others, has got to be the most important thing we can ever do.

Be willing to hear and follow God's voice. Every time you open the Bible or listen to a sermon, expect God to speak, and be ready to listen. He has so much to say; he wants to show us new truths, to remind us about old truths, to make specific applications, to encourage us, challenge us, rebuke us, direct us. If there's a barrier, it's generally on our side: we're not listening, we don't like what we hear, so we find some reason for rejecting it, or, as in the parable of the sower (Mark 4:2–20), as soon as we do hear it, it gets crowded out by other matters. A great phrase to keep in mind is the one Eli gave to Samuel: 'Speak, LORD, for your servant is listening' (1 Sam. 3:9).

Read the Bible as an instruction manual, not as an encyclopedia. God has given us the Bible not primarily to tell us about creation or the end of the age, or even to teach us theology. He's given it to us so that we can find him and know and follow him in every part of our lives. If we approach the Bible simply trying to discover historical or theological truths, we'll miss out on its main purpose. Too many people have got so bogged down trying to understand, say, the fine details of the first few verses of Genesis, that they've failed to hear what God is saying to them through these verses about his power and purpose as their Creator and Lord.

Handle the Bible wisely. We all know of sects and individuals who've taken verses out of context, stressed one passage at the expense of another, or taken too literally what is meant to be poetry or picture language, and as a result have gone off the rails. In these days we've got so many excellent commentaries available that it's easy to clear up any obscurity over the meaning of a passage. Wise biblical scholars, who love and respect the Scriptures, can show us how to interpret and apply them without being unfair to what these ancient writings originally meant and to what God wants to say to us through them today. A huge amount of the Bible's key teaching is in fact straightforward. We don't need lots of commentaries to understand that God is good, loving and mighty, that through Christ we have forgiveness and eternal life, or that he calls us to follow him and live loving, holy and obedient lives. If we just focused on the Bible's big themes, which are abundantly clear, we'd have plenty of material to keep us going for years!

Pray for the Holy Spirit. Make a conscious habit of this. We may accept in theory that it is the Spirit who both inspired the Scriptures and teaches them to us; but all too often we rush in with our own understanding or interpretation without stopping to ensure that it's God's voice we're listening for, not our ideas. In particular, ask the Holy Spirit to make the Word live to you. Take the experience of the two disciples on the Emmaus road as your goal. Familiar Scriptures, which they'd known for years, became alive when Jesus talked with them. 'Were our hearts not burning within us while he talked with us on the road and opened the Scriptures to us?' (Luke 24:32).

Study the Bible at first hand as well as at second hand. Second-hand study is when we listen to sermons or tapes, or read books, in which other people expound and explain what the Bible is saying. There's nothing wrong with this; indeed, it's a great way of learning and growing as a Christian, and God frequently uses these means to speak to us personally. But we also have the privilege of getting to grips ourselves with the words of Scripture, and of being alone with the Bible and the Holy Spirit, without even the intervention of our daily Bible-reading notes.

Use a variety of ways of studying the Bible. Here are seven suggestions.

1. *Sit down for an hour or two and read a long section.* This is great for getting an overall view, and for immersing yourself in the story or teaching of that part of the Bible. You could read an Old Testament historical book or a Gospel in about an hour (less for Mark). All of Paul's letters would take a couple of hours. You could read the whole of the New Testament in a day; it's the equivalent of two and a half Agatha Christie stories in length.

2. *Focus on just one word.* In contrast to taking a long passage, pick just one of the great Bible words, unpack its meaning and let it warm your heart and challenge you. Try 'holy', 'shepherd', 'light', 'grace', 'peace', 'forgiveness', 'joy', 'redemption', 'serve', 'trust', 'obey', 'repent', or any of the dozens of others. You may already have sufficient understanding of the concept to be able to delve into its treasures, or you may need to start by looking it up in a Bible dictionary and checking some of the passages where it occurs. Again, don't just work out its nuances of meaning; make it your primary aim to hear what God is saying to you through this one word.

3. *Read a passage of Scripture every day.* There are lots of Bible-reading plans and notes available that set a passage for each day. These are useful in providing a ready-made structure to follow, and often give helpful explanatory notes. But you could work out your own plan, or simply go at your own speed, working day by day through a book, some days covering two or three chapters, and sometimes taking most of a week to digest a single verse. It's not generally helpful to have no structure at all; just opening the Bible at random and reading the first passage you come across may be all right on occasion, but it's hardly likely to give you a consistent and balanced understanding and application.

4. *Try a team approach.* Married couples can read and study a passage together. Doing Bible study in a small group can give you all sorts of insights you wouldn't get on your own. You could try arranging with a Christian colleague at work for each of you to read the same passage first thing in the morning, and then discuss it together over lunch.

5. *Try meditating.* Don't let the fact that yoga and eastern religions meditate put you off; meditation is a thoroughly biblical practice. Take a biblical truth, story, person or concept and spend

time with it. Don't hurry; don't get distracted; be relaxed in the presence of God. Look at it from all sorts of angles, admiring its many facets. Chew it over slowly, extracting its full flavour and nutrition. Listen to it, the song it's singing, the way it's calling, the truths it's speaking. Ask it questions; use your imagination; let it get you excited. Write down your thoughts if you find this helpful. Above all, let the Spirit speak to you through your meditation.

6. *Work through a book of the Bible with a devotional commentary.* You can go at your own pace, on a daily or weekly basis. Again, remember to listen to what the Holy Spirit is saying specifically to you, as well as to what the commentator is saying.

7. *Tie your Bible study in with the teaching programme of your church.* Have another look at the passage preached on in the Sunday morning service or set for the house groups. Recall what the preacher or others said; dig deeper; apply the teaching to your personal situation.

Don't get bogged down. 'I started reading through the Bible but got to Leviticus and gave up.' 'I tried Revelation, but it blew my mind.' Paul's letters 'contain some things that are hard to understand' (2 Pet. 3:16). Of course, we ought to have the goal of plumbing the depths of every bit of the Bible if we live long enough. But there's not much point in spending lots of time and energy struggling with sections that we don't understand when there's so much else waiting for us that we can cope with. That's not to say we should never read Leviticus or Revelation; they're both great books. But, if we find them turning us off Bible study, it's best to finish them quickly and get on with something that is helpful to us. Don't miss out on the glories of the gospel because of Numbers, Deuteronomy or the ramblings of Job's friends.

Write things down. Whether or not you use other people's notes, write your own notes to record what God says to you. Don't attempt to write a commentary; rather, make it more like a personal journal. Writing things down fixes them in our minds; we state in black and white what God has said to us today. It can also be helpful to go back, say after a week or a month, to make sure we've not forgotten what he said, and to check that we're putting it into practice.

Listen for God in sermons. Theoretically, in a sermon the

preacher is expounding and applying a passage or theme of Scripture. Sadly, some sermons don't sound quite like that, and may seem to be little more than the preacher outlining his or her ideas. But even in the not-so-special sermons there may be places where God speaks, his truth shines out and his Spirit is at work. The sad thing is that many congregations miss them. Maybe they're half asleep, thinking about Sunday lunch, or so used to boring and irrelevant sermons that they can't recognize God's voice when he speaks through one. Get rid of the idea that in a sermon one person does all the work and the congregation does nothing. Be prepared to put in as much effort as the preacher. Be determined to hear God's voice every time you listen to a sermon. Pray for the preacher. Listen. Concentrate. Be aware that preaching is God's chosen way of speaking to his people and working in them. Pray for yourself, that you will hear God's voice. Pray for the rest of the congregation, that the Spirit will move among them all.

CARS AND TRANSPORT

There are well over twenty million cars in the UK. They travel a total of over 200 billion miles each year, and cost the average adult more than £1,000 annually. Statistically, the average father spends seven minutes driving his car for each minute he spends talking to one of his children.

Like all the products of contemporary technology, cars both enrich and threaten the quality of our lives. The ease of transport they provide opens up a huge range of potential benefits. But at the same time they can add to life's pressures, both because driving itself is often stressful, and because they enable us to rush from one place to another, packing more than is good for us into each day. Additionally, they threaten our health, not just through pollution, but by discouraging many of us from getting sufficient exercise.

If I'd lived a century or two ago, I'd have spent quite a bit of time walking or horse-riding from one place to another. I'd have passed a lot of people doing the same. Almost all of them I would have known; we'd have stopped to talk, or at the very least greeted one another. Now, when I travel by car, though I pass thousands of people, I never stop to greet them. Perhaps I don't even think of them as people; they are just 'cars going the other way'. We're all insulated in our little boxes, cut off from real relationships.

And how about my driving? We all think we're good drivers. Doubtless we're better than some. But what's happening when we get angry with other drivers? How about risk-taking, carelessness, or driving after drinking or when sleepy? What about the speed limits? It's common to see cars with 'fish' signs doing 80 on the motorway. Maybe we all need a sign in the back of our cars saying, 'Jesus is driving this car.'

Some Bible principles

Do not conform any longer to the pattern of this world (Rom. 12:2).

Everyone must submit himself to the governing authorities (Rom. 13:1).

... whatever you do, do it all for the glory of God (1 Cor. 10:31).

Be very careful, then, how you live – not as unwise but as wise, making the most of every opportunity, because the days are evil. Therefore do not be foolish, but understand what the Lord's will is. Do not get drunk ... Instead, be filled with the Spirit ...
Submit to one another out of reverence for Christ (Eph. 5:15–18, 21).

... as aliens and strangers in the world ... Live such good lives among the pagans that, though they accuse you of doing wrong, they may see your good deeds and glorify God on the day he visits us.

Submit yourselves for the Lord's sake to every authority instituted among men (1 Pet. 2:11–13).

What could I do?

Give every aspect of this area of your life over to God. Don't just pray for safety in travelling and then drive like those who aren't Christians. Ask the Holy Spirit to be in charge of the money you spend, the model of vehicle you buy, how you use it, how you drive, and how you react to other drivers, as well as your safety.

Be a truly Christian driver. Don't model your driving on other drivers. Think out how being a Christian should affect your driving, and put this into practice. You might find it helpful to imagine how you'd drive if Jesus was in the seat next to you – and then remember he's there!

Check periodically in case you're unconsciously being sucked into our materialistic culture's mindset. You could ask yourself:

• Why do I have a car? Because everyone else has one? To impress my friends? For essential transport? To use for the Lord?
• Can I justify the difference in price between an expensive model and a cheaper one, or between a new model and a used one? Do I really need all those gadgets? Could I go for the cheaper option and send the money saved to feed several starving families for a year?

Keep an eye on the environmental and health aspects of our car-dominated lifestyle. Ask yourself:

• Do I really need to use my car for those shorter journeys? Could I walk, or go by bike?
• Could I use public transport more?
• Could I choose a more environmentally friendly car?
• Does my use of the car mean I don't get enough exercise?
• Is my use of my car, or the way I drive, adding to the stress I'm under? If so, what can I do about it?

Check your driving habits. Here's a five-star opportunity to show how being a Christian affects every part of your life. How do you react to other drivers, especially bad drivers? Are you driven by a need to be out in front, to show the other guy who's boss, or to impress people with how much you matter or how clever you are? Do you find yourself driving faster than you need to or than what optimizes fuel consumption?

Check your attitude to the law. Christians who would be strict about making honest tax returns are often surprisingly lax about keeping the law while driving. Are the claims 'Most people use mobile phones while driving' or 'Everyone exceeds the speed limits' sufficient justification for you to do so? What about driving when you're tired or have been drinking? We all know that if everyone obeyed the law in these respects hundreds of lives would be saved and the pain and suffering of thousands of accidents would be avoided. Again, it may help to imagine you've got Jesus sitting in the seat next to you – or, if that doesn't work, in the police car following you!

Church 1: Choosing a local church

In New Testament days choosing a church would have been a non-issue. Nobody chose their church. All Christians simply accepted that they belonged to the local body of believers in their area. There was neither need nor opportunity to do any choosing.

But we live in very different times. For almost all of us the choice is real, and often bewildering. No longer do we have just one local church. There's the local Anglican church, the local Baptist, the local Roman Catholic, and the local 'New' church. What's more, there's the local charismatic Anglican, the local traditional Anglican, and the local socially involved Anglican. In fact, 'local' itself has been redefined. Some friends of mine have recently been commuting 80 miles each way to a church they've found particularly helpful. In our highly mobile society, most of us have dozens if not hundreds of churches within striking distance.

What's more, our mindset is very different from that of those who lived in the first century. The attitude of the consumer society around us makes us particularly choosy. The question 'Lord, which church do you want me to join?' is often overlaid with questions like 'Which church do I feel at home in?', 'Which church satisfies my needs?', 'Where do I get the greatest blessing?' or 'Which church offers a worship style that suits me?'

In an ideal world there wouldn't be lots of different denominations and styles of church structures and activities. But God has a great way of bringing good out of a less than perfect situation. We are all different, and at different stages of our Christian journey. So the church that is right for one person may well not be right for another, and what is right for me at one time may not be right for me a few years later. If I'm a young Christian, God may put me in a church where I get good teaching, so that I grow and become strong. But then he might guide me to a church where the teaching is very poor, but where I can lead a house group and give to others what I have received. A couple who attend a church with a vigorous youth work while their children are growing up may, when the children get older, be called by God to leave that church and go to help a small, struggling one.

What could I do?

Put God in charge of the decision. Forget the consumer society and the priority of your own desires or needs. Start with God. 'Lord, I'm willing to go anywhere you want me to go.' Accept that God may want you in a church that belongs to a different tradition or is of a very different size from what you're used to.

Analyse what you can offer. Once you've put God in charge of the decision, you can start assessing yourself. But don't start with your needs; start with what you can give. Be realistic here, neither too modest nor overestimating your skills and gifts. Make a list.

Some strengths, such as 'prayer', will be relevant in any church. But others, such as 'catering' or 'leading worship' may not be, either because the church in question doesn't go in for those kinds of activities, or because they've already got a surfeit of caterers and worship-leaders.

Analyse what you need. Again, make a list. Perhaps as a new or struggling Christian you do need particularly good teaching. Or you know you couldn't worship in anything but the style you're used to. Since we all tend to be too consumer-orientated, it might be wise, in compiling this list, to differentiate between the items you feel are essential and those you would prefer, and to keep giving them all over to God.

Check out the possible churches. Join them in worship. Get the 'feel' of the place. Talk to the people. Again, remember that the question 'Lord, is this where you want me to serve you?' is more important than 'Do I like this place?'

Get advice. Talk to people who know you, and, where possible, who know the churches you're looking at. They can't tell you where to go, but they may offer some helpful, objective comments or suggestions.

Keep listening for the call of God. Remember, he may surprise you.

Make your decision. In some circumstances it may be right to commit yourself to attending for a trial period, to make sure you've made the right choice. But generally it's better to be fully committed from the start, and to let the church know, so that you can get on and be fully involved as quickly as possible.

CHURCH 2: BELONGING TO A LOCAL CHURCH

At least two elements of our culture run counter to the biblical concept of belonging to a local church. One is the rejection of commitment; the other is our consumer mentality. Both are rooted in human selfishness: 'I won't get too involved in case I find it too costly and I want to pull out. I want a church that does something for me; if it doesn't do that, I'll leave.'

The Bible teaches that every Christian is called to a deep commitment of love and service to the local community of believers, and that our primary motivation in belonging is the good of others, not our own benefit. We belong to give, not just to get.

Quite apart from being countercultural, the concept of belonging to a church is out of favour today because many people have had a bad experience of the church. Tragically, all too often, people use words such as 'irrelevant', 'uncaring' and 'hypocritical' to describe the churches they've attended; they find the people critical, divided, and complaining about each other and their leaders.

None of that takes away our responsibility to belong to a local church. God clearly calls us to commitment and to selfless service of others and of Christ, even if the church he puts us in has as many faults as those in Corinth or Galatia, to which Paul wrote.

Though our motivation in belonging to a church is to give rather than to get, the benefits, of course, are huge. We receive love, encouragement, help and teaching; we are blessed by the prayers and practical support of others; and together we are able to serve and witness to the people in our local community much more effectively than we could as isolated believers.

Some New Testament teaching on belonging to a church

'Now that I, your Lord and Teacher, have washed your feet, you also should wash one another's feet. I have set you an example that you should do as I have done for you ... A new command I give you: Love one another. As I have loved you, so you must love one another. By this all men will know that you are my disciples, if you love one another' (John 13:14–15, 34–35).

... in Christ we who are many form one body, and each member belongs to all the others. We have different gifts, according to the grace given us. If a man's gift is prophesying, let him use it in proportion to his faith. If it is serving, let him serve; if it is teaching, let him teach; if it is encouraging, let him encourage; if it is contributing to the needs of others, let him give generously; if it is leadership, let him govern diligently; if it is showing mercy, let him do it cheerfully ... Be devoted to one another in brotherly love. Honour one another above yourselves. Never be lacking in zeal, but keep your spiritual fervour, serving the Lord (Rom. 12:5–8, 10–11).

Accept him whose faith is weak, without passing judgment on disputable matters.

... make up your mind not to put any stumbling-block or obstacle in your brother's way.

... make every effort to do what leads to peace and to mutual edification ...

We who are strong ought to bear with the failings of the weak and not to please ourselves. Each of us should please his neighbour for his good, to build him up ...

May the God who gives endurance and encouragement give you a spirit of unity among yourselves as you follow Christ Jesus, so that with one heart and mouth you may glorify the God and Father of our Lord Jesus Christ.

Accept one another, then, just as Christ accepted you, in order to bring praise to God (Rom. 14:1, 13, 19; 15:1–2, 5–7).

I appeal to you, brothers, in the name of our Lord Jesus Christ, that all of you agree with one another so that there may be no divisions among you and that you may be perfectly united in mind and thought (1 Cor. 1:10).

Now to each one the manifestation of the Spirit is given for the common good ...

The body is a unit, though it is made up of many parts; and though all its parts are many, they form one body. So it is with Christ. For we were all baptised by one Spirit into one body ... and ... were all given the one Spirit to drink ...

Now you are the body of Christ, and each one of you is a part of it ...

Follow the way of love and eagerly desire spiritual gifts, especially the gift of prophecy ...

But everything should be done in a fitting and orderly way (1 Cor. 12:7, 12–13, 27; 14:1, 40).

You, my brothers, were called to be free. But do not use your freedom to indulge the sinful nature; rather, serve one another in love (Gal. 5:13).

Carry each other's burdens, and in this way you will fulfil the law of Christ (Gal. 6:2).

... live a life worthy of the calling you have received. Be completely humble and gentle; be patient, bearing with one another in love. Make every effort to keep the unity of the Spirit through the bond of peace.

... speaking the truth in love, we will grow up into him who is the Head, that is, Christ. From him the whole body, joined and held together by every supporting ligament, grows and builds itself up in love, as each part does its work (Eph. 4:1–3, 15–16).

Submit to one another out of reverence for Christ (Eph. 5:21).

Whatever happens, conduct yourselves in a manner worthy of the gospel of Christ (Phil. 1:27).

If you have any encouragement from being united with Christ, if any comfort from his love, if any fellowship with the Spirit, if any tenderness and compassion, then make my joy complete by being like-minded, having the same love, being one in spirit and purpose. Do nothing out of selfish ambition or vain conceit, but in humility consider others better than yourselves. Each of you should look not only to your own interests, but also to the interests of others.

Your attitude should be the same as that of Christ Jesus (Phil. 2:1–5).

... as God's chosen people, holy and dearly loved, clothe your-selves with compassion, kindness, humility, gentleness and patience. Bear with each other and forgive whatever grievances you may have against one another. Forgive as the Lord forgave you. And over all these virtues put on love, which binds them all together in perfect unity.

Let the peace of Christ rule in your hearts, since as members of one body you were called to peace. And be thankful. Let the word of Christ dwell in you richly as you teach and admonish one another with all wisdom, and as you sing psalms, hymns and spiritual songs with gratitude in your hearts to God. And whatever you do, whether in word or deed, do it all in the name of the Lord Jesus, giving thanks to God the Father through him (Col. 3:12–17).

... respect those who work hard among you, who are over you in the Lord and who admonish you. Hold them in the highest regard in love because of their work. Live in peace with each other ... warn those who are idle, encourage the timid, help the weak, be patient with everyone. Make sure that nobody pays back wrong for wrong, but always try to be kind to each other and to everyone else.

Be joyful always; pray continuously; give thanks in all circum-stances ...

Do not put out the Spirit's fire; do not treat prophecies with contempt. Test everything. Hold on to the good. Avoid every kind of evil (1 Thess. 5:12–22).

Let us not give up meeting together, as some are in the habit of doing, but let us encourage one another – and all the more as you see the Day approaching (Heb. 10:25).

Remember your leaders, who spoke the word of God to you. Con-sider the outcome of their way of life and imitate their faith ...

Obey your leaders and submit to their authority. They keep watch over you as men who must give an account. Obey them so that their work will be a joy, not a burden, for that would be of no advantage to you (Heb. 13:7, 17).

My brothers, as believers in our glorious Lord Jesus Christ, don't
show favouritism ...

Don't grumble against each other ...

... confess your sins to each other and pray for each other so
that you may be healed (Jas. 2:1; 5:9, 16).

... you are a chosen people, a royal priesthood, a holy nation, a
people belonging to God, that you may declare the praises of
him who called you out of darkness into his wonderful light (1
Pet. 2:9).

Above all, love each other deeply, because love covers over a
multitude of sins. Offer hospitality to each other without grumbling. Each one should use whatever gift he has received to serve
others, faithfully administering God's grace in its various forms.
If anyone speaks, he should do it as one speaking the very words
of God. If anyone serves, he should do it with the strength God
provides, so that in all things God may be praised through Jesus
Christ. To him be the glory and power for ever and ever. Amen.
(1 Pet. 4:8–11).

He who has an ear, let him hear what the Spirit says to the
churches (Rev. 2:7, etc.).

What could I do?

See belonging to a church the way the New Testament sees it. Forget
the prejudices and fads of the world around us. Get excited about
your high calling to be part of the body of Christ.

Accept your local church. Remember, 'Christ loved the church and
gave himself up for her' (Eph. 5:25). If he accepts and loves it, so can
you. Of course it's got faults, and none of the people are anywhere
near perfect. But what would you expect? It's made up of very
different and very human people, all from different backgrounds and
at different stages of their spiritual journey. If necessary, repent of
your critical attitude towards it or towards specific individuals. Seek
God's forgiveness and cleansing. Ask him to fill you with the grace
to accept and love even the people you find most difficult.

Accept your belonging as a call from God. He has put you there. Belonging isn't an option; it's his command.

Settle it in your mind that you belong in order to give, not just to get. Ask God to purge you of the consumer mentality. You may feel there's not much you can give or will be allowed to give; if so, ask God to show you two or three possible contributions to start with, such as getting alongside one specific person, believing prayer or a joyful spirit. Above all, ask him to enable you to show true, Christlike love.

Refuse to get drawn into anything that is un-Christlike. Make a point of turning away from gossip, criticism and grumbling.

Pray. Pray for the whole church. Pray for the leaders. Pray for the moving of the Spirit. When you enter the building on a Sunday, spend time praying for the powerful presence of the living God in everything that is done.

Be a real worshipper. If necessary, blow the mind of the worship-leader or preacher. If they should look out over the congregation expecting to see people singing songs with little thought for the meaning of the words, or settling down to listen to the sermon with an attitude of bored resignation, make sure they see at least one person who's really in touch with God and hungry to hear his voice.

Wash feet. Regularly do something that you feel is rather demeaning and that, really, somebody else ought to do. It could be stacking the chairs after a meeting, anonymously cleaning the toilets or picking up the litter. Instead of moaning about the mess the youth group has left in the kitchen, get in there and clear it up yourself – without telling anybody.

Encourage others to recognize and exercise their gifts. Be a great encourager. Be quick to spot embryonic giftings and to help people to develop them. Be patient; remember that learners aren't experts. Make a point of thanking people for what they do.

Find and exercise your own gifts. If you feel that you're not being given the opportunity to exercise a specific gift, talk the issue through with one of the church leaders. You may have to be patient; if the church already has twenty people exercising the gift of preaching, there may not be much space left on the rota for you to exercise yours! You may be able to think of some other way of using your gift, such as offering to speak in the local school assembly.

Think highly of others. Practise Christlike humility in your attitude to everyone in the church. Work hard at honouring others above yourself (Rom. 12:10) and considering others better than yourself (Phil. 2:3). Never look down on anyone in the church; remember Jesus' words about the first being last and the last first (Matt. 19:30). Fight the attitude that you're more spiritual or more committed than the other person. Follow the example of Christ: 'humble' yourself and make yourself 'nothing' (Phil. 2:5–8).

Keep your spiritual fervour (Rom. 12:11). Perhaps the biggest cause of problems in a local church is loss of spiritual fervour. People get weary and jaded, take their eyes off the Lord and settle for less than the best. Whatever you do, don't let this happen to you. Continue to be filled with the Spirit, on fire for the Lord and a means through which God can bless and encourage and inflame others. If you should feel that most of the others are spiritually cold, don't use your fervour to attack them. Instead, let it drive you to powerful prayer and redoubled love.

Have a special ministry to those 'whose faith is weak' (Rom. 14:1). Don't criticize them for being weak; pour so much love into their lives that they become strong. Remember Paul's teaching that where there is a conflict between the spiritually weak and the spiritually strong, it's the spiritually strong who should be prepared to give way (Rom. 14:13–21).

Work at promoting unity and peace. Inevitably, a local church contains such a mix of people that there are innumerable points at which disagreement and conflict may arise. But God not only calls us to unity and peace; he provides in Christ the way we can achieve them. You'll never agree with everybody; there will always be things that you don't like about other people in the church. But allow Christ's grace and love to enable you to accept and love them, and, where you disagree, to do so creatively and in overall harmony of purpose.

Support and encourage the leaders. Pray for them. Thank them. Show love to them in practical ways. Wherever possible, accept their leadership and follow it enthusiastically. If you are unhappy with aspects of it, talk with them about it; never grumble about the issues behind their backs. If others criticize them, politely refuse to listen, and suggest they follow Jesus' teaching in Matthew 18:15–17.

Be Christ-centred. Do all you can to make your contribution and the life of the church in general full of Jesus. Refuse to be sidetracked. Refuse to major on petty issues. It's Christ's church, and he's the one who really matters.

CHURCH 3: LEADERSHIP IN A LOCAL CHURCH

Leadership in the church can take several forms. There's the overall leading of the church, sometimes by a minister, or by a team, perhaps of elders. Then there's leadership of a specific activity of the church, such as a house group, a youth club or a soup run. And then there's a form of leadership exercised not so much by virtue of holding office, but as a result of who the person is. Whether they're aware of it or not, Christians who are mature and full of the Lord will be watched and followed by others, who, consciously or unconsciously, will look to them as models of true Christlikeness and Christian behaviour.

Being a leader, and being followed by others, is a big responsibility. Mercifully, there's no shortage of relevant teaching in the New Testament. Jesus was training his disciples to be leaders; Paul and the other letter-writers were concerned to encourage and instruct the young churches in every aspect of church life, particularly leadership. Three of Paul's letters, 1 and 2 Timothy and Titus, were specifically written on this theme.

Some New Testament teaching about leadership in the church

'You know that the rulers of the Gentiles lord it over them, and their high officials exercise authority over them. Not so with you. Instead, whoever wants to become great among you must be your servant, and whoever wants to be first must be your slave – just as the Son of Man did not come to be served, but to serve, and to give his life as a ransom for many' (Matt. 20:25–28).

'... you are not to be called "Rabbi", for you have only one Master and you are all brothers. And do not call anyone on earth "father", for you have one Father, and he is in heaven. Nor are you to be called "teacher" for you have one Teacher, the Christ. The greatest among you will be your servant. For whoever exalts himself will be humbled, and whoever humbles himself will be exalted' (Matt. 23:8–12).

'... do you truly love me? ... Feed my lambs ... Take care of my sheep ... Feed my sheep' (John 21:15–17).

Keep watch over yourselves and all the flock of which the Holy Spirit has made you overseers. Be shepherds of the church of God, which he bought with his own blood (Acts 20:28).

... the overseer must be above reproach, the husband of but one wife, temperate, self-controlled, respectable, hospitable, able to teach, not given to drunkenness, not violent but gentle, not quarrelsome, not a lover of money. He must manage his own family well ... He must not be a recent convert ... He must also have a good reputation with outsiders ...

Deacons, likewise, are to be men worthy of respect, sincere, not indulging in much wine, and not pursuing dishonest gain. They must keep hold of the deep truths of the faith with a clear conscience (1 Tim. 3:2–4, 8–9).

Don't let anyone look down on you because you are young, but

set an example for the believers in speech, in life, in love, in faith
and in purity ... devote yourself to the public reading of
Scripture, to preaching and to teaching. Do not neglect your gift
... Be diligent in these matters; give yourself wholly to them, so
that everyone may see your progress. Watch your life and
doctrine closely (1 Tim. 4:12–16).

... pursue righteousness, godliness, faith, love, endurance and
gentleness. Fight the good fight of the faith ... guard what has
been entrusted to your care (1 Tim. 6:11–12, 20).

... fan into flame the gift of God, which is in you ... be strong in
the grace that is in Christ Jesus ... Endure hardship with us like
a good soldier of Christ Jesus ... pursue righteousness, faith, love
and peace, along with those who call on the Lord out of a pure
heart. Don't have anything to do with foolish and stupid arguments, because you know they produce quarrels. And the Lord's
servant must not quarrel; instead, he must be kind to everyone,
able to teach, not resentful. Those who oppose him he must
gently instruct, in the hope that God will grant them repentance
leading them to a knowledge of the truth (2 Tim. 1:6, 2:1, 3,
22–25).

Preach the Word; be prepared in season and out of season;
correct, rebuke and encourage – with great patience and careful
instruction ... keep your head in all situations, endure hardship,
do the work of an evangelist, discharge all the duties of your
ministry (2 Tim. 4:2, 5).

Since an overseer is entrusted with God's work, he must be
blameless – not overbearing, not quick-tempered, not given to
drunkenness, not violent, not pursuing dishonest gain. Rather
he must be hospitable, one who loves what is good, who is self-
controlled, upright, holy and disciplined. He must hold firmly
to the trustworthy message as it has been taught, so that he can
encourage others by sound doctrine and refute those who
oppose it (Titus 1:7–9).

In everything set them an example by doing what is good. In your teaching show integrity, seriousness and soundness of speech that cannot be condemned (Titus 2:7–8).

Be shepherds of God's flock that is under your care, serving as overseers – not because you must, but because you are willing, as God wants you to be; not greedy for money, but eager to serve; not lording it over those entrusted to you, but being examples to the flock (1 Pet. 5:2–3).

What could I do to be an effective leader?

Model your leadership on Jesus. You may well be able to learn a lot from other leaders, but make being like Jesus your priority, and test all other approaches by him. Study his way of ministering to people; get close to him so that you know his heart in any given situation.

Enable the people to follow Jesus in you. There's quite a bit of debate about the issue of authority in leadership. Jesus warned clearly against the wrong sort of authority, but there are still several differing views on what sort of authority Christian leaders should exercise. The best answer is summed up in the words of John the Baptist: 'He must become greater; I must become less' (John 3:30). Our concern is not that people should follow us, but that they should follow Jesus. So our priority is that they should see more and more of Jesus in us, and that they should follow our lead, not because we are in authority over them, but because they are following Jesus as they see him in us.

Pray for your people. Remember Samuel's words, 'far be it from me that I should sin against the LORD by failing to pray for you' (1 Sam. 12:23).

Keep watch over yourself (Acts 20:28). You're in the front line of a spiritual battle. 'Satan has asked to sift you as wheat' (Luke 22:31). You can be sure that the powers of darkness will do all they can to wreck your ministry, preferably bringing you down with such a crash that many others will be wrecked in the process. We all know of horror stories of trusted Christian leaders who have fallen into serious sin. Don't think, 'It could never happen to me.' They probably thought that, too. Rather, take to heart Paul's words 'if you think you are standing firm, be careful that you don't fall!' (1 Cor. 10:12). Be especially careful in the sexual area. As leaders, we express love and care for our people and involvement with them in their various needs and situations, but it's all too easy for this to slide into the wrong sort of involvement. If you should find this beginning to happen to you, take drastic steps to stop it (Matt. 5:29–30). Watch other aspects of your life as well. Some leaders are particularly prone to pride and arrogance. Others lose their spiritual fervour, and operate just on the human level. Others exploit their position to their own advantage. Make sure it doesn't happen to you.

Expect people problems. People today don't like being led. We all have a tendency to want to do things our way. Authority is a dirty word. Criticizing and grumbling about our leaders is a national sport. Not surprisingly, the attitudes of those around us rub off on Christians' attitudes to those in leadership in the church. When people problems arise:

- *Do everything you can to take them in your stride.* Don't offer your resignation. Don't let them sidetrack you from your real work. Try not to let them take up too much time or emotional energy.
- *Hand them over to the Lord.* He's much better at coping with them than you are, and is willing to carry the pain of them for you.
- *Pray.* Pray for your reaction, that it will be Christlike. Pray for wisdom in the response you make. Pray for the person or people concerned, that God will do good things in their lives (Matt. 5:44).
- *Beware of rushing to defend yourself.* In some situations it may be wise graciously to clear up any misunderstandings, but, as a rule, if you follow an attack by a defence you're much more likely to get a second attack than if you follow the example of Jesus and simply refuse to defend yourself (Matt. 26:62–63; Is. 53:7).
- *Try not to take criticisms and grumbles too personally.* Every leader gets criticized; it's part of the price we have to pay. We're

walking the way Jesus walked. No servant is greater than his master. If they criticized Jesus, they'll criticize you. If they failed to follow Jesus, they'll fail to follow you (John15:20).

- *Beware of self-pity.* 'I do all this for them, and that's the way they treat me.' Try instead following the Beatitude 'Blessed are you when people insult you, persecute you and falsely say all kinds of evil against you because of me. Rejoice and be glad, because great is your reward in heaven, for in the same way they persecuted the prophets who were before you' (Matt. 5:11–12).
- *Check to see if there is anything you can learn from the criticisms or grumbles.* Even if they're largely unfounded, they may give you a clue to how you might do things better. Be humble enough to learn even from those who oppose you.
- *Respond with redoubled love and grace.* Make it your aim to win over those who are against you by your Christlike response and loving attitude. Go out of your way to say positive things about them to others. 'If your enemy is hungry, feed him; if he is thirsty, give him something to drink' (Rom. 12:20).
- *Keep a careful eye on your own reaction.* It can be all too easy for Christian leaders to bottle up feelings of hurt, anger and resentment, while seeking to show love and grace. If you do have these feelings, find a way of dealing with them that doesn't do anybody any damage. Take them to the Lord; tell him exactly how you feel; his shoulders are broad enough to take it. Talk it all through with a wise Christian friend, who will let you offload your feelings and help you to do so creatively. Go for a long walk; play rugby; go for a workout in the gym; take a break.

Think seriously about having a 'mentor'. If you have responsibility for others, it's reasonable that you should be responsible to someone. In some contexts this arises naturally: a children's worker is responsible to the youth pastor, or a house-group leader to the pastoral elder. In other situations you may have to approach someone to fulfil this role. Be honest with your 'mentor'. Share your burdens. Talk through issues. Pray together. Accept help. Receive encouragement. Be willing to be corrected.

Every now and then, lose a battle. It's not healthy for any leader to get his or her own way all the time. For your own good, and for the good of the people you're leading, you periodically need to cope with being overruled, admit you got it wrong and climb down. This shows all concerned that you're human, fallible, and haven't yet reached perfection. It also gives you a great opportunity to demonstrate how Christians should react when they are overruled. After all, that's something that's happening all the time; whenever you as leader make a decision you will be disappointing somebody who wanted it to go a different way. So take it as part of your leadership that you show them how to express grace and humility when you are disappointed and things don't work out your way. Accept the setback graciously and cheerfully; back the alternative decision enthusiastically. Your people will be watching to see how you react and will learn valuable lessons.

Take sabbaticals. Leadership is demanding and costly. Spiritual battles take their toll. Far too many Christian leaders get weary and jaded. Make sure that doesn't happen to you. Follow the biblical teaching and take periodic breaks, when you're free from leadership pressures and can be refreshed and renewed and build up your strength for the next tasks.

Work at making yourself dispensable. One of the reasons some leaders work themselves into the ground is that they believe they are indispensable: if they don't do the job, everything will collapse. Avoid thinking that way. Adopt, rather, the line Paul urged to Timothy: 'the things you have heard me say in the presence of many witnesses entrust to reliable men who will also be qualified to teach others' (2 Tim. 2:2). Always be on the lookout for people who have the beginnings of leadership gifts; remember they may not necessarily be the most obvious people. Give them opportunities to develop those gifts. Guide and train them; if necessary, work yourself out of your job.

CONFLICT

Conflict is a fact of life. No two people are the same. We all see things from different angles. We each bring our background, beliefs, experiences, values and ways of looking at things to bear on each situation, and, inevitably, we often come to different conclusions.

But conflict doesn't have to be negative or destructive. Ideally, conflict is positive and constructive. He thinks walking in the hills is an ideal way to spend a holiday; she thinks there's nothing better than lying on a beach. Rather than spending all their holiday arguing, they agree to spend alternate days hill-walking and lying on the beach – and end up having the best holiday ever. The over-fifties want to sing Wesley and Watts and Sankey; the under-fifties want all the latest hits. Instead of a church split, the worship is enriched by having a mixture of old and new.

The New Testament has two great words that we need to hear when we find ourselves in conflict situations. The first is 'reconcile'. At the heart of the gospel is the incredible truth that God has stepped into the biggest conflict of all time – the human race v. the living God – and has brought the conflict to an end. He has done this not by wiping out his opponents, but by giving his Son to be broken on a cross. Through Christ the conflict is ended; God and sinners are reconciled.

We are a reconciled people. What's more, we have a message and ministry of reconciliation (2 Cor. 5:18). Inevitably, then, reconciliation must be our priority in any conflict. Others may say that their main aim is to win the argument, or at the very least to come to a face-saving compromise. But our main aim is to be reconciled to our opponent. Compared with that, the issue we're arguing about fades into insignificance. In his great discussion of a conflict in Romans 14, Paul makes it quite clear that he person-ally was prepared to let go a deeply held theological principle if sticking to it was a stumbling-block or obstacle to another person (Rom. 14:13–23).

That brings us to the second great word: 'submit'. Conflicts arise and are perpetuated because each side insists on sticking by its principles, holding its ground, doing things its way. The only exit from the impasse is for one or both sides to climb down, give way, submit. And the New Testament teaching is that we as Christians must be the ones who take the lead in submitting. In this we are simply following the example set by God in Christ. He didn't demand that we submit to him; instead, he chose to submit himself to us, even to the point of letting us kill him.

Submission is something most of us find very hard. As a conflict develops, it gets harder. Once we've taken up a position, stated our case and given our reasons, and everybody knows about it, it's very costly to give way and climb down. It's for this reason we need to deal with conflicts as soon as they begin to arise. 'Settle matters quickly with your adversary,' said Jesus. Sort things out before he gets you to the courthouse. If you don't, the whole thing will escalate right out of control (Matt. 5:25).

Of course, there will be exceptions to the principle of submission. When Peter and the apostles were in conflict with the Sanhedrin, who had ordered them to stop teaching in the name of Jesus, their reply was, 'We must obey God rather than men!' (Acts 5:29). Martin Luther hardly submitted to the Diet of Worms. There will be times when submitting to God will mean standing firm against our human opponents. But these occasions will be in the minority. In most cases, to submit to God will mean obeying his command to humble ourselves and submit to our opponent.

As a rule, then, the Christian response to conflict is humble submission. That's not easy, since it goes against all our natural human reactions. But maybe it's even harder to decide whether or not the situation we're facing is one where, exceptionally, we shouldn't submit and where we need to stand firm – still, of course, in a humble spirit, at the clear command of God.

The problem is that when we're personally and emotionally involved, it's hard to get a true perspective. When we see two people arguing over how they should spend their holidays or which songs they should sing in church, we quite rightly feel that the issues at stake are hardly worth the energy that's being put into the conflict. Whichever way they decide, we know the sky won't fall in. But when it's we who are embroiled in a conflict, it's far more difficult to get things in perspective. All the issues tend to look major. And even if they don't, we have all sorts of ways of making molehills look like mountains. We argue that 'This is the thin end of the wedge,' or, 'There's a principle at stake.' 'I know that singing the occasional Wesley hymn doesn't seem much of a problem, but once we allow one or two older songs into our worship, there'll be no way of stopping it. We'll all end up singing Latin plainsong!' 'There's a principle at stake: are we or are we not going to use old-fashioned and unintelligible language in our worship?' Often we need to stop and ask questions. Are the issues really that important? Does it really matter that I get my way? Can I back down in this conflict without disobeying God?

Some Bible teaching on issues related to conflict

'Blessed are the peacemakers,
   for they will be called sons of God' (Matt. 5:9).

'You have heard that it was said to the people long ago, "Do not murder, and anyone who murders will be subject to judgment." But I tell you that anyone who is angry with his brother will be subject to judgment ...

   'Therefore, if you are offering your gift at the altar and there remember that your brother has something against you, leave your gift there in front of the altar. First go and be reconciled to your brother; then come and offer your gift' (Matt. 5:21, 23–24).

'You have heard that it was said, "Eye for eye, and tooth for tooth." But I tell you, Do not resist an evil person. If someone strikes you on the right cheek, turn to him the other also. And if someone wants to sue you and take your tunic, let him have your cloak as well. If someone forces you to go one mile, go with him two miles. Give to the one who asks you, and do not turn away from the one who wants to borrow from you.

   'You have heard that it was said, "Love your neighbour and hate your enemy." But I tell you: Love your enemies and pray for those who persecute you, that you may be sons of your Father in heaven' (Matt. 5:38–45).

'If your brother sins against you, go and show him his fault, just between the two of you. If he listens to you, you have won your brother over. But if he will not listen, take one or two others along, so that "every matter may be established by the testimony of two or three witnesses." If he refuses to listen to them, tell it to the church; and if he refuses to listen even to the church, treat him as you would a pagan or a tax collector' (Matt. 18:15–17).

Bless those who persecute you; bless and do not curse ...

Do not repay anyone evil for evil. Be careful to do what is right in the eyes of everybody. If it is possible, as far as it depends on you, live at peace with everyone. Do not take revenge, my friends, but leave room for God's wrath, for it is written: 'It is mine to avenge; I will repay,' says the Lord. On the contrary:

'If your enemy is hungry, feed him;
    if he is thirsty, give him something to drink.
In doing this, you will heap burning coals on his head.'

Do not be overcome by evil, but overcome evil with good (Rom. 12:14, 17–21).

Let us therefore make every effort to do what leads to peace and mutual edification ...

We who are strong ought to bear with the failings of the weak and not to please ourselves (Rom. 14:19; 15:1).

I appeal to you, brothers, in the name of our Lord Jesus Christ, that all of you agree with one another so that there may be no divisions among you and that you may be perfectly united in mind and thought (1 Cor. 1:10).

God ... reconciled us to himself through Christ and gave us the ministry of reconciliation: that God was reconciling the world to himself in Christ, not counting men's sin against them. And he has committed to us the message of reconciliation (2 Cor. 5:18–19).

... live a life worthy of the calling you have received. Be

completely humble and gentle; be patient, bearing with one another in love. Make every effort to keep the unity of the Spirit through the bond of peace (Eph. 4:1–3).

Submit to one another out of reverence for Christ (Eph. 5:21).

If you have any encouragement from being united with Christ, if any comfort from his love, if any fellowship with the Spirit, if any tenderness and compassion, then make my joy complete by being like-minded, having the same love, being one in spirit and purpose. Do nothing out of selfish ambition or vain conceit, but in humility consider others better than yourselves. Each of you should look not only to your own interests, but also to the interests of others. Your attitude should be the same as that of Christ Jesus:

Who, being in very nature God,
    did not consider equality with God something to be grasped,
but made himself nothing,
    taking the very nature of a servant,
    being made in human likeness.
And being found in appearance as a man,
    he humbled himself
    and became obedient to death – even death on a cross!
    (Phil. 2:1–8).

Therefore, as God's chosen people, holy and dearly loved, clothe yourselves with compassion, kindness, humility, gentleness and patience. Bear with each other and forgive whatever grievances you may have against one another. Forgive as the Lord forgave you. And over all these virtues put on love, which binds them all together in perfect unity.

Let the peace of Christ rule in your hearts, since as members of one body you were called to peace (Col. 3:12–15).

What causes fights and quarrels among you? Don't they come from your desires that battle within you? You want something but don't get it. You kill and covet, but you cannot have what you want. You quarrel and fight ...

... Scripture says:

> 'God opposes the proud
>   but gives grace to the humble.'

Submit yourselves, then, to God. Resist the devil, and he will flee from you. Come near to God and he will come near to you. Wash your hands, you sinners, and purify your hearts, you double-minded ... Humble yourselves before the Lord, and he will lift you up.

Brothers, do not slander one another ... who are you to judge your neighbour? (Jas. 4:1–2, 6–8, 10–12).

What could I do when I find myself in a conflict situation?

Love. There are no two ways about it; the priority for a Christian in any conflict must be to show the love of Jesus. Whether the conflict is with a fellow Christian, a family member, a colleague at work, or an enemy who is persecuting you, the command is the same: to love, and to demonstrate that love in action. Showing true *agapē* (love) is, in fact, the exact opposite of our natural re-action in a conflict situation. Naturally, we want to assert ourselves and our needs and ideas in opposition to the other person. But *agapē* has as its primary concern the other person's good. According to the Bible, no other principle or factor is of greater importance than the principle of love. Whatever else you do in a conflict, make sure you show love.

Forbear. A cluster of New Testament words make it clear that as Christians we should have a very high tolerance level. They're vari-ously translated as 'forbearance', 'patience', 'longsuffering', 'endurance', 'tolerance' and 'bearing with'. They describe a quality found primarily in God (Rom. 2:4; 3:25), expressed in Jesus (1 Pet. 2:23) and commanded in his followers (Eph. 4:2; Col. 3:12–13). They call us to put up with a lot without retaliating; indeed, if we follow the example of Jesus, to be prepared to put up with anything. Most of us have a fairly low tolerance level; we can take so much, but then comes 'the last straw', and the balloon goes up. By the grace of God and the power of the Spirit, whose fruit is 'patience' (literally 'longsuffering') and 'self-control' (Gal. 5:22), push that tolerance level as high as you possibly can.

If at all possible, submit. Ask yourself, 'Would the way of Jesus be to give way in this situation? Is this an issue it's essential to fight over? Am I sure I need to stand my ground here? There are perhaps three situations in which it would be wrong to give way and submit. One is when to do so would damage the other person. A parent should not submit to little Johnny when he demands a large bar of chocolate; the way of love is to stand firm. A second is when we're standing up for someone else who is particularly weak and vulnerable; here it's not our own interests that are at stake, but the well-being of the vulnerable person. A third is when to submit would break a command of God.

If the situation is such that you choose not to submit:

- *Fight the issue, not the person.* It's not the boss you're opposed to; it's her dishonest way of running the department. Hate the sin, but keep loving the sinner. 'Love your enemies and pray for those who persecute you' (Matt. 5:44). Go out of your way to show that love. If you complain to your colleagues about her practices, go out of your way to say something positive and loving about her as well. Do your utmost to prevent the issue becoming divisive. 'This thing is not going to drive us apart, but bring us closer together.'
- *Study the Bible's teaching on conflict, and its principles for resolving it.* Matthew 18:15–17 is particularly important: always make sure you go directly to the person concerned before you complain about the issue to others.
- *Commit yourself to resolving the conflict constructively.* Your goal is not to get your own way, or to win, but to enable all those involved to find the best way of going forward at this time, given all the complexities of the situation and of the people involved.
- *Pray.* Pray for yourself and for those who agree with you. Pray for the other side. Pray for the wisdom and grace of the Holy Spirit. Pray for the mind of Christ. Pray that both sides will be protected from anything that would grieve the Spirit in this conflict.

- *Accept that the insights of the other side mixed with yours will be richer than your insights alone.*
- *Where there is a complex range of issues, try selecting one at a time to deal with.* Pick one of the less difficult issues. Talk it through; plan specific, practical steps. When one has been sorted out, go on to another.
- *Check all your assumptions.* Everyone makes assumptions.
- *Confine the conflict.* Don't let it spread. Resist the temptation to bolster your case by drawing in allies.
- *Where necessary, call in someone acceptable to both sides to help to resolve the conflict.* It's vital to trust and follow this person's advice, even if it seems biased towards the other side.

Take special care to avoid the standard pitfalls of conflicts:

- *Feelings of self-pity, anger, resentment, hurt, victimization and rejection.* These may be inevitable to some extent, but do all you can to avoid letting them control your attitudes and relationships.
- *Being pushed, or pushing the other person, into an extreme position.* You need to emphasize common ground and to be working towards agreement, not getting further apart.
- *Failing to understand the other person's point of view, or misrepresenting, exaggerating or caricaturing it.* It's always easier to knock down a 'man of straw', or to justify our position by misrepresenting the opposing one. Take special care to listen to the other side, to do everything you can to understand and empathize and to present its case accurately.
- *Refusing to give way because 'a principle is at stake'.* Many 'principles' are not worth sticking up for at the cost of a major conflict. After all, people matter more than principles, and love must be the overriding principle at all times (Col. 3:14). Give the 'principle' over to God and let him take care of it.
- *In a conflict with fellow Christians, abusing the Bible or theological or 'spiritual' arguments.* Of course, we want to show how biblical or theological or spiritual we are. But church history is full of conflict situations where both sides have been convinced that the Bible and theology and God were on their side, and have spent their time using them to fight other Christians. The

Bible verses you're tempted to use as ammunition were almost certainly not written with your particular conflict in mind. 'Theological' principles can notoriously be applied in more than one way. And claims like 'God told me in a dream that we must do it this way,' 'God won't bless our church unless we do it that way,' or, 'I'm the minister, so you must do it my way,' though they may look very spiritual, are in fact a very dangerous form of manipulation.

Don't take seriously what is said in the heat of the moment. When people are worked up they exaggerate their case or say things they are sorry for afterwards. Make allowances. Don't store up such statements to use as ammunition later.

Accept that the future is more important than the past. Never rake up the past. Love 'keeps no records of wrongs' (1 Cor. 13:4). Concentrate on building a good foundation for the future. Work hard at forgiving and forgetting.

Check to see if external factors are causing or exacerbating the conflict. These might be tensions and stresses from other sources, poor working conditions or inadequate communication. Do what you can to make sure these are addressed.

Check to see whether at least part of the cause of conflict lies in you. This is especially important if you find yourself frequently getting into conflicts. It could be that something in you makes you specially vulnerable to conflict, such as insecurity, fear or difficulty in coping with certain situations or relating to certain people. You may need to access the wisdom of others on this; if you decide there is an issue here, do everything you can to deal with it.

DEATH

The Bible is realistic about both the awfulness of death and the wonder of God's victory over it through Christ. Through his resurrection the power of death to destroy is broken; it has been changed from disaster to the gateway to glory. But it remains an 'enemy' (1 Cor. 15:26). It still brings pain, sorrow and loss.

Many of those around us seek to cope with death by ignoring it or by desperately seeking to put it off as long as possible. As Christians we can face death with peace and confidence, knowing that the Lord Jesus is the Living One, who has passed through death and conquered it, and who holds the keys of death and of life beyond death (Rev. 1:18).

In some ways, experiencing the death of a loved one is harder to bear than facing our own death. Watching someone else suffering can bring as much pain as suffering ourselves; and when it is a loved one who dies, though we know their suffering is over, we are the ones who are left to cope with the sorrow and loss of bereavement. Being a Christian doesn't take away the grief and loneliness; these are inevitable if we lose someone close to us. But God offers us great comfort in our sadness, and promises us his grace to bring us through.

Some of the Bible's teaching on death

> Even though I walk
>   through the valley of the shadow of death,
> I will fear no evil,
>   for you are with me;
> your rod and your staff,
>   they comfort me (Ps. 23:4).

> The Spirit of the Sovereign LORD is on me,
>   because ...
> He has sent me to bind up the broken-hearted,
> to ... provide for those who grieve in Zion –
>   to bestow on them a crown of beauty
>   instead of ashes,
> the oil of gladness
>   instead of mourning,
> and a garment of praise
>   instead of a spirit of despair (Is. 61:1, 3).

'Blessed are those who mourn,
   for they will be comforted' (Matt. 5:4).

... they went and told Jesus [of the death of John the Baptist].
   When Jesus heard what had happened, he withdrew by boat privately to a solitary place (Matt. 14:12–13).

... none of us lives to himself alone and none of us dies to himself alone. If we live, we live to the Lord; and if we die, we die to the Lord. So, whether we live or die, we belong to the Lord (Rom. 14:7–8).

Christ has indeed been raised from the dead, the firstfruits of those who have fallen asleep.
   ... the perishable must clothe itself with the imperishable, and the mortal with immortality. When the perishable has been clothed with the imperishable, and the mortal with immortality, then the saying that is written will come true: 'Death has been swallowed up in victory.'

'Where, O death, is your victory?
   Where, O death, is your sting?'

... thanks be to God! He gives us the victory through our Lord Jesus Christ (1 Cor. 15:20, 53–55, 57).

Praise be to the God and Father of our Lord Jesus Christ, the Father of compassion and the God of all comfort, who comforts us in all our troubles, so that we can comfort those in any trouble with the comfort we ourselves have received from God. For just as the sufferings of Christ flow over into our lives, so also through Christ our comfort overflows (2 Cor. 1:3–5).

... we know that the one who raised the Lord Jesus from the dead will also raise us with Jesus ...
   Therefore we do not lose heart. Though outwardly we are wasting away, yet inwardly we are being renewed day by day ... we fix our eyes not on what is seen, but on what is unseen.

... if the earthly tent we live in is destroyed, we have a building from God, an eternal house in heaven ... while we are in this tent, we groan and are burdened, because we do not wish to be unclothed but to be clothed with our heavenly dwelling, so that what is mortal may be swallowed up by life. Now it is God who has made us for this very purpose and has given us the Spirit as a deposit, guaranteeing what is to come.

Therefore we are always confident and know that as long as we are at home in the body we are away from the Lord. We live by faith, not by sight. We are confident, I say, and would prefer to be away from the body and at home with the Lord (2 Cor. 4:14, 16, 18; 5:1, 4–8).

I eagerly expect and hope that I will in no way be ashamed, but will have sufficient courage so that now as always Christ will be exalted in my body, whether by life or by death. For to me, to live is Christ and to die is gain. If I am to go on living in the body, this will mean fruitful labour for me. Yet what shall I choose? I do not know! I am torn between the two: I desire to depart and be with Christ, which is better by far; but it is more necessary for you that I remain in the body (Phil. 1:20–24).

Brothers, we do not want you to be ignorant about those who fall asleep, or to grieve like the rest of men, who have no hope. We believe that Jesus died and rose again and so we believe that God will bring with Jesus those who have fallen asleep in him ... so we will be with the Lord for ever. Therefore encourage each other with these words (1 Thess. 4:13–14, 17).

[Jesus] shared in their humanity so that by his death he might destroy him who holds the power of death – that is, the devil – and free those who all their lives were held in slavery by their fear of death (Heb. 2:14–15).

'Do not be afraid. I am the First and the Last. I am the Living One; I was dead, and behold I am alive for ever and ever! And I hold the keys of death and Hades' (Rev. 1:17–18).

I saw a new heaven and a new earth ... I heard a loud voice from
the throne saying, 'Now the dwelling of God is with men, and
he will live with them. They will be his people, and God himself
will be with them and be their God. He will wipe every tear
from their eyes. There will be no more death or mourning ... for
the old order of things has passed away' (Rev. 21:1–2, 3–4).

The book of Psalms contains many passage written by people
passing though darkness and grief; the writers are very honest about
their feelings, but always they come back to the faithfulness of God
who will in the end bring them through. See, for example, Psalms
6; 22; 31; 57; 69; 71; 90; 130. Here's a selection from two of them.

> My God, my God, why have you forsaken me?
>> Why are you so far from saving me,
>> so far from the words of my groaning?
> O my God, I cry out by day, but you do not answer,
>> by night, and am not silent ...
> ... you brought me out of the womb;
>> you made me trust in you
>> even at my mother's breast ...
> Do not be far from me,
>> for trouble is near
>> and there is no-one to help ...
> I am poured out like water,
>> and all my bones are out of joint.
> My heart has turned to wax;
>> it has melted away within me ...
> But you, O LORD, be not far off;
>> O my Strength, come quickly to help me ...
> I will declare your name to my brothers;
>> in the congregation I will praise you.
> You who fear the LORD, praise him!
>> All you descendants of Jacob, honour him!
>> Revere him, all you descendants of Israel!
> For he has not despised or disdained
>> the suffering of the afflicted one;
> he has not hidden his face from him

but has listened to his cry for help
(Ps. 22:1–2, 9, 11, 14, 19, 22–24).

Save me, O God,
for the waters have come up to my neck.
I sink in the miry depths,
where there is no foothold.
I have come into the deep waters;
the floods engulf me.
I am worn out calling for help;
my throat is parched.
My eyes fail,
looking for my God ...
But I pray to you, O LORD,
in the time of your favour;
in your great love, O God,
answer me with your sure salvation.
Rescue me from the mire,
do not let me sink ...
Answer me, O LORD, out of the goodness of your love;
in your great mercy turn to me.
Do not hide your face from your servant;
answer me quickly, for I am in trouble ...
I will praise God's name in song
and glorify him with thanksgiving ...
The poor will see and be glad –
you who seek God, may your hearts live!
(Ps. 69:1–3, 13–14, 16–17, 30, 32).

What could I do when facing illness and the prospect of death?

Go gently on yourself. Accept that you will experience a wide range of emotions in your reaction to your illness and to the prospect of dying and pain. These are the natural responses of your body and your emotions to what you are going through. Seek to take them in your stride; don't be afraid of them; God will give you the strength you need for each new situation.

Draw near to God. Make sure that your relationship with him is untainted. Kneel again at the cross, and let Jesus deal with all your sin. Put yourself, your life and your death into his hands. Take the opportunity of getting things in the right perspective, of putting the Lord at the centre of everything and of enjoying his presence and goodness in a way you've never experienced before.

Settle your accounts. Take the opportunity to put right all you can think of from the past. Restore broken relationships; write letters of apology; make reparation; draw very near to your family and friends.

Relive and enjoy the good things of the past. Look through old photograph albums and diaries. Talk about old times with your loved ones. Don't worry if it upsets you; there's nothing wrong with having a good cry.

Remember that through Christ the future is bright. Death has been transformed into the gateway to glory. God is preparing for you a new resurrection body, free from all suffering and pain. Seek to follow Paul's example and find strength for the present by focusing on the future (2 Cor. 4:16 – 5: 1).

Find and do something really worthwhile in your last days. Write a poem or a journal incorporating what you've learnt from life. Paint a picture. Befriend a lonely or hurting person. Help somebody to faith in Jesus.

Remember that this is a tough time for those nearest to you and those who care for you. Do everything you can to encourage and help them. Be quick to apologize when pain or the strength of your feelings makes you short-tempered or grumpy.

Where necessary, talk about your feelings and fears with a minister, or counsellor or someone who will understand. Be honest, and be willing to receive help in facing your feelings and the prospect of death. You don't have to walk this path alone; let others walk it with you and carry some of the burden.

Talk through plans for the future with those closest to you. These may include funeral arrangements, but remember too to equip your loved ones to face the future without you.

Pray. You will very likely want to pray for healing, knowing that God could deal with the illness and give you more years to live. Get others to pray for your healing as well, possibly following

James's advice and getting the elders of the church to anoint you and pray for you in the Lord's name (Jas. 5:14). But remember to leave the final decision in God's hands (Matt. 26:39). In any of our prayers, we must not tell God what to do. Rather, we tell him what we would like him to do, and leave the doing to him. And don't just pray for healing. Pray, with Paul, that Christ will be exalted 'whether by life or by death' (Phil. 1:20). Pray for those caring for you, for your witness, for other sufferers. If you find it hard to pray, don't worry; get others to hold you before God in their prayers, while you just put yourself and all your struggles into God's gracious and powerful hands.

What could I do when going through bereavement?

Allow yourself to grieve. True, our grieving is different from the hopelessness of those who don't know Christ (1 Thess. 4:13). But losing someone we love through death is still a most shattering experience. Even though we know there is life after death, we still have to go through the pain of parting, the sense of loss, and the grieving process. Don't underestimate the shock and sadness the death of a loved one brings. Weep, as Jesus wept at the tomb of Lazarus (John 11:35). Forget about a 'stiff upper lip'. Tears and grieving are a God-given and beautiful expression of the extent to which we loved the one who has died, and how much we miss him or her.

Remember that grieving takes time. The intensity of our grieving and the time it takes for us to work through the process will vary greatly. In some situations death is something we welcome, a merciful release, or the timely closing of a long and good life. In those circumstances the pain of loss and grieving will be less. At other times the pain will be greatly increased by, say, the suddenness or the circumstances of the death, or because the person is young or has died tragically. Let the process of grieving follow its natural course. Accept that you'll have good days and bad days. Expect mood swings and steps 'backwards' in the grieving process; you may feel fine one week and then have to go through a bad patch the next. As in the case of a bodily wound or illness, healing will come gradually, at the right pace. If you should feel that you are making no progress in the process of healing, talk to someone who can help you.

Accept help. There's an independent streak in most of us. Maybe you don't like to admit to others that you are struggling. But when you're passing through bereavement, others want to help you. Let them show their love, concern and support. Many people find that they go through all sorts of feelings and emotional experiences during grieving, including anger, self-pity, guilt, depression and despair. If you're struggling with your feelings, find someone you can talk to honestly and openly, who will support you and give you wise advice. You won't be able to pour out your innermost feelings to everyone, but there are times when it will be a great help to talk through your anger, fears and loneliness with someone who will listen and understand. Consider getting help and support from a local bereavement network.

Don't worry if you have vivid dreams or strange experiences of the person being near you. When we've been used to having someone around for years, the mind takes time to adjust to his or her absence. But resist the temptation to fantasize or to try to get in touch with your loved one. However hard it is, you need to adjust to the reality of your loss.

Talk about the person to others. Treasure memories. Relive the good experiences of the past. Give thanks to God for all he gave you together. But don't get stuck in the past; use it as a foundation to build a good future.

If possible, avoid major changes in the early days of bereavement. It might be unwise, for example, to move to a new area and thus lose a supportive circle of friends.

Have someone who is willing to let you make contact at any time if you are feeling particularly low. This person doesn't need to be a professional counsellor – just someone who will listen, provide a shoulder to cry on, make you a cup of tea and generally stand by you in your need.

Keep trusting God. At times all sorts of questions will arise in your mind, and you may well feel like crying, with Jesus, 'My God, my God, why have you forsaken me?' (Mark 15:34). As in so many situations in life, it's virtually impossible at the time to understand why God is allowing sadness and loss into our lives.

Maybe one day we'll be able to look back and see how he has worked it all into his perfect and beautiful plan, but at the time we have to keep trusting him even when we don't know the answers to our questions. This is faith. It's not blind faith, but faith founded on the firmest of foundations: the love, power and promises of a God who has broken the power of death and who has said he'll never leave or forsake us (Heb. 13:5).

As time goes by, work at developing new interests and friendships.

EDUCATION

There are several possible answers to the question 'What is the purpose of education?' Perhaps the commonest is, 'To get a good job.' Clearly, there's some wisdom in this, but there are alarming statistics of those who have gone through a university education but can't find a job, or at least not the kind of job their education was supposed to be preparing them for.

A less pragmatic answer is, 'To enrich life.' We study history or literature not primarily with a view to getting a good job, but because they are part of our heritage as human beings, and studying them helps us to learn about the world and about ourselves, broadening our horizons, expanding our ideas and understanding and enriching our lives.

Sadly, for many who are seeking education a significant motive is status. Our society seems to brand those who leave school early or don't go on to university as failures. All too often parents seem to be driven by the need to see their children doing well and gaining qualifications, apparently assuming that if this doesn't happen others will look down on them.

Undoubtedly, too, there are commercial interests involved in promoting education. Education is big business; the competition to enlist students is fierce. Even top Oxford and Cambridge colleges now work hard at persuading promising students to apply for places so that they can climb higher in the university league tables.

Education in Bible times was very different from what it is today. Perhaps there are three elements in it, however, from which we could have something to learn. The first is the primary role of parents and the family or community. There's a tendency today to assume that education is the responsibility of the educators; it's the job of teachers to teach, or of the church's youth workers to train our children in Christian truth; parents can and should leave the job to them. In the Bible the task belongs specifically to the parents, helped by the wider family, local community and church.

A second element is the broad practical nature of education in the Bible. This included the skills training handed on from parents to children that would enable them to work for a living, but it was also education on how to live, and how to follow the commands of God and the teaching of Jesus. Facts and theories had a place; children learnt about the mighty acts of God, the history of the Hebrew nation, the stories of Jesus, and as much of the theology of Paul as they could cope with. But all this was with a view to living as the people of God. Knowing was not an end in itself; it was a means to the greater ends of living and being.

Linked to these two elements was a third. The primary means of learning was living with someone who modelled what was being taught. This was true, of course, of parents; and it is particularly seen in the training Jesus gave his disciples. The call was not 'Learn from my teaching,' but 'Follow me.'

Bible teaching relevant to education

Fix these words of mine in your hearts and minds; tie them as symbols on your hands and bind them on your foreheads. Teach them to your children, talking about them when you sit at home and when you walk along the road, when you lie down and when you get up. Write them on the door-frames of your houses and on your gates, so that your days and the days of your children may be many in the land (Deut. 11:18–21).

> Listen, my son, to your father's instruction
> and do not forsake your mother's teaching
> (Prov. 1:8).

> Listen, my sons, to a father's instruction;
>   pay attention and gain understanding.
> I give you sound learning,
>   so do not forsake my teaching.
> When I was a boy in my father's house,
>   still tender, and an only child of my mother,
> he taught me and said,
>   'Lay hold of my words with all your heart;
>   keep my commands and you will live' ...
> My son, pay attention to what I say;
>   listen closely to my words.
> Do not let them out of your sight,
>   keep them within your heart;
> for they are life to those who find them
>   and health to a man's whole body.
> Above all else, guard your heart,
>   for it is the wellspring of life
>   (Prov. 4:1–4, 20–23).

[Jesus'] disciples came to him, and he began to teach them (Matt. 5:1–2).

Fathers, do not exasperate your children; instead, bring them up in the training and instruction of the Lord (Eph. 6:4).

All Scripture is God-breathed and is useful for teaching, rebuking, correcting and training in righteousness, so that the man of God may be thoroughly equipped for every good work (2 Tim. 3:16).

What could I do to provide an education for my children?

Be the key educator in your children's lives. More important than choosing the right school is accepting your responsibility to teach them true values and to model true godliness. Be determined that your children will be able to say, 'I learnt more about the things that really matter from my parents than from all my teachers.'

Start at the beginning. Give priority time to your children. Play with them; talk to them; read to them. Take them for walks and give them a love of nature and of the world around us. Talk to them about God, Jesus and the truths of the Bible. Pray with them – real prayers, not just childish prayers. Let them learn from you what it means to be a real person.

Keep up the interest. When they do go to school, continue to be involved in what they're learning. Talk about it with them. Keep it going when they get to secondary school; they'll teach you a lot, but you can still go on influencing them. Remember the horrific statistic that the average child spends only three minutes a day talking with his or her father; be determined that your children will get something far better.

Seek God's guidance about the right school. Choosing schools is a big responsibility, but remember that it's not a matter of life and death. God can and does use both state and private schools, inner-city and elitist schools, secular and Christian schools. Provided the basis in the home is secure, a child will be able to cope with antagonism in the classroom, as many Christian families experienced under the communist regimes in eastern Europe.

Points to consider in choosing a school include:

- *The nature of the school.* Check carefully the values on which the school operates and teaches its pupils. Use the opportunity to talk with the staff on open evenings and the like. Talk with other parents whose children are there. The fact that it's a state school doesn't necessarily mean that it is opposed to Christian values; many state schools have excellent Christian staff. If its values are largely anti-Christian, how will you counter these in your child's education?
- *The specific strengths of the school.* Some elements of what the school provides may be particularly suited to your child's need or abilities, such as a focus on music, sport or a specific academic subject.
- *The school's teaching philosophy and priorities.* These are worth exploring. Most schools have an impressive mission statement; find out how and to what extent this is put into practice. In these days of financial constraints, check the school's priorities.

Do smart buildings or the latest equipment come first, or is the emphasis on small classes? Is it more interested in getting pupils into Oxbridge than in developing every child's potential to the full? Are the staff enthusiastic about the school? Is there a high turnover of staff?

- *Access and transport.* There may be a better school further away, but does it justify the cost and hassle of transport?
- *The cost of a private school.* Can you afford it? Is it justifiable in today's world? Will the education there necessarily be better than in a state school? Is it possible to get a scholarship or bursary?
- *The benefits of being involved in a local school and so in the local community.*
- *The benefits of a specifically Christian school.* These would particularly include the provision of a relatively secure environment and the promotion of Christian values and teaching. How will you cope with the possible disadvantage of a narrow education and inadequate preparation for life in a generally secular world?

What could I do to further my own education?

Decide whether further or higher education is for you. Think through the reasons for and against further or higher education. Don't go to college just because that's what everyone else is doing, because your parents or teachers push you, or because it's a standard way of gaining status these days. What is it you want out of your education? Write down the pros and cons. Balance them up. Pray over them.

Consider the possibility of postponing higher education. Take a 'gap' year or two, or more. There are plenty of Christian and secular organizations that will welcome the contribution you could make and can offer you a range of interesting experiences. Or spend a year or two earning some money to see you through college. Delaying your higher education often means that you appreciate it more when you undertake it; your life experience enriches your studies. If you do plan a gap time in some remote part of the world, it's wise to secure your university place before you go; putting in an application from a remote Nepali village can be difficult!

Choose your subject with care. It's much better to select a subject that you'll enjoy studying for three years than one that you're good at but find boring. You may feel that usefulness for your future career is the primary consideration, or you may decide on some broader topic of study that will enrich you as a person, without necessarily giving you money-making skills.

Choose your college or university. Once you've decided what you'd like to study, decide where it's best to study it. Most schools are well equipped to help you with basic information on this, but the task of finding out about courses and visiting prospective universities is up to you. When visiting a university, take the opportunity to get the feel of it and of the community in which it's set. Talk with students and prospective tutors. University life isn't all study; check out its social and community aspects. Find out whether there's a Christian Union in the university or college, and what the churches are like in the area; is there one where you would feel at home and which you could make your spiritual base?

Think about a Christian college. Consider the possibility of a specifically Christian degree course that will strengthen you as a Christian and equip you for effective Christian service, whatever particular career you may follow. Most Bible colleges now offer university-validated degree courses. These are often degrees specifically in theology, but an increasing number include other major elements, such as music, sport, youth work and counselling. Like Christian schools, Christian colleges have both advantages and disadvantages that need to be carefully weighed up.

Work out how you're going to finance your course. Most first-degree courses still attract a mandatory grant, but this does not cover all the expenses of the course. Are your parents able to help? Could you work part time or in the vacations to support yourself? Or would you be happy going for a student loan?

Home or away? One way of saving on cost may be to go to a local college or university so that you can live at home. In some countries, such as France, this is the accepted thing to do. Besides saving you money, living at home will enable you to keep in touch with your circle of friends and your home church. Conversely, the course you want may not be available locally, or you may feel it's time to leave home, to make a new life for yourself, to develop new friends and to explore a different church.

Environmental issues

Some Bible teaching relevant to environmental issues

In the beginning God created the heavens and the earth ...

> So God created man
> in his own image,
> in the image of God
> he created him;
> male and female
> he created them.

God blessed them and said to them, 'Be fruitful and increase in number; fill the earth and subdue it. Rule over the fish of the sea and the birds of the air and over every living creature that moves on the ground' ...

God saw all that he had made, and it was very good (Gen. 1:1, 27–28, 31).

'For six years you are to sow your fields and harvest the crops, but during the seventh year let the land lie unploughed and unused. Then the poor among your people may get food from it, and the wild animals may eat what they leave. Do the same with your vineyard and your olive grove.

'Six days do your work, but on the seventh do not work, so that your ox and your donkey may rest and the slave born in your household, and the alien as well, may be refreshed' (Exod. 23:10–12).

'Do not pollute the land where you are. Bloodshed pollutes the land, and atonement cannot be made for the land on which blood has been shed, except by the blood of the one who shed it. Do not defile the land where you live and where I dwell, for I, the LORD, dwell among the Israelites' (Num. 35:33–34).

Do not muzzle an ox while it is treading out the grain (Deut. 25:4).

> The heavens declare the glory of God;
>> the skies proclaim the work of his hands.
> Day after day they pour forth speech;
>> night after night they display knowledge ...
> Their voice goes out into all the earth,
>> their words to the ends of the world (Ps. 19:1–2, 4).

> The earth is the LORD's, and everything in it,
>> the world, and all who live in it;
> for he founded it upon the seas
>> and established it upon the waters (Ps. 24:1).

> Love and faithfulness meet together,
>> righteousness and peace kiss each other.
> Faithfulness springs forth from the earth,
>> and righteousness looks down from heaven.
> The LORD will indeed give what is good,
>> and our land will yield its harvest (Ps. 85:10–12).

> Let the heavens rejoice, let the earth be glad
>> let the sea resound, and all that is in it;
>> let the fields be jubilant, and everything in them.
> Then all the trees of the forest will sing for joy;
>> they will sing before the LORD, for he comes,
>> he comes to judge the earth.
> He will judge the world in righteousness
>> and the peoples in his truth (Ps. 96:11–13).

> The wolf will live with the lamb,

the leopard will lie down with the goat,
the calf and the lion and the yearling together;
    and a little child will lead them.
The cow will feed with the bear,
    their young will lie down together,
    and the lion will eat straw like the ox ...
They will neither harm nor destroy
    on all my holy mountain,
for the earth will be full of the knowledge of the LORD
    as the waters cover the sea (Is. 11:6–7, 9).

The earth is defiled by its people;
    they have disobeyed the laws,
violated the statutes
    and broken the everlasting covenant.
Therefore a curse consumes the earth;
    its people must bear their guilt (Is. 24:5–6).

'Woe to him who piles up stolen goods
    and makes himself wealthy by extortion! ...
... you have plundered many nations ...
You have plotted the ruin of many peoples ...
The stones of the wall will cry out,
    and the beams of the woodwork will echo it ...

'For the earth will be filled with the knowledge
    of the glory of the LORD,
    as the waters cover the sea' (Hab. 2:6, 8, 10, 11, 14).

'Your kingdom come,
your will be done
    on earth as it is in heaven' (Matt. 6:10).

'Are not five sparrows sold for two pennies? Yet not one of them
is forgotten by God' (Luke 12:6).

The creation waits in eager expectation for the sons of God to
be revealed. For the creation was subjected to frustration, not by

its own choice, but by the will of the one who subjected it, in
hope that the creation itself will be liberated from its bondage to
decay and brought into the glorious freedom of the children of
God. We know that the whole creation has been groaning as in
the pains of childbirth right up to the present time. Not only so,
but we ourselves, who have the firstfruits of the Spirit, groan
inwardly as we wait eagerly for our adoption as sons, the
redemption of our bodies. For in this hope we were saved (Rom.
8:19–24).

... long ago by God's word the heavens existed and the earth was
formed out of water and by water. By these waters also the world
of that time was deluged and destroyed. By the same word the
present heavens and earth are reserved for fire, being kept for the
day of judgment and the destruction of ungodly men.
　... the Day of the Lord will come like a thief. The heavens will
disappear with a roar: the elements will be destroyed by fire, and
the earth and everything in it will be laid bare.
　Since everything will be destroyed in this way, what kind of
people ought you to be? You ought to live holy and godly lives
as you look forward to the day of God and speed its coming.
That day will bring about the destruction of the heavens by fire,
and the elements will melt in the heat. But in keeping with his
promise we are looking forward to a new heaven and a new
earth, the home of righteousness (2 Pet. 3:5–7, 10–13).

'The time has come for judging the dead,
　and for rewarding your servants the prophets
and your saints and those who reverence your name,
　both small and great –
and for destroying those who destroy the earth' (Rev. 11:18).

I saw a new heaven and a new earth, for the first heaven and the
first earth had passed away, and there was no longer any sea
(Rev. 21:1).

The environmental crisis we face today on planet Earth was un-
known in Bible times, so it's unsurprising that it's not specifically

addressed. Nevertheless, the Scriptures teach that the Earth is God's creation, that he cares for it, that he's concerned for all aspects of it, and that the damage brought about by human sin cries out for redemption. There is a very strong awareness in the Bible of the impact of human actions on the world around us. We can pollute the land, not just by pouring noxious chemicals into its rivers, but by oppressing its inhabitants or by practising greed or selfish extortion; human sin leaves its mark wherever it is committed. The fall of humanity drags the world around us down with it.

But, equally, God's purposes of redemption and salvation include the natural order. The world (that is, the whole natural order), too, will be redeemed and recreated. Just what form the 'new heavens and new earth' will take is open to debate; the vision so graphically described in Isaiah 11 (for example) may well have to be taken metaphorically rather than literally. But the underlying truth is sure: God is concerned for the world that he has made, and he promises that, just as he'll create a new humanity, he'll create a new world, free from all the blemishes of this present one.

Does this mean, then, that we can be absolved from any responsibility to care for this world in which we live? Is it to be treated as a 'write-off' and so either neglected or exploited at will? By no means. Such a negative attitude to the world was fairly widespread in the pagan thought of the early Christian centuries, and at times Christians have been tempted to follow it. But the Bible's doctrine of creation and of God's care for all that he has made makes it impossible for Christians to do so. If God cares for what he has made, so much that he pays the price of the cross to redeem it as well as to redeem humanity, then our attitude towards it must reflect the value he places on it. It must be the object of our care, love and goodness, not of our exploitation, selfishness and greed.

Even though the Bible writers didn't address the current environmental issues, the passages quoted above illustrate several basic biblical principles for Christians to follow today.

1. *We have a God-given responsibility towards the world around us.* In Genesis 1 this is expressed as 'ruling over' it. For Christians,

'ruling' in any context can't be an excuse for selfishness or exploit-ation. Rather, it means taking the responsibility to use our skills and opportunities for the good of whatever we're ruling over. For example, parents or church leaders 'rule' over their children or church community, not in a selfish or dictatorial way, but out of love and concern for the well-being of those God has entrusted to them. Since we are called by God to 'rule over' the world around us, we must exercise our skills and opportunities for its well-being.

2. *We treat the world as God's world; we look on it as God looks on it.* For Christians, the motivation for caring for the world around us is not our own ultimate self-interest ('If we damage and destroy the environment the human race will suffer'), nor some New Age concept that the world, God and ourselves are all basi-cally one. Instead, we love and care for the world because it is God's world. He loves it, and cares for it and calls us to be like him in our attitude towards it.

3. *Human interests aren't the only ones that we should be concerned about.* Though we legitimately benefit from the world around us, we must take specific steps to avoid exploiting it, even though we find this costly. Doubtless it was inconvenient for the Israelites to follow the commands about observing fallow years and resting their animals. And any sensible farmer would put a muzzle on an ox to stop it eating the corn that was, after all, due for human consumption. But it is all too easy to follow our own selfish inter-ests, so from time to time we need to check ourselves and take action that may well inconvenience us, but will benefit the wider world, such as refusing to buy cheap food that has been produced by abusive farming methods.

4. *The primary issues are moral rather than environmental.* The land, says Isaiah, suffers from sin, and not just from exploitation. Indeed, it's human sin that lies at the root of environmental abuse. Moral pollution needs to be fought just as fiercely as environ-mental pollution. Sometimes our generation seems to get matters out of proportion. Animal-rights activists maim children in calling attention to their cause. At the time of writing, a war in the Democratic Republic of Congo is said to have claimed two mil-lion lives; but media interest has been virtually non-existent – in

contrast, say, to that given to the debate over the issue of genetically modified crops.

5. *The coming of God's kingdom 'on earth as it is in heaven' (Matt. 6:10) is the answer to all environmental issues, including our present crisis.* The coming of God sets the whole world right. Joy and peace are key elements of his vision for the world. Where he is, mountains and hills sing for joy; the trees of the forests clap their hands; the wolf and the lamb live together in harmony. But joy and peace spring from righteousness, love and faithfulness, and these are the hallmarks of the coming of God's kingdom. 'Your kingdom come, your will be done on earth as it is in heaven' is the key environmental prayer.

6. *We leave the last word to God.* As in other areas, God does not, as a rule, prevent the evil that results from human abuse of our responsibility to care for the world; if we spoil our world we have to live with the results of our sin. But he promises that in his good time he will do two things. He will 'destroy those who destroy the earth' (Rev. 11:18). And he will recreate the universe, putting right all that has been spoilt. This is the ultimate fulfilment of our prayer and work for the coming of God's kingdom.

What could I do?

Get a biblical understanding of environmental issues. Don't just pick up the concerns and fashions of the people around you, however good they may be. Test all things by the Bible; see issues as God sees them; seek to have the mind of Christ.

Accept God's call to you as an individual to behave responsibly towards the environment. Check your lifestyle and, where possible, follow environmentally friendly practices: recycle, use chemicals wisely in the home and garden, shop discerningly, support nature conservation.

Take seriously the call of God to the whole human race. For the most part, our culture rejects many of the principles that God laid down for the whole of humanity, such as the ways in which we should express our sexuality. By contrast, concern for the environment is a biblical principle that most people in our culture would agree with. So we can join with others in fighting for 'green' issues by attempting to influence government and industrial policies.

Do what you can to promote good environmental policies in the local and wider church. There are all sorts of ways of doing this. How about re-laying the church car park with honeycomb plastic that allows grass and wild flowers to grow instead of masses of tarmac? Some churches have organized litter clean-ups in their areas. Others have supported petitions over specific issues.

Maintain a holistic view. Keep the biblical emphasis on moral pollution and its relationship to environmental pollution. See both the problem and the answer the way God sees it. This will save you from getting things out of proportion.

Maintain basic Christian principles in the ways you fight for environmental issues. Don't get corrupted by the methods adopted by some organizations in order to make their voice heard. This doesn't mean that you shouldn't belong to pressure groups. Indeed, membership may provide a good basis for you to have a positive influence on policies you're not happy with. But remember that there are several Christian organizations that campaign on environmental issues and seek to follow specifically Christian principles.

Work and pray for the coming of God's kingdom. Foundational to this is proclaiming the good news of Jesus. Ultimately, the only answer to greed, selfishness and exploitation is the love of God overflowing from hearts and lives that have been transformed by his grace.

EUTHANASIA

The debate over euthanasia is often obscured by a failure to clarify just what we mean by the term. Some use it to describe any act by which a person's life is humanely brought to an end. This would include allowing a very frail elderly person to die, even though we have the drugs and medical technology to keep him or her alive.

Others use it to mean a deliberate act of causing death, which would not otherwise happen.

Since Christians don't share the belief held by some that death is to be avoided at all costs, allowing 'nature' to take its course and to bring a life to its close would seem an acceptable option in many situations. Indeed, there is something offensive in keeping a frail old person 'artificially' alive when her or his earthly body has clearly come to the end of its span of natural life, and it's time for it to be folded away like a tent and replaced by something rather better (2 Cor. 5:1).

What is much less acceptable is the possibility of bringing a life to a close when, in the course of nature, it seems likely it could continue for a reasonable time, maybe even for years. This is actually killing, rather than allowing to die. The arguments for it are often put very subtly, playing on our natural compassion for those whose quality of life is very poor, and on our concern at the burden they place on those near to them. There have been well-publicized cases in which it's not just been a matter of relatives wanting to end a person's life out of compassion; the patients themselves have begged to be killed.

Nevertheless, from a Christian point of view, there are serious difficulties in the way of allowing someone, in effect, to kill someone else, or encouraging someone to commit suicide. It appears to go against the commandment not to kill, and to put ourselves in the place of God in deciding when a life should close. Given the availability of painkilling drugs, it is always possible that a way can be found to relieve the person's suffering other than by ending his or her life.

An additional factor is the extreme difficulty of drawing up legislation on euthanasia that would be sure to prevent abuse. During the debate on legalizing abortion, campaigners in favour of abortion used graphic and heart-rending examples in which the prohibition of abortion caused pain and suffering and greatly diminished women's quality of life. However, once the legislation was through, it was used to allow a virtually unlimited number of abortions, the vast majority of which were simply matters of convenience and not vital to prevent major suffering or great loss of quality of life. Almost certainly, euthanasia, where it is legalized, will be open to similar abuses.

Even where euthanasia is illegal, difficult decisions have to be taken from time to time, such as whether to switch off a life-support machine, give increasing doses of a painkilling drug although it will eventually hasten the person's death, or accede to the request of an old person with pneumonia to be allowed to stay at home, when taking her or him into hospital would artificially prolong life. In these situations there is no obvious Christian principle to make the issues clear cut. We need to weigh them up carefully, seeking through prayer God's special guidance and grace.

What could I do when faced with such a decision about a loved one?

Pray. Put the whole situation in God's hands and trust him. He knows all its complexities. He is wise and merciful. If you trust in him, he'll not let you make a terrible mistake.

Talk with others. Don't carry the burden of the decision alone. Talk with other family members and close friends. Talk with wise Christian leaders and friends. Consult the doctor or medical team. They may not all agree, but discussion with them will help clarify issues for you.

Make the decision. Remember, in these circumstances it's not so much a matter of choosing between a right way and a wrong way, but of deciding which of two equally acceptable paths is the best to follow.

Leave everything with God. Once the decision been made, let God carry the burden. Don't keep wondering, 'Have I done the right thing?', and going over things again and again in your mind. You prayed for guidance; you trusted God to guide; now trust that he has guided. 'Cast all your anxiety on him because he cares for you' (1 Pet. 5:7).

Bible teaching relating to euthanasia

'You shall not murder' (Exod. 20:13).

None of us lives to himself alone and none of us dies to himself alone. If we live, we live to the Lord; and if we die, we die to the Lord. So, whether we live or die, we belong to the Lord.

For this very reason, Christ died and returned to life so that he might be the Lord of both the dead and the living (Rom. 14:7–9).

All things are yours, whether ... the world or life or death or the present or the future – all are yours, and you are of Christ, and Christ is of God (1 Cor. 3:22–23).

You are not your own; you were bought at a price. Therefore honour God with your body (1 Cor. 6:19–20).

'Do not be afraid. I am the First and the Last. I am the Living One; I was dead, and behold I am alive for ever and ever! And I hold the keys of death and Hades' (Rev. 1:17–18).

FAITH 1: DEVELOPING FAITH

In an age of scepticism and cynicism, faith is under pressure. Our educational system trains us to practise questioning and doubting as virtues. Our scientific worldview tells us that only the phenomena that the scientists can test and prove are worthy of our belief. Christianity is looked on by many around us as a myth or as the product of wishful thinking, which we choose to believe in just the same way as some people choose to believe that Elvis is still alive or that Martians have landed. Even within the Christian church we are still reeling from the impact of sceptical liberal theology, which seemed determined to undermine all the foundational truths on which Christianity has been built. And on a more personal level, our faith is often challenged by the suffering and pain of life, by unanswered prayer, or by pressures and problems.

Maybe it has never been easy to have faith. Surrounded by incredible miracles, amazing teaching, and the manifest presence of God in the Lord Jesus Christ, the twelve disciples still had a problem. They were aware that, compared with Jesus, at any rate, their faith was very small; indeed, on a number of occasions Jesus rebuked them for their 'little faith' (Matt. 6:30; 8:26; 14:31; 16:8). But when they asked him to increase their faith (Luke 17:5), he gave a rather strange response: 'If you have faith as small as a mustard seed, you can say to this mulberry tree, "Be uprooted and planted in the sea," and it will obey you' (Luke 17:6).

It's hard to escape the impression that Jesus wasn't entirely happy with the disciples' request. Perhaps there was something wrong in their motive in asking: maybe they wanted extra faith so that they could perform spectacular miracles and get a lot of glory. Perhaps he felt they were asking for a short cut; growing to be spiritual giants with great faith takes time, but the disciples wanted instant gianthood. Or perhaps he was saying that the faith they already had was much more powerful than they realized.

Is it wrong, then, to want to grow in faith? It can't be, since Paul wrote with approval of the way the faith of the Thessalonians was growing (1 Thess. 1:3). But it's interesting to note that growth in faith is not included in Paul's prayer requests for the people he was writing to. The nearest he gets to it is in Ephesians 3:17, where he prays for the power of the Spirit to work in their inner beings 'so that Christ may dwell in your hearts through faith'.

Maybe this gives us the key. It puts faith in its right place. It's a means to an end, not an end in itself. What matters is Christ, Christ living in us. True, it's through faith that we receive Christ, but, amazingly, we don't need to be faith giants for that to happen. We can come trembling, crying, 'I do believe; help me overcome my unbelief!' (Mark 9:24). The way to receive God's kingdom is as a child (Mark 10:15), not as a giant. And that's because it's God's grace and power and love that matter, not the size of our faith. 'For it is by grace you have been saved, through faith – and this is not from yourselves, it is the gift of God' (Eph. 2:8).

Perhaps that's what Jesus was saying. It's not the size of our faith that matters, but the size of the grace and power of God. A mustard-seed-sized bit of faith (that's about as small as you can get) allied with a great and glorious God can do anything.

Some key Bible passages on faith

'Have faith in God' (Mark 11:22).

'... have faith in our Lord Jesus' (Acts 20:21).

I am not ashamed of the gospel, because it is the power of God for the salvation of everyone who believes ... For in the gospel a righteousness from God is revealed, a righteousness that is by faith from first to last, just as it is written: 'The righteous will live by faith' (Rom. 1:16–17).

'... the promise comes by faith, so that it may be by grace' (Rom. 4:16).

... faith comes from hearing the message, and the message is heard through the word of Christ (Rom. 10:17).

Christ lives in me. The life I live in the body, I live by faith in the Son of God, who loved me and gave himself for me (Gal. 2:20).

... since we have confidence to enter the Most Holy Place by the blood of Jesus ... let us draw near to God with a sincere heart in full assurance of faith ...
   Now faith is being sure of what we hope for and certain of what we do not see. This is what the ancients were commended for ...
   Therefore, since we are surrounded by such a great cloud of witnesses, let us throw off everything that hinders and the sin that so easily entangles, and let us run with perseverance the race marked out for us. Let us fix our eyes on Jesus, the author and perfecter of our faith (Heb. 10:19, 22; 11:1–2; 12:1–2).

... faith by itself, if it is not accompanied by action, is dead (Jas. 2:17).

... build yourselves up in your most holy faith (Jude 20).

What could I do to develop my faith?

Focus on God, not on your faith. To focus on your faith is to look at yourself and, very probably, to get discouraged. If we turn away from ourselves and focus on God we'll probably find that our faith is growing without our noticing it. We'll realize how great God is, how powerful, how loving. We'll see how utterly trustworthy he is, and how he promises to keep us in every situation and to work all things together for good for those who love him. We'll be reminded of the ways he has worked in the past, bringing good out of seeming disasters, providing, guiding, keeping. And the more we focus on him and take on board all that he is, the stronger our faith will become.

Get very close to Jesus. We tend to think that the main point of faith is to enable us to cope with doubts and the difficult questions of life. But, according to the Bible, the main point of faith is that we should live in a close relationship with God through Christ. Exercising faith, according to the New Testament, is not, at heart, giving intellectual assent to certain truths, but rather living in Christ. Remember that the New Testament words generally translated 'faith' and 'believe' can equally be translated 'trust'. Trust is something we exercise in a relationship; to live a life of faith is to trust Jesus in each situation.

Whatever faith you've got, give it plenty of exercise. Muscles grow with exercise. If we say to God, 'Lord, increase my muscle power', he's likely to say to us, 'Go for a run,' or, 'Try some weightlifting.' Muscles that are never used atrophy. Faith that isn't accompanied by action, says James, is dead (Jas. 2:17). So a good way of developing faith is to go through a few experiences that make us put faith into practice. Many of us live such safe lives that this might be something strange and new; surrounded by security and plenty and soft living, we've never needed to exercise faith. To pray 'Give us today our daily bread' is meaningless when the fridge is packed with food. So take a risk. Go out on a limb. Give away the money you've saved for your holiday, and see how God provides. Obey his command or call in a specific area of your life, and see how he blesses. Get stuck in to telling others about Jesus, however hard it may be, and watch him use you.

Feed your faith. 'Faith comes from hearing the message,' says Paul, and that message is 'the word of Christ' (Rom. 10:17). So keep reading and keep feeding your faith on the gospel, especially the stories and teaching of Jesus. Read, too, the story of God's mighty works, recorded elsewhere in the Bible. Read the great stories of the book of Acts. Read, too, the ongoing story, particularly the biographies of God's people down through the centuries who have continued in the succession of the great heroes of faith listed in Hebrews 11.

Share with others in developing faith. Find ways of encouraging others in the faith; be encouraged and strengthened by them. Give up cynical and negative comments. 'Do not let any unwholesome talk come out of your mouths, but only what is helpful for building others up' (Eph. 4:29). When Jude called on his readers to build themselves up in their most holy faith (Jude 20), he was almost certainly meaning that we should be building each other up, not each sitting in her or his small corner trying hard to grow. Use every opportunity to encourage the faith of others, and to let your own be strengthened by them.

FAITH 2: LOSING FAITH

Our Christian faith is a living thing. As such it sometimes grows and is strong; but at other times it goes through a bad patch and begins to wilt. Occasionally, maybe due to a combination of factors, it looks as though it has disappeared altogether.

We sometimes look on losing faith as a matter of the intellect. Up to a specific point, we might feel, we have a certain set of beliefs that we accept; after that point we reject those beliefs and adopt a new set. But Christianity is (or should be) much more than the acceptance of a set of beliefs. Far more than our intellect is involved. Being a Christian involves our emotions, our will, our principles or standards of behaviour, our relationships, our body, and our soul or spirit, as well as our mind or intellect. Pressures and problems in any of these areas can have an adverse effect on our faith.

Our feelings and experiences, including those linked with faith, though very meaningful to us in our Christian lives, are not the basis for the existence of God or of our relationship with him. That basis, of course, lies in God himself – in his reality, his love, his truth, his saving grace and his promises. If tomorrow I decide to give up believing in God, that will be very meaningful to me, but it won't make the slightest bit of difference to God's actual existence.

Some Bible passages relevant to losing faith

When John [the Baptist] heard in prison what Christ was doing, he sent his disciples to ask him, 'Are you the one who was to come, or should we expect someone else?'

Jesus replied, 'Go back and report to John what you hear and see: The blind receive sight, the lame walk, those who have leprosy are cured, the deaf hear, the dead are raised, and the good news is preached to the poor. Blessed is the man who does not fall away on account of me' (Matt. 11:2–6).

The devil said to him, 'If you are the Son of God, tell this stone to become bread.'

Jesus answered, 'It is written: "Man does not live on bread alone"'...

The devil led him to Jerusalem and had him stand on the highest point of the temple. 'If you are the Son of God,' he said, 'Throw yourself down from here ...'

Jesus answered, 'It says: Do not put the Lord your God to the test"' (Luke 4:3–4, 9, 12).

'This is the meaning of the parable [of the sower]: The seed is the word of God. Those along the path are the ones who hear, and then the devil comes and takes away the word from their hearts, so that they may not believe and be saved. Those on the rock are the ones who receive the word with joy when they hear it, but they have no root. They believe for a while, but in the time of testing they fall away. The seed that fell among thorns stands for those who hear, but as they go on their way they are choked by life's worries, riches and pleasures, and they do not mature. But the seed on good soil stands for those with a noble and good heart, who hear the word, retain it, and by persevering produce a crop' (Luke 8:11–15).

... fight the good fight, holding on to faith and a good conscience. Some have rejected these and so have shipwrecked their faith (1 Tim. 1:18–19).

The love of money is a root of all kinds of evil. Some people, eager for money, have wandered from the faith and pierced themselves with many griefs (1 Tim. 6:10).

Here is a trustworthy saying:

> If we died with him,
>   we will also live with him;
> if we endure,
>   we will also reign with him.
> If we disown him,
>   he will also disown us;
> if we are faithless,
>   he will remain faithful,
>   for he cannot disown himself ...

Hymenaeus and Philetus ... have wandered away from the truth. They say that the resurrection has already taken place, and they destroy the faith of some. Nevertheless, God's solid foundation stands firm, sealed with this inscription: 'The Lord knows those who are his,' and, 'Everyone who confesses the name of the Lord must turn away from wickedness' (2 Tim. 2:11–13, 17–19).

Demas, because he loved this world, has deserted me (2 Tim. 4:10)

My brothers, if one of you should wander from the truth and someone should bring him back, remember this: Whoever turns a sinner from the error of his way will save him from death and cover over a multitude of sins (Jas. 5:19).

What could I do if I'm losing my faith?

Be honest with yourself. What is it that has knocked your faith? Have you prayed earnestly for something and found that God's answer has not been what you wanted? Have you grown weary of living the Christian life and decided that being a non-Christian looks more attractive? Has your relationship with God faded, so that he has become distant and unreal? Has another Christian let you down or done something that has upset you? Have you been faced with an intellectual problem you can't resolve? Or does one of the factors in the Scripture passages quoted above apply: disappointment, 'life's worries, riches and pleasures', a bad conscience, 'the love of money', doctrinal error, or the attractiveness and pressures of 'the world'? A number of factors may have come together to put pressure on your faith. Write them down. Think them through. Each of them is doubtless significant, but do they justify giving up on Christianity? Do they establish that the whole of the Christian message is false? Do they prove that God doesn't exist, or that he hasn't come to us in Jesus? Perhaps you already know the answers to some of these issues; for instance, that God's answers to prayer are always wiser than our ideas, or that it's unfair to judge the truth of Christianity on the failings of individual Christians.

Be honest with God. Tell him where you're at. It may well be a case of saying, 'Lord, I'm not at all sure if you're there, but this is where I am.' But still ask him to show you reality and truth, and be willing to follow what he shows you.

Get help. Don't struggle on your own. Many Christians have faced the same issues you're facing, and have found answers. Talk to a wise and experienced Christian leader or friend. Read a book that deals with the issue that's concerning you. Get others to pray for you.

Keep in touch with your Christian friends. You need their help and encouragement at this time. Don't stop going to church, even if much of what goes on there is hard for you to cope with.

Church is for those who are struggling just as much as for those who are strong.

Don't rush into a decision to give up. Someone I know prayed earnestly for the healing of a friend who had cancer. When the friend died, he gave up being a Christian. Some time later he returned to Christianity and is now a very strong Christian. He now realizes that his giving up Christianity was part of his emotional reaction at the death of his friend, a way of expressing his grief and anger at the awfulness of death. At the time, he was unable to think clearly or to make an objective assessment of the truth or otherwise of the claims of Christianity. With hindsight he would now say that he was unwise to declare himself an unbeliever; he should have waited until he could see things in true perspective. The devil is very subtle; he attacks when we're down, just as he tempted Jesus to doubt when he was hungry. It's rarely wise to make life-changing decisions under the pressure of circumstances.

Remember: facts cannot be changed. However much our feelings and experiences may change, Christianity, more than any other religion, is firmly rooted in historical fact, right from the fact of creation (where else did the world come from?) to the facts of the life, death and resurrection of Jesus. Our attitude to these facts may change, but that in no way affects their truth. If the universe was created by God, but I choose to believe it's the product of chance, the universe remains God's creation. My belief or lack of belief can't make any difference to the facts.

Remember that all Christians have to cope with times of special satanic attack. It's what happened to Jesus (Luke 4:1–13) and to Peter (Luke 22:31–32). But God allows our faith to be tested only because he wants to bring something infinitely worthwhile out of the process. Peter wrote about 'all kinds of trials' that God allows to prove the genuineness of our faith (1 Pet. 1:6–9), and both Paul and James list some of the good things God may bring about through a time of testing (Rom. 5:3–5; Jas. 1:2–4).

Make a choice. The Bible teaching is clear: God allows our faith to be tested in order to refine and strengthen it. We, of course, can choose to let the problems destroy our faith, or we can choose the opposite. Whatever you're going through, however tempting it is to give up Christianity, choose to stay with God, and be determined that after going through the fire, you'll come out stronger and in a deeper relationship with him.

Take whatever steps you can to reverse your loss of faith. Focus on God, not on your feelings, experiences or doubts. If you can, cry, 'I do believe; help me overcome my unbelief!' (Mark 9:24). See the section on developing faith.

FAMILY ISSUES 1: FAMILY RELATIONSHIPS

God's purpose is that we should live in families, and find there the security, acceptance and love that we need in order to cope with living in the world. In Bible times, family units tended to be larger than today, extending to wider family relationships. Thus a family would be a small community, in which each person would have an accepted role and place.

Families today still frequently fulfil God's purpose and provide love and security for each of their members. Relationships are deep and strong. Each family member finds acceptance, trust, faithfulness, encouragement, and a sense of belonging and value. Our families are places where we can relax and be ourselves, where we can ask for and offer help, and where we can share burdens and face all sorts of experiences together.

Family relationships can be beautiful. But they can also be ugly. Perhaps because the relationships are so close, and because in the family we can 'be ourselves', we can hurt one another deeply. Family rows are notorious for their vehemence; husbands and wives shout at each other in ways they'd never dare to with anyone else. Anger, resentment and broken relationships can last for years; individuals, especially children, can bear the scars for life.

To an extent, in the New Testament the local church replaced the family as the key unit to which we belong. This was partly because, in times of persecution, becoming a Christian often meant being rejected by your family. Jesus talked about this when he sent his disciples out to evangelize: 'I have come to turn "a man against his father, a daughter against her mother, a daughter-in-law against her mother-in-law – a man's enemies will be the members of his own household"' (Matt. 10:35–36). Indeed, this was his own experience; for a time his mother and brothers opposed his ministry (Mark 3:21), leading him to say, 'Who are my mother and my brothers?' Looking at those seated around him, he answered, 'Here are my mother and my brothers! Whoever does God's will is my brother and sister and mother' (Mark 3:33–35). Among the believers love, security, a sense of belonging and all the ideals of the family unit were to be found.

This is not to say that the natural family is redundant. The New Testament continued to teach the value of deep and rich family relationships, where these were possible. In effect, the Christian now has two families, the natural family and the church family. Each is patterned to a large extent on the other; the principles and pattern of behaviour that the New Testament gives for the local church should, wherever possible, apply to our family relationships, and the directions given for family life are to be lived out in the local church.

Some Bible passages relevant to family relationships

'Honour your father and your mother, so that you may live long in the land the LORD your God is giving you' (Exod. 20:12).

Love must be sincere. Hate what is evil; cling to what is good. Be devoted to one another in brotherly love. Honour one another above yourselves (Rom. 12:9–10).

Submit to one another out of reverence for Christ.
    Wives, submit to your husbands as to the Lord ... Husbands, love your wives, just as Christ loved the church and gave himself up for her ... each one of you also must love his wife as he loves himself, and the wife must respect her husband.

Children, obey your parents in the Lord, for this is right ...

Fathers, do not exasperate your children; instead, bring them up in the training and instruction of the Lord (Eph. 5:21–22, 25, 33; 6:1, 4).

Wives, submit to your husbands, as is fitting in the Lord.

Husbands, love your wives and do not be harsh with them.

Children, obey your parents in everything, for this pleases the Lord.

Fathers, do not embitter your children, or they will become discouraged (Col. 3:18–21).

If anyone does not provide for his relatives, and especially for his immediate family, he has denied the faith and is worse than an unbeliever ...

If any woman who is a believer has widows in her family, she should help them and not let the church be burdened with them, so that the church can help those widows who are really in need (1 Tim. 5:8, 16).

What could I do?

Resist the temptation to take your family for granted. Commit yourself to doing all you can to build up your family relationships, not only for your own benefit but also for that of all the other members of the family. Spread the love of Jesus right through the family.

Do what you can to heal any broken relationships there may be in your family. In some circumstances full reconciliation may not be possible or desirable, such as when a broken marriage has been followed by remarriage to someone else. Nevertheless, as Christians we are called to do what we can to restore broken relationships whenever possible. If you're part of the broken relationship, take all the personal steps you can to restore it from your side. If you have been hurt or wronged, seek God's grace to forgive, even if you have to pray, 'Lord, I forgive; help me overcome my unforgiveness' (compare Mark 9:24). If you're not directly involved, you may have to proceed with a degree of caution – family quarrels are strange things! Pray for God's wisdom; show love and respect to all concerned; refuse to take sides; speak highly of everyone; and trust that God will give you an opportunity to be a 'peacemaker', a true child of God (Matt. 5:9).

Spend time with your family. The average child spends far more time watching TV than with her or his father. Work takes up many more hours than family. Some families rarely or never eat together. Many families find Christmas and annual holidays very difficult to cope with because they've forgotten how to relate to each other. Don't let this happen to you. Do all you can to spend quality time with your family.

Enjoy your family. They're God's gift to you. Find ways of bringing them joy; learn to find joy in them.

Think through the contemporary application of the biblical concepts of 'honouring', 'submitting' and 'respecting'. Our culture is very different from that of Bible times, but there is still a place for these concepts in today's families. The concept of 'submission' is often misunderstood. There are two important things the New Testament does *not* say about submission. First, it does not say that only wives should be submissive; rather, it says we should all give way, where appropriate, to each other (Eph. 5:21). Secondly, it does not say that anyone has a right to require or even to expect anyone else to submit to them; submission is a voluntary act of love, not obedience to a demand.

Where appropriate, give family members space. Part of respecting each other is allowing each person to live his or her own life. Because families are close, one member might start trying to control another. This can happen in a marriage relationship – a husband attempts to control his wife, or the wife her husband, or each tries to control the other. It is also common between parents and grown-up children; after eighteen years of control, parents find it hard to allow their offspring to be adults and to make their own decisions. Most 'in-law' problems arise from this. If you are a parent, settle it in your mind that, once your children are adults, you will treat them as adults; respect their ability and their right to live their own lives, even if you are sure you know better. The element of control can also work the other way: children can attempt to control the lives of their parents, particularly as they grow older. Check to make sure you're not trying to be in a position of control in any of your family relationships. If you find yourself a victim of inappropriate control, graciously refuse to let it continue. Accept that God calls you to be responsible for your decisions and life; don't let anyone take that from you.

Foster your extended family. Keep in touch with those who've moved away. Plan holidays together. Get together for special occasions such as anniversaries and weddings.

FAMILY ISSUES 2: PARENTING

Being a parent gives us the incredible privilege of doing and being something very Godlike. We create something in our own image. We love, we nourish, we care. We weep, we laugh, we rejoice, we are hurt, we sacrifice. We watch our children grow in love and understanding; our relationship with them deepens and grows – or it does the opposite. We work, we give, we long, we teach, we encourage, we give ourselves. And sometimes it's all infinitely worthwhile. But sometimes it seems as though it's all a waste of time. In all this we are experiencing something that is at the heart of the Father God.

The Bible gives some teaching on parenting, and a number of examples of both good and bad parenting. Despite the different social context, and the fact that children in biblical times were brought up in the context of the wider family rather than in our much smaller 'nuclear' or single-parent family, there are basic principles we can draw from it.

Some Bible passages relevant to parenting

'Abraham will surely become a great and powerful nation, and all nations on earth will be blessed through him. For I have chosen him, so that he will direct his children and his household after him to keep the way of the LORD by doing what is right and just' (Gen. 18:18–19).

Fix these words of mine in your hearts and minds; tie them as symbols on your hands and bind them on your foreheads. Teach them to your children, talking about them when you sit at home and when you walk along the road, when you lie down and when you get up. Write them on the door-frames of your houses and on your gates, so that your days and the days of your children may be many in the land (Deut. 11:18–21).

> Listen, my son, to your father's instruction
> and do not forsake your mother's teaching (Prov. 1:8).

'... the Father loves the Son and shows him all he does ... I live because of the Father ... I honour my Father ... My Father ...glorifies me ... the Father knows me and I know the Father ...' (John 5:20; 6:57; 8:49, 54; 10:15).

Fathers, do not exasperate your children; instead, bring them up in the training and instruction of the Lord (Eph. 6:4).

Fathers, do not embitter your children, or they will become discouraged (Col. 3:21).

What could I do?

Use all the help you can get. Parenting is a huge task. Not only does it take many years, but the demands and stresses change as you go along. Parenting a teenager is very different from parenting a baby. Though you may pick up a lot of skills and experience from your own parents and from watching others around you, you need to tap into every possible resource to make sure you do as good a job as you can. Read books; go to Christian seminars on parenting; talk through issues with other parents or with those who have special knowledge or training. Use the wider resources of your church and your extended family. Have a policy of always learning. Don't be afraid to admit that an issue is too big for you to cope with alone, and to seek others' help.

Pray. Pray for your children and yourselves. Get others to pray for you. Spiritual battles are being fought over our children today;

fight with spiritual weapons. Keep giving your parenting and your children to God. Pray continually. Put the children in God's hands and trust him with them.

Think through the principles on which you are operating in your parenting. Don't just muddle along, reacting to circumstances and making decisions according to your feelings.

Found your relationship with your children on unconditional love. Keep demonstrating it; children need to be constantly reassured that their parents love them. Tell them verbally, in your attitudes and in your actions. When you have to discipline them, or do something they find difficult to accept, be sure to surround it with love. Pattern your love on the love of God.

Be consistent. Don't say one thing one day and something different the next. Don't allow the children to play off one parent against the other. Even if your approaches differ, as they often may, always back the other up.

Be prepared to go against the fashion – and help your children to do so. Children are under tremendous pressure to conform. Some of it comes from their peers, but much comes from commercial interests, some comparatively innocent, but others decidedly sinister. Right from the start, teach your children how to be different and how to cope with being different. Explain to them why, for instance, they're not given unbridled access to TV or the Internet.

Accept your children for who they are. Don't expect them to react like adults. Don't blame an adolescent for behaving like an adolescent. Respect them as persons. Study them. Empathize. Try to understand them as far as you can, particularly how they feel in various situations. Put yourself in their position. Be open with them about yourself.

Get close to your children and stay close. Develop the deepest love and trust on both sides. Make the relationship between Jesus and his Father your model.

Talk a lot with your children. Make it your aim that they will spend more time talking with you than watching TV. Talk about their day and their concerns. Explain to them why you do what you do. Take their questions seriously, and give them good answers. Read to them. Discuss issues with them. Do this from childhood, and right through adolescence.

Walk with them through all their experiences. Be especially sensitive to potentially traumatic experiences, such as the death of a pet or of a grandparent. Love and support them through everything.

Affirm your children. Never belittle them, either in front of them or behind their backs. Praise them. Thank them for what they do. Tell them often that they mean a lot to you, and show it in the way you speak to them and treat them. But also affirm them as individual persons. Don't smother or attempt to control them. Respect their individuality and decisions. Demonstrate that you trust them. Let them be themselves. Be prepared to let them go; run risks with them. Your aim is to enable them to grow into whole people, not to keep them as children for ever.

Give them clear structures within which to operate. Children need to know the rules; they need the security of a structure they can understand. They will, of course, try going outside the structure, and pushing the boundaries to test your reaction. Show wisdom, love and grace in dealing with this, but continue to keep the boundaries in place.

Accept that you'll make mistakes. All parents do. Learn to cope quickly with mistakes, to say sorry, to sort things out, and to explain in ways the children can understand.

FAMILY ISSUES 3: CARING FOR AGEING PARENTS

Some Bible teaching

'Honour your father and your mother, so that you may live long in the land the LORD your God is giving you' (Exod. 20:12).

'Rise in the presence of the aged, show respect for the elderly and revere your God. I am the LORD' (Lev. 19:32).

... parents are the pride of their children (Prov. 17:6).

Near the cross of Jesus stood his mother, his mother's sister, Mary the wife of Clopas, and Mary Magdalene. When Jesus saw his mother there, and the disciple whom he loved standing near by, he said to his mother, 'Dear woman, here is your son,' and to the disciple, 'Here is your mother.' From that time on, this disciple took her into his home (John 19:25–27).

If anyone does not provide for his relatives, and especially for his immediate family, he has denied the faith and is worse than an unbeliever ...

If any woman who is a believer has widows in her family, she should help them and not let the church be burdened with them, so that the church can help those widows who are really in need (1 Tim. 5:8, 16).

There are perhaps four main sources of care for those who are growing older and can no longer care for themselves, the local community, the church, their near relatives (especially their children) and the state.

In New Testament times there was no state care for the elderly, and the expectation was that, once they were unable to care for themselves, care would be undertaken by the family and the local community. From earliest days the local church community accepted the responsibility of caring for those in need, though Paul's instructions in 1 Timothy 5 make it clear that he felt that the primary source of care should be family; the church should take the responsibility only when no family care was available.

As a result of ever-improving healthcare, people are today living longer than ever before, and the problems posed by the need to care for them as they become increasingly frail are becoming acute. Government policy in Britain has meant that the state has handed much of its former responsibility to care for the elderly over to the private sector. Though a number of private organizations provide care on a not-for-profit basis, many are essentially commercial undertakings, seeking a financial return for those who have invested in them. But costs have risen greatly, partly because, as people live longer, the proportion of very frail people needing extra care has increased considerably, and partly because of the demands made by ever-increasing regulations. As a result, many residential and nursing homes for the elderly have ceased to be financially viable and have had to close.

Quite apart from a widespread attitude that 'welfare' of any sort is the responsibility of the state, the general weakening of the concept of the family has meant that fewer and fewer elderly people are actually being cared for by their children. Indeed, where families have broken up, children may with some justification feel that they are under no obligation to care for parents who so signally failed to care for them. Additionally, most people find that life is so full and hectic they do not have the time to care. In a highly mobile society, the family may well be scattered over the country and even over the world. There is also the limitation of space. With the growth of affluence, we have come to need larger homes and more room per person. In the first half of the twentieth century it was quite common for Gran to move in with the family, even though Mum and Dad and the kids were already crammed into a small terraced house. Now, we all feel we need our space, and we have many more possessions and activities to accommodate. Taking in an ageing parent is seen as requiring the costly addition of a granny flat or a move to a larger property.

Even so, there can be no doubt that the basic biblical principle still stands: the primary responsibility for caring for parents when they can no longer care for themselves rests with their immediate family, and so, in most cases, with their children. That care can, of course, be exercised indirectly as well as directly. Generally, the most satisfactory approach is to enable the parents or parent to maintain their home and independence as long as possible by arranging appropriate support. Social Services can provide a great deal of advice and help, as can local voluntary organizations and clubs. Good neighbours and caring people in the local church provide friendship and support, and are often the front-line resource if a problem or emergency arises.

One way in which an older person can retain a high degree of independence is by moving to a warden-assisted flat, bungalow or housing complex. Many of these schemes were started by

Christian groups, and they have proved successful in allowing people to live in their own home and to remain independent with the security of immediate help on hand should they need it.

What could I do?

Obey the command to honour your parents. This is foundational to all else. It is one of the Ten Commandments, and it is picked up by Paul in Ephesians 6:2. Even if you think they have been bad parents, the command still stands. Though you may find it hard to feel respect or affection for them, you're still called to show them Christlike love. Remember that, for at least some of his ministry, Jesus' mother, Mary, misunderstood and opposed him. But he still accepted and fulfilled his responsibility to her as her son, even when on the cross. Check to see if you are giving your parents the right level of honour and love, and work out how you can set right any deficiencies.

Talk with your parents about any possible arrangements. Don't wait till a crisis happens and then have to decide in a hurry. Encourage them to think of possibilities such as moving to a single-storey home or a warden-assisted complex before this becomes essential. Have emergency plans in place in case they should be taken ill. Remember to respect their wishes in all the decision-making, and to preserve their dignity in all the arrangements.

Talk with other family members. These will include those who might share the responsibility of caring, and your own immediate family, who might be affected by the arrangements you make.

Plan the arrangements carefully if you decide that your parent or parents should come and live with you. Find ways of giving each generation space. Do what you can to retain a reasonable level of independence for them and for you. In Bible times it was common for the extended family to spend all their lives together in community. In our culture we're used to living in much smaller units, and suddenly having to share our home, even with close relatives, can raise many problems. Talk with other people who've had elderly parents living with them. Take steps to minimize the effect of any problems before they arise.

If your parents decide to go for a residential home, do everything you can to make the transition easy. The trauma of such a move can be very great, involving loss of independence, separation from neighbours, friends, home and treasured possessions, a radical change of life pattern, and, in some homes, a loss of dignity. Do all you can to minimize these problems. Ideally, help them to find a home where you and other members of the family can visit regularly. It's staggering how many people in residential homes for the elderly go for weeks without a family visitor. Such visits don't need to be long, provided they are frequent; it can mean a great deal to a parent to know that each day you'll be popping in for five minutes 'just to see that you're all right'. Continue to visit even if declining abilities mean that your parent doesn't recognize you. Even a person with advanced Alzheimer's will have some periods of comparative lucidity; in any case, you will want to continue to show love although there is little response. Even the best residential homes can be depressing places; make a point of taking your parent out regularly for a meal, a ride in the car or some other special activity. Remember that staff in such homes have an unenviable job and are often poorly paid; do what you can to encourage and help them.

FOOD

Some of the Bible's teaching on food

God said, 'I give you every seed-bearing plant on the face of the whole earth and every tree that has fruit with seed in it. They will be yours for food' (Gen. 1:29).

God blessed Noah and his sons, saying to them ... 'Everything that lives and moves will be food for you. Just as I gave you the green plants, I now give you everything.

   'But you must not eat meat that has its lifeblood still in it' (Gen. 9:1, 3–4).

'When you reap the harvest of your land, do not reap to the very edges of your field or gather the gleanings of your harvest. Do not go over your vineyard a second time or pick up the grapes that have fallen. Leave them for the poor and the alien. I am the LORD your God' (Lev. 19:9–10).

'Give us today our daily bread' (Matt. 6:11).

Therefore I tell you, do not worry about your life, what you will eat or drink; or about your body, what you will wear. Is not life more important than food, and the body more important than clothes? Look at the birds of the air; they do not sow or reap or store away in barns, and yet your heavenly Father feeds them. Are you not much more valuable than they? ...
　'But seek first his kingdom and his righteousness, and all these things will be given to you as well' (Matt. 6:25–26, 33).

John answered, 'The man with two tunics should share with him who has none, and the one who has food should do the same' (Luke 3:11).

'When you enter a town and are welcomed, eat what is set before you' (Luke 10:8).

Jesus said to his host, 'When you give a luncheon or dinner, do not invite your friends, your brothers or relatives, or your rich neighbours; if you do, they may invite you back and so you will be repaid. But when you give a banquet, invite the poor, the crippled, the lame, the blind, and you will be blessed. Although they cannot repay you, you will be repaid at the resurrection of the righteous' (Luke 14:12–14).

Jesus then took the loaves, gave thanks, and distributed to those who were seated as much as they wanted. He did the same with the fish.
　When they had all had enough to eat, he said to his disciples, 'Gather the pieces that are left over. Let nothing be wasted.' So they gathered them and filled twelve baskets with the pieces of

the five barley loaves left over by those who had eaten (John 6:11–13).

Share with God's people who are in need. Practise hospitality (Rom. 12:13).

One man's faith allows him to eat everything, but another man, whose faith is weak, eats only vegetables. The man who eats everything must not look down on him who does not, and the man who does not eat everything must not condemn the man who does, for God has accepted him ...

I am fully convinced that no food is unclean in itself ... the kingdom of God is not a matter of eating and drinking, but of righteousness, peace and joy in the Holy Spirit ... All food is clean, but it is wrong for a man to eat anything that causes someone else to stumble. It is better not to eat meat or drink wine or to do anything else that will cause your brother to fall (Rom. 14:2–3, 14, 17, 20–21).

... about eating food sacrificed to idols ... food does not bring us near to God; we are no worse if we do not eat, and no better if we do ...

... if what I eat causes my brother to fall into sin, I will never eat meat again, so that I will not cause him to fall (1 Cor. 8:4, 8, 13).

Eat anything sold in the meat market without raising questions of conscience, for, 'The earth is the Lord's, and everything in it.'

If some unbeliever invites you to a meal and you want to go, eat whatever is put before you without raising questions of conscience (1 Cor. 10:25–27).

Our culture tends to assume that food is essentially a human product, something that we create and control. The Bible's outlook is different. Food is very much a gift of God, and something he creates. We ask and thank him for it. It is something to be shared, since it is God's gift to all, his provision so that all may live. In particular, the Bible carefully stipulates that those who have food should share it with those who have none.

There were controversies over food in New Testament times, and some of the passages have a contemporary ring, speaking as they do of vegetarianism and abstinence from alcohol. The core issue was eating meat that might have been offered in sacrifice to pagan idols. Paul's line on this was clear: there was no need for Christians to be concerned about this; all foods, including those that were 'unclean' for Jews, were God's gift to us and to be accepted with thanksgiving, even if they had been used in pagan sacrifices. But there was something more important than considerations of food – our concern for the well-being of each other. If our attitude towards food causes a 'weaker' Christian to sin, then we should let it go; people matter more than principles.

In Bible times, eating a meal together was more than a convenient way of feeding. It was a significant social occasion, which drew the participants together in a spiritual bond. It was this that made the horror of Psalm 41:9, applied by Jesus to Judas in John 13:18, all the more acute: 'He who shares my bread has lifted up his heel against me.' The pressures of contemporary living, and the temptation to take a snack in front of the TV, mean that in many homes this potentially significant aspect of eating food is lost.

Similarly, the decline in the practice of 'saying grace' has removed a valuable element from meals. 'Grace' in this context is linked with the Latin word for 'thanks'. The equivalent Greek word has come down to us in 'eucharist'. Giving thanks together at the start of a meal is not just acknowledging that the food is God's gift, significant though that is. For Christians, it is fulfilling the command of Jesus to remember him whenever we eat or drink together.

The food industry and its methods raise a host of issues in today's world. As in Romans 14, Christians come down on different sides in the debates over organically grown or genetically modified food, as they do over vegetarianism and abstinence from alcohol. But there are two underlying issues on which all Christians may agree.

One we've already seen: people matter more than principles. We've all been in the difficult position where a poor person in generosity and love offered us food that, we suspect, was prepared in less than hygienic conditions. But we take it and eat it (maybe with a quick prayer that God will see it safely through) because we know that by doing so we are showing our respect and love for that person. Our convictions and scruples over food may be important to us, but they must never become more important than other people.

A second, related, issue is obedience to the Bible's command to make sure that the poor have enough to eat. We may feel we can do little to help those suffering from hunger in distant parts of the world. But, of course, we can do a lot. We can be responsible with what we've got. We can eat simply and give what we save to feed others. We can cut down on waste. And we can take other practical steps, such as those mentioned below, to help to change the inequality in the world distribution of food.

What could I do?

Sort out your 'theology' of food. How do you view it? Do you think about it the same way as non-Christians do? What sort of difference should being a Christian make to your attitude towards food? What about things like greed, self-indulgence, over-eating, and faddishness? Get to grips with what the Bible says about food and try to reshape your thinking into a biblical attitude towards it.

Enrich your mealtimes. Eat more often with your family or with others, instead of letting everyone eat to suit themselves or snacking in front of the TV. Start each meal with prayer, giving thanks for the food and remembering Christ. Talk together; encourage each other; feed your minds and spirits as well as your bodies.

Practise hospitality. Invite others for meals. Every now and then, try following Jesus' instruction in Luke 14:13 and make a banquet for those in need.

Shop wisely. There are many factors besides getting the best bargain that may influence you, such as supporting the small, local trader over against big business and supermarkets, supporting 'fairly traded' initiatives and refusing food produced in unacceptable ways.

Eat responsibly. For many of us this may well mean eating less. It will certainly mean avoiding foods that will damage our health. Cut down on waste.

Remember the hungry. Do what you can to feed them. Support and pray for organizations such as Tearfund and Christian Aid. Campaign for measures that will bring about a fairer world distribution of wealth and food.

Keep your scruples over food in their proper place. It's fine to have convictions about hygiene or diet, or to refuse on principle to eat certain products. But such convictions can degenerate into self-centredness or faddishness, or could even be a form of attention-seeking. Be prepared sometimes to follow Jesus' and Paul's instructions (Luke 10:8; 1 Cor. 10:27) and eat what is set before you without asking any questions.

FRIENDSHIP

Friendship was a central theme in the debates and writings of the ancient world and the medieval period. By comparison, our society seems little interested in it. Perhaps our excessive individualism is partly to blame. Maybe, too, the competitiveness of our society is a factor; it's hard to develop a true friendship with someone when your constant desire is to come out on top. Many would say that the widespread breakdown of relationships in our culture has made it hard to form real friendships; someone who has been hurt early in life, say, through the break-up of a marriage and family, will find it difficult to develop close, trusting friendships with anybody.

The New Testament doesn't draw a strict line between friendship and love. Indeed, it calls us to express love (*agapē*) in all our relationships, even towards our enemies (Matt. 5:44). So its teaching on the type of love to be expressed in all our various human relationships takes us to the heart of true friendship.

Mutuality is a key feature of friendship. If I love my enemy, the love is one-way; she or he doesn't love me back. So, although we might say I befriend my enemy, the relationship can't be one of friendship. By contrast, our relationship with our friends is marked by two-way love; we love them and they love us. We enrich their lives and they enrich ours.

Some biblical passages relevant to friendship

Jonathan became one in spirit with David, and he loved him as himself ... And Jonathan made a covenant with David because he loved him as himself ...

... they kissed each other and wept together – but David wept the most.

Jonathan said to David, 'Go in peace, for we have sworn friendship with each other in the name of the LORD' ...

> [David said] 'I grieve for you, Jonathan my brother:
>   you were very dear to me.
> Your love for me was wonderful,
>   more wonderful than that of women'
> (1 Sam. 18:1, 3; 20:41–42; 2 Sam. 1:26).
>
> A friend loves at all times ...
>   there is a friend who sticks closer than a brother ...
> Wounds from a friend can be trusted
> (Prov. 17:17; 18:24; 27:6).

'As the Father has loved me, so have I loved you. Now remain in my love ... I have told you this so that my joy may be in you and that your joy may be complete. My command is this: Love each other as I have loved you. Greater love has no-one than this, that he lay down his life for his friends. You are my friends if you do what I command. I no longer call you servants, because a servant does not know his master's business. Instead, I have called you friends, for everything that I learned from my Father I have made known to you' (John 15:9, 11–15).

I will show you the most excellent way ...

Love is patient, love is kind. It does not envy, it does not boast, it is not proud. It is not rude, it is not self-seeking, it is not easily angered, it keeps no record of wrongs. Love does not delight in evil but rejoices with the truth. It always protects, always trusts, always perseveres.

Love never fails (1 Cor. 12:31; 13:4–8).

... clothe yourselves with compassion, kindness, humility, gentleness and patience. Bear with each other and forgive whatever grievances you may have against one another. Forgive as the Lord forgave you (Col. 3:12–13).

Now that you have purified yourselves by obeying the truth so that you have sincere love for your brothers, love one another deeply, from the heart (1 Pet. 1:22).

The elder,

To my dear friend Gaius, whom I love in the truth.

Dear friend, I pray that you may enjoy good health and that all may go well with you, even as your soul is getting along well (3 John 1–2).

What could I do?

If you find it difficult to know where to start, try these basic steps in cultivating a friendship.

- *Perform simple kindnesses.* Smile. Encourage. Thank.
- *Spend time together.* Invite the person you're befriending for coffee. Go for a walk together.
- *Without going over the top, check that you're at your attractive best* – clean and tidy, suitably dressed, fun to be with. But once you've checked, forget about yourself. Relax; focus on the other person, and simply be yourself.
- *Give people an opportunity to talk.* Make sure that you don't dominate the conversation. Draw them out; be a good listener.
- *Avoid talking too much about yourself.* They'll want to know about you; when they ask questions, give them what they ask

for, but don't let it trigger ten minutes of you talking about your problems and interests. Talking about yourself all the time is a good way of putting other people off. Stop the flow after a minute or two, with, 'That's enough about me; what about you?' If they really want to hear more about you, they'll tell you.

• *Eat together.* Sharing a meal is one of the oldest and best ways of showing friendship. You could take them for a meal out, though there's a lot to be said for a meal that you prepare. If you do the cooking, for the first time or two make it a relatively simple meal; don't go for the advanced stuff; it could get you all hassled, and you would be embarrassed if it didn't turn out right.

Work at friendships. Any relationship will wilt if it isn't cared for and strengthened. Keep in good contact. Make extra efforts to affirm, encourage, thank and help.

Make it easy for people to express loving friendship to you. Accept acts of friendship in a right spirit. Some people find it hard to let others do nice things for them, and, consciously or unconsciously, make it difficult for their friends to show true friendship and love. If someone does something good to you, don't feel you're necessarily under obligation to respond by matching (or even beating!) their kindness. Be careful about using the phrase 'You shouldn't have done that.' When a person has done something for you out of love and friendship, it's better to say, 'That was a beautiful thing to do. It really meant a lot to me.'

Develop friendships with people who aren't Christians. As Christians we often become so involved with a huge number of Christian friends that our friendships with non-Christians get neglected. Try to avoid this, not simply because you want to share Jesus with them, but for the sake of your non-Christian friends themselves. As far as possible, model your friendships with those who aren't Christians on Christian friendship. Don't behave one way with your Christian friends and a totally different way when you're with your non-Christian friends. After all, they'll know you're a Christian, and will expect you to behave like one. Relating to them with the love and goodness of Jesus can itself make a powerful impact, quite apart from your words of witness.

In Christian friendships, enrich one another spiritually as well as in other ways. Encourage each other's faith and spiritual growth. Pray together. Put into practice the verse in Hebrews: 'let us consider how we may spur one another on towards love and good deeds' (Heb. 10:24).

Watch for the friendless. God has a special concern for the rejects of society, such as the aliens and the poor in the Old Testament, and tax collectors and 'sinners' in the New Testament. He calls us to follow his example. Even in churches, particularly larger churches, people can get overlooked and be very lonely. Watch out for them. Don't spend all the coffee-after-the-service time talking to those you know. Spot those who are on their own, or even those who slip away straight after the service because drinking coffee alone is too painful for them.

Be diverse in your friendships. Cultivate friendship with people of different generations, backgrounds and experiences. Don't just mix with people you're familiar with. Try new ground; explore new territory. It may take more effort, but you'll find it enriching.

Beware of selfish elements creeping into your relationships with your friends. Friendship is a two-way relationship, so you will receive much from the relationships, as well as giving much. But don't give in order to get. We've all had experiences of people who suddenly appear very friendly, and go out of their way to do us a good turn or two; and then we discover that they're only doing it in order to get something out of us. That's manipulation, not friendship. Avoid it; it's a most effective way to kill a friendship.

Watch out for the pitfall of an exclusive friendship, characterized by possessiveness, and by jealousy if the other person takes an interest in anyone else. Be consciously generous in your friendships; you want to have many friends, and you want your friends to have many friends too.

Beware of the sexual pitfall. Partly because we're sexual beings, and partly because of the way we're constantly being indoctrinated by our culture with the idea that love must mean sex, what starts as a beautiful and holy friendship can begin to develop sexual overtones and end up in intercourse, whether with the opposite sex or the same sex. Make absolutely certain this doesn't happen to you. Remember that this kind of thing can be so insidious that you're hardly aware it's happening until it's too late. Guard against any possibility of it happening with you, and be determined to deal ruthlessly with any such elements as soon as they start to arise. Take Paul's guidelines seriously: 'among you there must not be even a hint of sexual immorality, or any kind of impurity, or of greed, because these are improper for God's holy people. Nor should there be obscenity, foolish talk or coarse joking, which are out of place, but rather thanksgiving' (Eph. 5:3–4).

Be a loyal and consistent friend. Of course, your relationships will go up and down. You'll do things that upset each other; you'll disagree over issues; you'll make mistakes. But let these test and strengthen your friendships, rather than harm them. Be quick to forgive, or to admit you were wrong. Learn to accept 'wounds from a friend' (Prov. 27:6).

If you struggle with loneliness, be determined not to let it conquer you. Get help; try working through the 'Twelve steps to conquering loneliness' on pp. 339–340.

If you find it hard to make friends, try working through this check-list:

1. Is there a simple cause that I could put right easily, such as bad breath or body odours, or never making time to cultivate a friendship?

2. Is there some other relatively external factor that is a barrier? You may be living in an alien culture, or among people who speak a different language from you. You may have a disability, or people may believe things about you that make them unfriendly. If this is the case, don't give up. You'll have to work harder at forming and cultivating friendships than many other people, but it's perfectly possible, with God's help, for you to do so. After all, you have so much to give, as well as to receive.

3. Is the barrier deeper and more inward? Do you find it hard to be open with others, to trust people and to run risks in rela-tionships? Do you find yourself withdrawing into yourself when relationships do begin to develop? Are you afraid of being committed in a relationship? If so, do everything you can to get to the root of these feelings and to sort them out. God doesn't want you to be like that. He wants you to be able to love and trust and form deep and secure relationships. Talk your feelings through with a wise Christian friend or counsellor. It may be that they go

back to bad experiences in the past – to an insecure childhood, or to the pain of some broken relationship. God doesn't want bad experiences in the past to cast their shadow over the rest of our lives. He wants us to find healing. Set yourself to work the issues through, with the help of others; and seek God's special grace and healing, maybe through a time of prayer ministry.

'FULL-TIME' CHRISTIAN SERVICE

Every Christian is called to serve Christ, and no two calls are the same. Many are called to serve in the contexts of their daily jobs, to do their work for the glory of God, and to witness to the Lord Jesus to those around them. Some are called to give up their working careers, a step which may involve considerable financial sacrifice, and devote their working hours to specific Christian service.

Traditionally, there have been two main forms of 'full-time' Christian service: cross-cultural missionary work, and church-based pastoral ministry, usually through 'ordination'. These were seen as lifetime callings, generally requiring a period of training and lasting until (and often beyond) retirement. More recently, concepts of 'full-time' service have broadened considerably. Many Christians have wanted to spend some part of their lives serving God in this way without feeling called to a lifetime's commitment. All sorts of 'short-term' ministries have been developed, ranging from a period of a few months to several years, taking a variety of forms and using a whole range of skills, from piloting a mission ship or digging wells to ministering to homeless people in the inner city.

The concept of a lifetime call to ministry has also been broadened and enriched. Traditional concepts of 'being a missionary' and 'being ordained' have been widened, allowing a variety of cross-cultural or church-based ministries to be exercised.

All forms of 'full-time' service require preparation. Organizations that arrange short-term opportunities generally build preparation and training into their programmes. This is especially important, since the time of service is short and needs to be as effective as possible. For longer-term service, college training is generally expected. 'Traditional' denominations require a period of study for those wishing to be ordained; the Church of England, for example, requires study at an Anglican theological college, usually for three years. Bible colleges offer a range of courses, generally centred on study of the Scriptures, but also providing training in various skills and giving the opportunity for the student to grow as a Christian as well as in understanding.

How might you know whether or not God wants you to be involved in 'full-time' Christian work? As you would expect, there's no set formula for finding this out; God calls and leads every individual in a unique way. But here are three factors that can act as indicators:

1. *An inner urging or personal awareness that God is leading you this way.* This may come clearly on a specific occasion, or it may be a gentle prompting experienced over a period of time. It may come and go, but it won't go away altogether. It's probably at its strongest when you are in close touch with the Lord.

2. *Evidence that you have gifts and abilities, at least in embryonic form, that God can use in the ministry you are considering.* It seems hardly likely that God will call someone who can't stand children to work among the street children in South America, or someone who's never told anybody about Jesus to be an evangelist.

3. *Confirmation by others of the leading of God.* Talk with Christian friends who know you well, and especially with your church leaders. Be careful not to consult just those you know will be affirming; talk also to those who will be honest about your weaknesses and failings. Organizations and training colleges all operate candidate assessment and interview programmes to satisfy themselves that God is truly leading.

The financing of full-time ministry, and of the training for it, is often a major issue. Some organizations and denominations guarantee a subsistence income. Others expect you to raise the support you need. Promises of financial support from individuals and churches and, perhaps, grant-making bodies, can be a good confirmation that God is leading you forward. In other circumstances, Christian workers may be self-supporting or partly self-supporting. An older person, for instance, who has taken early retirement, may be supported by her or his pension and savings. Or those with specific skills may work, say, a couple of days a week to earn enough to support themselves or to supplement the support others are giving.

Some Bible teaching relevant to 'full-time' service for Christ

'Come, follow me,' Jesus said, 'and I will make you fishers of men.' At once they left their nets and followed him (Mark 1:17–18).

Jesus went up on a mountainside and called to him those he wanted, and they came to him. He appointed twelve – designating them apostles – that they might be with him and that he might send them out to preach and to have authority to drive out demons (Mark 3:13–15).

'You yourselves know that these hands have supplied my own needs and the needs of my companions. In everything I did I showed you that by this kind of hard work we must help the weak, remembering the words the Lord Jesus himself said: "It is more blessed to give than to receive"' (Acts 20:34–35).

Paul, a servant of Christ Jesus, called to be an apostle and set apart for the gospel of God ...
    ... called to be an apostle of Christ Jesus by the will of God ...
    ... sent not from men nor by man, but by Jesus Christ and God the Father, who raised him from the dead ...
    ... an apostle of Christ Jesus by the command of God our Saviour and of Christ Jesus our hope ... (Rom 1:1; 1 Cor. 1:1; Gal. 1:1; 1 Tim. 1:1).

... offer your bodies as living sacrifices, holy and pleasing to God – this is your spiritual act of worship ...

We have different gifts, according to the grace given us. If a man's gift is prophesying, let him use it in proportion to his faith. If it is serving, let him serve; if it is teaching, let him teach; if it is encouraging, let him encourage; if it is contributing to the needs of others, let him give generously; if it is leadership, let him govern diligently; if it is showing mercy, let him do it cheerfully (Rom. 12:1, 6–8).

Now about spiritual gifts ...

There are different kinds of gifts, but the same Spirit. There are different kinds of service, but the same Lord. There are different kinds of working, but the same God works all of them in all men.

Now to each one the manifestation of the Spirit is given for the common good.

... in the church God has appointed first of all apostles, second prophets, third teachers, then workers of miracles, also those having gifts of healing, those able to help others, those with gifts of administration, and those speaking in different kinds of tongues (1 Cor. 12:1, 4–7, 28).

... to each one of us grace has been given as Christ apportioned it ...

It was he who gave some to be apostles, some to be prophets, some to be evangelists, and some to be pastors and teachers, to prepare God's people for works of service, so that the body of Christ may be built up (Eph. 4:7, 11–12).

What could I do about considering the possibility of 'full-time' Christian service?

Pray. Ask God to guide you. Put him in charge of the whole decision-making process, and ask him to help you to hear clearly what he is saying. But don't use prayer just to ask for things. Take the opportunity to get very close to God in a deep relationship of love and trust, so that you can feel his heartbeat and be lifted up and carried by his goodness and grace.

Be willing to do anything. It's no good saying to the Lord, 'I'm willing to serve you in Surbiton, but not in Tottenham,' or, 'I'll be a pastor, but don't ask me to be a missionary.' We have to be willing to say, 'Lord, I'll serve you anywhere, and do anything you want me to do.' But be reassured; if there is some place you couldn't stand going to or some task that you'd absolutely hate to have to do, it's extremely unlikely God would call you to it. He knows all about you, your likes and dislikes, and your strengths and weaknesses, and he graciously takes them all into consideration when he calls you. The best policy is to talk through with him your feelings and preferences, giving him permission to change you if there's anything in you that doesn't fit in with his gracious purposes.

Get all the information you can. Talk with as many people as you can who know about the sort of work you might be doing. Don't go into it with your eyes closed, or with an unrealistic concept of what it is to serve the Lord in this way. It will almost certainly be tough and costly. If a time of study is involved, talk with those who have done or are doing the course.

Share the decisions with your close family. The costs and pressures of serving God in this way will have many repercussions on those closest to you. If you are married, be sure your spouse is fully in agreement with the steps you're taking. If you have children or other family who will be affected, explain things clearly to them.

Check and pray through the three points listed above about recognizing the Lord's leading: an inner urging or conviction, evidence that you have gifts and abilities (at least in embryonic form) that God can use in the ministry you are considering, and confirmation by others.

Choose the right training. The organization you're thinking of working with may run its own course or require you to go to a specific college. Or they may advise you about the most suitable course. But in many cases the choice of course is left to you. Again, get all the information you can; send for prospectuses from a range of colleges. Be careful to select a course that will train you for the realities of ministry you'll be doing; a university degree in religious studies is fine, but it's unlikely to train you in, say, pastoral skills or preaching. Most universities offer generic courses up to degree level. Some colleges offer courses specializing in specific areas, such as children's or youth work, evangelism and church-planting, counselling, pastoral ministry, worship-leading and cross-cultural ministry. Another key factor to check is the college's emphasis on personal and spiritual growth during your training; it's vital that you let God use your time of preparation to build up your relationship with him.

Think through where the money's coming from. At this stage it's hardly appropriate to ask people for firm promises of support, but you still need to have a good idea of how your training and time of service are likely to be financed.

Send in applications. Making an application isn't a firm commitment to go forward. It's still up to the organization to turn you down, or to you to withdraw as you talk further with them. But applying is a key part of the process. Be honest in your application; don't fall to using the techniques advocated for landing a good secular job. Admit to your hesitations and doubts; be honest about your weaknesses as well as your strengths. And keep soaking the whole process in prayer.

Be prepared for setbacks. God doesn't promise us an easy ride, even when we're committed to following his leading. And the devil will do all he can to deflect you; remember what he did to Jesus when he was starting out on his ministry (Luke 4:1–13). Ask for God's strength to face each setback, and, as you come through them, thank him for giving you further confirmation that he is leading you. If a setback proves fatal for the plans you were making, go back to God and ask him for his alternative.

GIFTS AND MINISTRIES: RECOGNIZING AND DEVELOPING SPIRITUAL GIFTS

God has done a great job in planning and shaping the local church. He could have made it monochrome, with everybody the same and doing the same things. He could have arranged it that one or two really gifted and special people did all the exciting things while everybody else looked on.

But instead he's made it a fantastic mix of people, all different, and each with a special part to play. Just as he created a world where no two leaves are the same shape and no event is ever repeated in exactly the same way, so he's made each of us unique individuals and given us each unique gifts or giftings. In two or three places the New Testament gives lists of these gifts. Some writers have taken these lists, put them together, drawn up a definitive list of some thirty to forty gifts and ministries that Christians might have, and found ways for the individual Christian to work through that list in order to decide which of those gifts she or he has.

There is doubtless some value in this, but I suggest it's a mistake to assume that the New Testament sets out to give us a complete list of gifts and ministries. The three main lists that are given don't claim to be covering everything; what they're doing is mentioning examples. There are plenty of other gifts they could have mentioned. After all, it's a mistake to limit God's creativeness and originality to a mere forty giftings.

One of the fascinating things about the giftings mentioned in the Bible is the way 'spiritual' and 'practical' gifts rub shoulders together. We might be inclined to put gifts such as doing miracles or speaking in tongues into a 'spiritual' category, and others, such as administration and giving, into a much more 'practical' category. After all, we might think, we were administering and giving before we became Christians, so all we're doing is carrying on with our old 'natural' giftings; but to do miracles or to speak in tongues we need a special anointing of the Holy Spirit.

But the New Testament doesn't seem to see things that way. It views the gift or ministry of giving as every bit as much a spiritual gift as the gift or ministry of doing miracles or speaking in tongues. Nowhere does it call anything a 'natural' gift; if it's something given by God, whether before or after conversion, and offered back to God to be used by him for his glory, then it's just as 'spiritual' as any other gift.

Recognizing gifts and ministries isn't so much a matter of working through a list of some forty 'possibles' and deciding which ones fit best. Rather, it's a question of accepting who we are and recognizing those areas of our lives where God has given us something we can use for his glory.

New Testament passages on gifts and ministries

I urge you, brothers, in view of God's mercy, to offer your bodies as living sacrifices, holy and pleasing to God – this is your spiritual act of worship ... Do not think of yourself more highly than you ought, but rather think of yourself with sober judgment, in accordance with the measure of faith God has given you. Just as each of us has one body and many members, and these members do not all have the same function, so in Christ we who are many form one body, and each member belongs to all the others. We have different gifts, according to the grace given us. If a man's gift is prophesying, let him use it in proportion to his faith. If it is serving, let him serve; if it is teaching, let him teach; if it is encouraging, let him encourage; if it is contributing to the needs of others, let him give generously; if it is leadership, let him govern diligently; if it is showing mercy, let him do it cheerfully (Rom. 12:1, 3–8).

There are different kinds of gifts, but the same Spirit.

... to each one the manifestation of the Spirit is given for the common good. To one there is given through the Spirit the message of wisdom, to another the message of knowledge by means of the same Spirit, to another faith by the same Spirit, to another gifts of healing by that one Spirit, to another miraculous powers, to another prophecy, to another distinguishing between spirits, to another speaking in different kinds of tongues, and to still another the interpretation of tongues. All these are the work of one and the same Spirit, and he gives them to each one, just as he determines ...

God has arranged the parts in the body, every one of them, just as he wanted them to be.

... you are the body of Christ, and each one of you is a part of it. And in the church God has appointed first of all apostles, second prophets, third teachers, then workers of miracles, also those having gifts of healing, those able to help others, those with gifts of administration, and those speaking in different kinds of tongues (1 Cor. 12:4, 7–11, 18, 27–28).

... live a life worthy of the calling you have received ... keep the unity of the Spirit through the bond of peace. There is one body and one Spirit ...

... to each one of us grace has been given as Christ apportioned it ... It was he who gave some to be apostles, some to be prophets, some to be evangelists, and some to be pastors and teachers, to prepare God's people for works of service, so that the body of Christ may be built up (Eph. 4:1, 3–4, 7, 11–12).

... fan into flame the gift of God, which is in you (2 Tim. 1:6).

Each one should use whatever gift he has received to serve others, faithfully administering God's grace in its various forms. If anyone speaks, he should do it as one speaking the very words of God. If anyone serves, he should do it with the strength God provides, so that in all things God may be praised through Jesus Christ. To him be the glory and the power for ever and ever. Amen (1 Pet. 4:10–11).

What could I do?

Thank God for the brilliant way he's planned things. Thank him for giving you specific gifts and ministries. Forget about complaining that he's given more interesting or more up-front gifts to others and the duller and more mundane ones to you. What he's given you is his perfect choice for you as you are. For you to try to be an apostle when he's calling you to be an encourager or a church treasurer would be a disaster. If you really think you've had a raw deal, take comfort from Jesus' words 'Many who are first will be last, and the last first' (Mark 10:31).

Take a good look at the gifts God has given you. Take time over this – weeks rather than minutes. Ask the Holy Spirit to show you the specific abilities that he has put in you that he wants you to use for God's glory. By all means look through the lists given in

Scripture, but don't limit yourself to them. Check your specific skills. Ask others what gifts they can see in you. Remember that some gifts may be in embryonic form; the gift of church-planting or writing symphonies doesn't spring up complete overnight.

As you locate them, give each gift back to God. Do this specifically and solemnly. Write it down somewhere where you can keep it. 'Today I solemnly gave back to God my gift of playing the drums. I told him that from now on it's his to use in any way he chooses, and only for his glory. I asked him to sort me out if I start taking the gift back and begin using it my way and for my glory. I asked him to keep filling me and my playing with the Holy Spirit, to show me how to play in such a way that he is glorified, and to use my gift to help and build up others and to be a means of bringing in his kingdom.'

Ask God to open up ways for you to use your gifts. If he has created and given them to you in the first place, there has got to be some way of using them for his glory. Tell him you're keen to get on and serve him in any way he shows you.

Work at finding ways of using your gifts. Remember the parable of the talents and the mistake of the man who simply buried his talent in the ground (Matt. 25:24–30). Don't be put off if the way of using it isn't immediately obvious. Your gift of javelin-throwing may seem out of place in a Sunday service, or your vicar may be unable to use your gift of speaking Urdu. But our gifts are not just for use on Sundays. Maybe God is calling you to share his good news with someone in the athletics club, or to help an Asian woman learn English. In some cases you may have to be patient; your gift of playing the organ in the Sunday services may have to wait until the current organist moves on. But in most cases it's likely that if you look hard enough you'll find ways of using your gifts, even if only in a short-term way.

Keep renewing your commitment to use your gifts only for God's glory. The story of the Christian church has been plagued by gifted people abusing their gifts, from leaders who've used their leadership gifts to manipulate others for their own ends, or scholars who've used their intellectual gifts to discredit the Bible, to organists or flower arrangers who've got upset because they weren't given due credit for their wonderful contributions. Be determined this won't happen with you: 'whatever you do, do it all for the glory of God' (1 Cor. 10:31). However you use your gifts, keep remembering that it's God who matters, not you. Very often you won't be thanked; you may well be criticized or rejected. But you're not doing it so that you'll get the credit. To be criticized and rejected is standard for followers of Jesus. Keep the right perspective, and keep going.

Develop your gifts. Paul wrote to Timothy, 'Do your best to present yourself to God as one approved, a workman who does not need to be ashamed' (2 Tim. 2:15). The word he used for 'Do your best' has a sense of urgency about it; this, he says, is a priority. Don't get slack, or let things begin to drift. What God has entrusted to you as a gift is a key part of the bringing in of his kingdom, so keep working at it. Some gifts need specific training to develop them: a course at a Bible college to train as an evangelist; day conferences to sharpen your teaching or worship-leading skills. Others develop by constant practice. All need prayer; don't slip into the way of thinking that you've preached or given a stranger a lift so many times before that you don't need to surround this particular sermon or this hitch-hiker in prayer. Make sure you listen to what other people say; they won't always get things right, but you can learn something even from negative and destructive criticism. Ask wise and discerning Christian friends to comment and suggest how you can improve the use of your gift. Be a constant learner.

GIVING

There are a number of reasons why, as Christians, we should give. One is that giving is very Godlike. He is the supreme giver. He gives freely and generously, and invites us to follow his example.

Another reason is that giving greatly benefits us. It helps us to have the right perspective on possessions. It reminds us that they are not ours; they are the Lord's. We are stewards, not owners.

What's more, developing the ability to give helps to set us free from the bondage to things that is all too common in our society. And it enables us to express love, mercy and compassion. And, in addition, God promises to bless those who give.

A third reason why we should give is the need around us. We may be tempted to feel that our gifts are too small to make much difference, but that is demonstrably untrue. Even without the Bible stories of the loaves and fish (John 6:9–13) and the widow's offering (Luke 21:1–4), we can all think of ways in which even a small gift can make a big difference. We're surrounded with need, and God calls us to use what we have to answer that need.

I guess no Christian has any quarrel with the principle of giving, nor with the principle that giving includes the giving of money. Of course, it includes many other forms of giving as well, such as the giving of our home and possessions in hospitality, the giving of our time in work and service, and the giving of our skills to help and minister to others. But the giving of money is a key form of giving, and it's on that that we'll be focusing in the rest of this section.

Perhaps there are two key issues. We know we should give. But who should we give to, and how much?

Some Bible teaching on giving

'Be careful not to do your "acts of righteousness" before men, to be seen by them. If you do, you will have no reward from your Father in heaven.

'So when you give to the needy, do not announce it with trumpets, as the hypocrites do in the synagogues and on the streets, to be honoured by men. I tell you the truth, they have received their reward in full. But when you give to the needy, do not let your left hand know what your right hand is doing, so that your giving may be in secret. Then your Father, who sees what is done in secret, will reward you' (Matt. 6:1–4).

'Freely you have received, freely give' (Matt. 10:8).

'Then the King will say ... "Come, you who are blessed by my Father; take your inheritance, the kingdom prepared for you since the creation of the world. For I was hungry and you gave me something to eat, I was thirsty and you gave me something to drink, I was a stranger and you invited me in, I needed clothes and you clothed me, I was sick and you looked after me, I was in prison and you came to visit me."

'Then the righteous will answer him, "Lord, when did we see you hungry and feed you, or thirsty and give you something to drink? When did we see you a stranger and invite you in, or needing clothes and clothe you? When did we see you sick or in prison and go to visit you?"

'The King will reply, "I tell you the truth, whatever you did for one of the least of these brothers of mine, you did for me"' (Matt. 25:34–40).

'Give to everyone who asks you, and if anyone takes what belongs to you, do not demand it back. Do to others as you would have them do to you ...

'Give, and it will be given to you. A good measure, pressed down, shaken together and running over, will be poured into your lap. For with the measure you use it will be measured to you' (Luke 6:30–31, 38).

'Do not be afraid, little flock, for your Father has been pleased to give you the kingdom. Sell your possessions and give to the poor. Provide purses for yourselves that will not wear out, a treasure in heaven that will not be exhausted, where no thief comes near and no moth destroys. For where your treasure is, there your heart will be also' (Luke 12:32–34).

Now about the collection for God's people: Do what I told the Galatian churches to do. On the first day of every week, each one of you should set aside a sum of money in keeping with his income (1 Cor. 16:1–2).

Remember this: Whoever sows sparingly will also reap sparingly, and whoever sows generously will also reap generously. Each man should give what he has decided in his heart to give, not reluctantly or under compulsion, for God loves a cheerful giver. And God is able to make all grace abound to you, so that in all things at all times, having all that you need, you will abound in every good work. As it is written:

> 'He has scattered abroad his gifts to the poor;
> his righteousness endures for ever.'

Now he who supplies seed to the sower and bread for food will also supply and increase your store of seed and will enlarge the harvest of your righteousness. You will be made rich in every way so that you can be generous on every occasion (2 Cor. 9:6–11; see the whole passage from 2 Cor. 8:1 to 9:15).

See also the story of the rich young man in Matthew 19:16–30.

What could I do?

Start by giving all your money to God. You've probably already done that many times, but it's worth doing again. Since we belong to him, everything that is ours belongs to him as well. Tell him that it's his to use in any way he chooses.

Accept the responsibility of handling it for him. Once you've clarified that your money is actually God's money, he then trusts you to handle it wisely and well on his behalf. It's rather like your body. When you give your body to him (Rom. 12:1; 6:13) he doesn't take it away so that you never see it again. Instead, he gives it back to you to manage for his glory. So with your money; it's his, but he trusts you to use it wisely and well. (See the section on **money**.)

Ask him to guide you how to use your money. In particular, ask him to show you how much you should give away, and who to give it to.

Think through Paul's teaching about regularly giving a proportion of your income (1 Cor. 16:2). In the Old Testament the required proportion was one tenth. In the New Testament no precise proportion is named; it's not a question of having to give what the law requires, but rather of free and 'cheerful' giving (2 Cor. 9:7). Some Christians choose to give one tenth of their income; some give more, some less. Some work out the proportion according to their income before tax and other stoppages; others give a proportion of the actual money received. Talk it through with God. Think what would be the kind of proportion you'd like to give him. Then assess this in the light of your outgoings and responsibilities. If the two don't fit, consider possible ways of reducing your outgoings, possibly by living more simply. Then make a decision. Put it into practice. Every now and then, review it.

Decide what to give to. Do this prayerfully and with thought. There are so many worthy causes it's impossible to give to them all. So be selective, narrowing the field down to people and projects you can support not just financially, but with interest, prayer and perhaps even personal involvement. You will probably want to keep a balance between different types of causes, in this country and abroad: social, evangelistic, building up Christians, and so on. Probably a substantial part of your giving will be to your local church. Many churches operate schemes whereby a proportion of the income they receive is passed on to other individuals and organizations; they may also be willing to forward earmarked gifts. This enables you to channel all your giving through your local church, and makes life a lot simpler. Besides giving to organizations, consider making gifts to individuals: an elderly person struggling to make ends meet; a young person spending a 'gap' year doing some worthwhile voluntary work; someone who gives up a good job to go to a Bible college.

Every now and then, consider making a gift over and above your regular commitment. You might do so as an expression of thankfulness for something special that has happened in your life, in response to a special need, or simply because God prompts your heart.

Where possible, use one of the tax-effective means of giving. Payroll giving, Gift Aid and giving through Christian charities-aid organizations are means by which your chosen charity can reclaim the tax you've paid on the sum you give.

Keep quiet about your giving. It isn't really possible these days to keep our giving entirely secret. But as far as possible, keep it quiet.

Resist the temptation to let others know what a good Christian you are because of what you give (Matt. 6:2–4).

HAPPINESS

Many people seem to think happiness is the most important thing in life. What's more, they assume that the chief aim of Christianity is to make us happy, and the chief responsibility of God is to remove from our lives anything that diminishes our happiness. Though there are, of course, some grains of truth in this, it's much too facile a way of viewing matters. Not only is it a very superficial understanding of happiness; it isolates happiness from all the other elements that make life rich and good, as though it's the only thing that matters.

The Bible is full of teaching about happiness. Happiness is one of its most common themes. But its concept of happiness is gloriously deep and rich, so much so that the concepts of our contemporary culture seem but shadows in comparison. It's so rich that it takes a number of terms to describe it, including words generally translated 'blessed', 'joy', and 'peace'.

Many today find the meaning of the term 'blessed' hard to grasp. Perhaps the best way to understand it is to remember that the terms 'bless', 'blessed' and 'blessing' are used throughout the Bible both of God and of humans. We bless the Lord; he blesses us. Both he and we can be described as 'blessed'. So we can understand human blessedness in the light of God's blessedness. When we are blessed, we are sharing in something that belongs especially to God. We experience his happiness, joy and peace. We feel what God feels.

A number of Bible passages on both 'joy' and 'blessedness' are given below. For passages on 'peace' (*shalom*) see the section on **health**.

A key distinctive of biblical teaching is that the source of true happiness is God himself, not circumstances or things around us.

That, of course, is a radical reversal of most contemporary people's way of seeing life. They assume that having God with us limits our freedom to do what we like, and, since what we like to do is what makes us happy, having God in our lives necessarily limits our happiness.

The Bible's teaching is quite the opposite. Only God knows what will bring us the truest and greatest happiness; in love and mercy he has provided this for us through the salvation he has made possible through the work of Christ. We need to accept that our ideas of what we would like will not ultimately lead to happiness. So we need to turn from these things, denying ourselves where necessary (Luke 9:23–24), and maybe even suffering as a result (Rom. 5:1–5); and instead receive his salvation, which in effect means receiving him.

Out of this comes happiness on at least three levels. First, there is deep and lasting joy and peace that 'transcends all understanding' (Phil. 4:7) and is able to continue even when everything around us seems disastrous (Hab. 3:17–18; 2 Cor. 12:9–10). There is, secondly, the anticipation that our ultimate destiny is total joy in the presence of God, of which we may have a foretaste, but which will surpass all earthly joys as the sunrise surpasses the starlight.

And there's a third level that Paul and James talk about and that many miss. It is finding happiness, joy or peace not just *despite* problems and difficulties and suffering, but even, in a sense, because of them or arising from them. Paul was able to say that we 'rejoice in our sufferings' (Rom. 5:3), or 'I delight in weaknesses, in insults, in hardships, in persecutions, in difficulties' (2 Cor. 12:10). James started his letter with the extraordinary command to 'Consider it pure joy, my brothers, whenever you face trials of many kinds' (Jas. 1:2). Peter told his readers to 'rejoice that you participate in the sufferings of Christ' (1 Pet. 4:13). All three echo the words of Jesus when he told his followers to 'rejoice' and even 'leap for joy' when they face poverty, hunger, weeping, hatred, insults and rejection (Luke 6:20–23).

This is not, of course, a command to take a masochistic delight in suffering, any more than it's a call to force ourselves to say something cheerful through gritted teeth. Rather, it arises from a total confidence that if God has permitted hardship or suffering to come into our lives it is because he is going to do at least two things. First, he will give us the extra grace we need to get through it. Secondly, he will use it for some beautiful purpose, unattainable in any other way. This purpose may be something personal, such as growth in Christian character (Rom. 5:3–5; Jas 1:2–4) or an extra experience of God's grace and power (2 Cor. 12:7–10). Or it could be something that brings benefit to others: Paul suffered imprisonment and persecution so that others might find Christ and be built up in him (Col. 1:24). In every situation, therefore, we see the hand of God working 'for the good of those who love him', and enabling us to be 'more than conquerors', never for one moment separated from 'the love of God that is in Christ Jesus our Lord' (Rom. 8:28–39).

Some Bible passages on joy

'... the joy of the LORD is your strength' (Neh. 8:10).

You have made known to me the path of life;
    you will fill me with joy in your presence,
    with eternal pleasures at your right hand (Ps. 16:11).

God, my joy and my delight (Ps. 43:4).

... the city of our God ... the joy of the whole earth
(Ps. 48:1–2).

Restore to me the joy of your salvation (Ps. 51:12).

'With joy you will draw water
    from the wells of salvation' (Is. 12:3).

    ... the ransomed of the LORD will return.
They will enter Zion with singing;
    everlasting joy will crown their heads.
Gladness and joy will overtake them,
    and sorrow and sighing will flee away (Is. 35:10).

> Though the fig-tree does not bud
>> and there are no grapes on the vines,
> though the olive crop fails
>> and the fields produce no food,
> though there are no sheep in the pen
>> and no cattle in the stalls
> yet I will rejoice in the LORD,
>> I will be joyful in God my Saviour (Hab 3:17–18).

'Blessed are you when people insult you, persecute you and falsely say all kinds of evil against you because of me. Rejoice and be glad, because great is your reward in heaven' (Matt. 5:11–12).

'As the Father has loved me, so have I loved you. Now remain in my love ... I have told you this so that my joy may be in you and that your joy may be complete.
   '... no-one will take away your joy.
   '... the full measure of my joy' (John 15:9, 11; 16:22; 17:13).

... the disciples were filled with joy and with the Holy Spirit (Acts 13:52).

... we rejoice in the hope of the glory of God. Not only so, but we also rejoice in our sufferings (Rom. 5:2–3).

... the kingdom of God is ... righteousness, peace and joy in the Holy Spirit (Rom 14:17).

Out of the most severe trial, their overflowing joy and their extreme poverty welled up in rich generosity (2 Cor. 8:2).

The fruit of the Spirit is ... joy (Gal. 5:22).

Consider it pure joy, my brothers, whenever you face trials of many kinds (Jas. 1:2).

... you greatly rejoice, though now for a little while you may have had to suffer grief in all kinds of trials. These have come so that your faith – of greater worth than gold, which perishes even though refined by fire – may be proved genuine and may result in praise, glory and honour when Jesus Christ is revealed. Though you have not seen him, you love him; and even though you do not see him now, you believe in him and are filled with an inexpressible and glorious joy, for you are receiving the goal of your faith, the salvation of your souls (1 Pet. 1:6–9).

... do not be surprised at the painful trial you are suffering ... But rejoice that you participate in the sufferings of Christ, so that you may be overjoyed when his glory is revealed. If you are insulted because of the name of Christ, you are blessed, for the Spirit of glory and of God rests on you (1 Pet. 4:12–14).

Blessedness according to the book of Psalms and the Sermon on the Mount

Blessed is the man
    who does not walk in the counsel of the wicked ...
But his delight is in the law of the LORD
    and on his law he meditates day and night.
He is like a tree planted by streams of water,
    which yields its fruit in season
and whose leaf does not wither.
    Whatever he does prospers (Ps. 1:1–3).

Blessed is he
    whose transgressions are forgiven,
    whose sins are covered.
Blessed is the man
    whose sin the LORD does not count against him
    and in whose spirit is no deceit (Ps. 32:1–2).

Taste and see that the LORD is good;
    blessed is the man who takes refuge in him (Ps. 34:8).

Blessed is the man
  who makes the LORD his trust (Ps. 40:4).

Blessed are those you choose
  and bring near to live in your courts! (Ps. 65:4).

Blessed are those who dwell in your house;
  they are ever praising you.
Blessed are those whose strength is in you,
  who have set their hearts on pilgrimage ...
They go from strength to strength,
  till each appears before God in Zion ...
O LORD Almighty,
  blessed is the man who trusts in you (Ps. 84:4–5, 7, 12).

Blessed are those who have learned to acclaim you,
  who walk in the light of your presence, O LORD.
They rejoice in your name all day long;
  they exult in your righteousness.
For you are their glory and strength (Ps. 89:15–17).

Blessed are they who maintain justice,
  who constantly do what is right (Ps. 106:3).

Blessed is the man who fears the LORD,
  who finds great delight in his commands (Ps. 112:1).

Blessed are they whose ways are blameless,
  who walk according to the law of the LORD.
Blessed are they who keep his statutes
  and seek him with all their heart (Ps. 119:1–2).

Blessed are all who fear the LORD,
  who walk in his ways (Ps. 128:1).

'Blessed are the poor in spirit,
  for theirs is the kingdom of heaven.

Blessed are those who mourn,
>   for they will be comforted.
Blessed are the meek,
>   for they will inherit the earth.
Blessed are those who hunger and thirst for righteousness,
>   for they will be filled.
Blessed are the merciful,
>   for they will be shown mercy.
Blessed are the pure in heart,
>   for they will see God.
Blessed are the peacemakers,
>   for they will be called sons of God.
Blessed are those who are persecuted because of righteousness,
>   for theirs is the kingdom of heaven.

'Blessed are you when people insult you, persecute you and falsely say all kinds of evil against you because of me. Rejoice and be glad, because great is your reward in heaven, for in the same way they persecuted the prophets who were before you' (Matt. 5:3–12).

What could I do to experience true happiness?

Stop looking for happiness in the wrong places. Accept that though material possessions, good health, a problem-free life, popularity and success may all bring happiness, they aren't its real source, and we shouldn't make them our ultimate goals. To focus on them runs the risk of idolatry, worshipping something that takes the place in our lives that God should have.

Go for God. He *is* happiness, joy and peace, and many other things besides. But don't go for him as a means to an end: 'I'll follow you, Lord, so that you can make me happy.' Go for him because he is your God, your Creator, who loves you and gave Jesus to be your Saviour. Go for him for who he is, and let happiness follow (Matt. 6:33).

Develop the art of unselfish happiness. There's nothing wrong with selfish happiness, provided we don't make an idol of it. God wants us to happy when good things happen to us. But, for a

Christian, it can't be right to be happy when good things happen only to us; unselfish happiness is glad when something good happens to someone else, even if we miss out on it. Again, in our competitive and self-centred culture this is an art that few are really interested in or prepared to work at. Indeed, many psychologists seem to assume that it's impossible; we can only be happy in a selfish way, they would say. But Jesus has taught us something better.

Accept that there is no incompatibility between having a tough time and being truly happy. You may find this hard to take on board, and even harder to work out in your experience, but it is a profound biblical truth. Remember Jesus, facing the agony of Gethsemane and the cross, speaking of the fullness of his joy (John 17:13).

Work towards 'rejoicing in sufferings'. I like to think of it in terms of having a holiday in the English Lake District. Everyone loves it there when the weather is glorious, the sun shines and you can see for miles. But some learn the art of enjoying the Lake District when the clouds are low on the fells, the rain sweeps in from the sea, and every hillside runs with water. It's those who know how to enjoy both good and bad weather who have the best holidays. Learning to rejoice in sufferings takes some doing, but, by God's grace, it's within reach of us all. Here are some steps you might take towards it:

- *Ask God to teach you.*
- *Study the relevant passages in the New Testament.* Search out Paul's secret. Even more, focus on Jesus and the source of his joy.
- *Build up your trust in God.* There's a kind of scale, and we're all at different points. It ranges from 'I can trust God as long everything's going well' to 'Though he slay me, yet will I hope in him' (Job. 13:15). Reflect on his faithfulness, love, goodness and power. See how far up the scale you can get.
- *Try to look at your problems and suffering from God's angle.* Think of the possible reasons why God might have allowed them. You may have to use a bit of ingenuity, but, remember, God is ingenious, and has every conceivable resource at his disposal.

Let your imagination range over what good goals he might be working towards, such that one day you'll say, 'It was tough at the time, but now, in the light of what God has brought out of it, I see that it was worth every moment.' Of course, there's a fair chance that you won't hit on the outcome that God has in mind, so don't make the mistake of deciding what it's got to be and getting frustrated if things don't work out that way. Leave the final decision to him – he's committed to making the best choice.

Be thankful. There are plenty of biblical commands to give thanks. Thankfulness is a key element of letting God be God in our lives. If we think we're God, or that everything happens by chance, we won't be thankful for anything – a sure way to lose out on happiness. But if we see everything as God's gracious gift, and practise the art of saying thank you, we'll be tapping in to a rich source of joy.

Practise praise. Again, the Bible is full of commands to praise the Lord. If we fail to do this, we'll not only be holding back from God something he richly deserves; we'll be depriving ourselves of something that greatly enriches our lives. Make your worship in church a real act of praise; don't just sing the songs; praise God with all your being as you do so. Praise him day by day and in all circumstances; it's always possible to find something to praise him for. Praise him when praise wells up in you like a spring. But also praise him when the spring is replaced with a wet blanket; that's what the writer to the Hebrews meant by a 'sacrifice of praise' (Heb. 13:15). There's something special about our praise when it's a costly gift we bring to God. Praise and happiness are closely linked.

Get hold of hope. Thankfulness and praise are rich biblical concepts that are linked closely with happiness. So is hope. 'We rejoice in the hope of the glory of God,' said Paul (Rom. 5:2), and he followed it up with a command: 'Be joyful in hope' (Rom. 12:12). He's not talking, of course, about some vague and uncertain hope that things will eventually turn out all right. Rather, it's the assurance available to every Christian that God definitely will bring our lives and everything in them to a glorious climax, the full expression of our salvation, described as nothing less than the glory of God himself. The future isn't just bright; it's ablaze with glory. That's something to chase away the clouds.

Let happiness surprise you. If we think of happiness as a kind of right, something that we can demand from life, we'll often be disappointed and frustrated. But if we more or less forget about happiness and go for God and his purposes in our lives, we'll find happiness popping up in all sorts of unexpected places. In C. S. Lewis's phrase, we'll be 'surprised by joy'.

HEALTH

The biblical understanding of health is to be seen as part of its concern with *shalom*. This is a rich and broad concept; it covers so many aspects of human wholeness and well-being that it and its New Testament equivalent have to be translated by a variety of terms to draw out the full meaning. The most common translation is 'peace', but at times it needs to be translated as 'health', 'salvation', 'completeness', 'soundness', 'safety', 'well-being' or 'prosperity'.

Shalom describes human life as it ought to be, where all its aspects are right and in their right proportion. Thus it covers right relationships with God, with other people and with the world around; a balanced attitude towards ourselves; the proper functioning of our thoughts and feelings and of all that the Bible means by our 'heart'; and the right functioning of our bodies in physical health and vitality. Perfect *shalom* will entail full well-being in every aspect of life, but that doesn't mean that we can't experience a high level of *shalom* even in the imperfections of our human lives. It would be quite possible for someone, say, with a major physical disability or illness to have a high degree of 'health' or 'wholeness' in the broad sense of *shalom*.

Western culture's neurotic fascination with personal physical health arises largely from our narcissistic individualism: my most important priority is my bodily well-being. It is encouraged by the fact that, for the first time in human history, perfect health and everlasting bodily life seem within our grasp. Previous generations accepted that illness, ageing, and death were an inevitable part of being human. Thanks to the hype of scientific and media claims, many people now seem to believe that, with a bit more research and a lot of money, we'll be able to buy a cure for everything and live for ever. From that belief it's easy to slide into regarding perfect health as a right we can demand and should expect. An additional factor, the exact opposite of Paul's approach, is that this life is all we have, so we must make it as pleasurable and as lengthy as possible.

The Christian way of seeing health is very different. There are far more important things in life than bodily health. Experiencing pain, suffering, illness and ageing are part of what it means to be human in a fallen world. Death is by no means something to be feared and avoided at all costs; its sting has been drawn; it has been transformed by Christ into the gateway to glory. So a Christian view of health will be much wider than an exclusive interest in having a body that doesn't cause us pain or inconvenience and that does all we want it to do. True health has significant spiritual, mental, emotional and relational dimensions, as well as covering the proper functioning of our physical bodies.

Thus John prays for good health for his friend in the context of spiritual health, and 'that all may go well with you' (3 John 2). And Paul, when writing to Timothy, though he recognizes the value of taking exercise and keeping fit, takes care to get it in its right perspective. Keeping physically fit is valuable for this life, he says; but keeping spiritually fit is valuable both for this life and for the life to come (1 Tim. 4:8). We keep our focus on what lasts for ever, he says in 2 Corinthians 4:18; physically we may be 'wasting away' and 'groaning', but that's far outweighed by the spiritual reality that is ours both now and in heaven.

Because we reject the self-centred individualism of our culture, Christians view health as something to be sought in its totality for the whole of humanity. It's nothing less than the fulfilment of the prayer 'your kingdom come, your will be done on earth as it is in heaven' (Matt. 6:10). Though we shall be concerned to keep our own bodies fit and healthy, therefore, we shall also have a deep concern for the physical, spiritual, emotional and relational well-being of others throughout the world.

Some aspects of the biblical view of health

1. The biblical concept of shalom

The LORD said to Moses, 'Tell Aaron and his sons, "This is how you are to bless the Israelites. Say to them:

'"'The LORD bless you
    and keep you;
the LORD make his face shine upon you
    and be gracious to you;
the LORD turn his face towards you
    and give you peace [*shalom*].'"

'So they will put my name on the Israelites, and I will bless them' (Num. 6:22–27).

The LORD gives strength to his people;
    the LORD blesses his people with peace [*shalom*] (Ps. 29:11).

My son, do not forget my teaching,
    but keep my commands in your heart,
for they will prolong your life many years
    and bring you prosperity [*shalom*] (Prov. 3:1–2).

... to us a child is born ...
And he will be called
    Wonderful Counsellor, Mighty God,
    Everlasting Father, Prince of Peace [*shalom*].
Of the increase of his government and peace [*shalom*]
    there will be no end (Is. 9:6–7).

... he took up our infirmities
    and carried our sorrows ...

the punishment that brought us peace [*shalom*]was upon him,
and by his wounds we are healed (Is. 53:4–5).

2. Other Bible teaching relevant to health

Jesus went throughout Galilee, teaching in their synagogues,
preaching the good news of the kingdom, and healing every
disease and sickness among the people. News about him spread
all over Syria, and people brought to him all who were ill with
various diseases, those suffering severe pain, the demon-
possessed, those having seizures, and the paralysed, and he
healed them (Matt. 4:23–24).

I urge you, brothers, in view of God's mercy, to offer your
bodies as living sacrifices, holy and pleasing to God – this is
your spiritual act of worship (Rom. 12:1).

If only for this life we have hope in Christ, we are to be pitied
more than all men.
... as in Adam all die, so in Christ all will be made alive ...
But someone may ask, 'How are the dead raised? With what
kind of body will they come?'...
The body that is sown is perishable, it is raised imperishable;
it is sown in dishonour, it is raised in glory; it is sown in weakness, it is raised in power; it is sown a natural body, it is raised
a spiritual body.
... the perishable must clothe itself with the imperishable,
and the mortal with immortality (1 Cor. 15:19, 22, 35,
42–44, 53).

... we do not lose heart. Though outwardly we are wasting away,
yet inwardly we are being renewed day by day ... we fix our eyes
not on what is seen, but on what is unseen. For what is seen is
temporary, but what is unseen is eternal.
Now we know that if the earthly tent we live in is destroyed,
we have a building from God, an eternal house in heaven, not
built by human hands. Meanwhile we groan, longing to be
clothed with our heavenly dwelling (2 Cor. 4:16, 18; 5:1–2).

Physical training is of some value, but godliness has value for all things, holding promise for both the present life and the life to come (1 Tim. 4:8).

Is any one of you in trouble? He should pray. Is anyone happy? Let him sing songs of praise. Is any one of you sick? He should call for the elders of the church to pray over him and anoint him with oil in the name of the Lord. And the prayer offered in faith will make the sick person well; the Lord will raise him up. If he has sinned, he will be forgiven (Jas. 5:13–15).

Dear friend, I pray that you may enjoy good health and that all may go well with you, even as your soul is getting along well (3 John 2).

What could I do?

Work at broadening your thinking. Move away from a concept of health that focuses on 'me not being ill' to a vision of 'everyone in the world living *shalom*'.

Adopt a realistic view of suffering, ageing and death. Reject the implicit assumption of our culture that we have some sort of right to a pain-free life, perpetual youth, or endless life in this body. We all have to suffer pain, illness, the wearing out of our bodies and the decline of our faculties. Make up your mind that you will accept these experiences positively, and help others to do so.

Do what you can to promote true health worldwide. Pray for the coming of God's kingdom on earth, as it is in heaven. Work for it. Given the huge inequality of healthcare throughout the world, do what you can to promote its just distribution. There are all sorts of ways of doing this, ranging from financial and prayer support for a specific healthcare project or medical mission to campaigning for the cancellation of Third World debt.

Within the context of a broad biblical view of health, be a good steward of your body. The fact that we don't make perfect physical health and freedom from pain our priority doesn't mean we should neglect our bodies. They are a gift from God and it's our privilege to return them to be used for his glory (Rom. 12:1).

So we have a responsibility to care for them. In particular, we should not abuse or damage them through neglect, laziness, over-eating, drug or alcohol abuse, unhealthy diet or lack of exercise. See if there are ways you could be a better steward of your body, and put them into action.

Avoid the trap of making health an idol. Loss of physical health is not a disaster; be prepared to accept it if God entrusts you with it. Good diet, healthy foods and good physical exercise are all excellent in their place, but keep them in their right place; don't let them become an obsession or an overruling concern in your life. Use the benefits that contemporary medicine and surgery provide, but keep a right perspective on them; remember that, for example, in Africa 8,000 children die every day from hunger or easily treatable diseases such as measles. If you choose to use complementary medicines and therapies, make sure that your use of them is free from any spiritual elements that run counter to Christianity; given that, the principle expressed in 1 Timothy 4:4–5 can be applied.

Check that you have a Christlike attitude to those who suffer poor health. Our society still tends to exclude the ill, those with disabilities and the frail elderly as though they were somehow less than fully human. Christians have always rejected this attitude, and followed the example of Jesus in making such people a special focus for love and care. Indeed, for much of the last 2,000 years in the West, the vast majority of projects and institutions for care of those who are ill or in need has been the work of Christians. Keep up this tradition; go out of your way to love, support, care and bring healing.

Remember to support those who care for those who are ill. This includes medical staff and support staff in hospitals and in nursing homes for the elderly, but don't forget relatives and carers, who often feel they are struggling alone with a long-term problem they are helpless to solve.

If you lose your health, seek to retain a positive attitude to your illness or disability. Remember the words of Job, 'The LORD gave and the LORD has taken away; may the name of the LORD be praised' (Job 1:21). Guard against self-pity. Pray that God will use the illness for good and for his glory. Tell him that, like Paul, you're even willing to rejoice in your sufferings (Rom. 5:3), because you believe that he will bring good things out of them. Avoid being too independent; let others show their love for you by caring for you. Be aware that pain and suffering may make you short-tempered and that those close to you may find this difficult to cope with. If this happens, talk with them about it and do what you can to minimize the problems that might arise.

HOUSE AND HOME

We use different words to describe the place in which we live and the people who live there. In biblical times only one word was used. A 'house' wasn't just a building; it was the community of people that lived there. In our materialistic culture the focus tends to be on the building, the furnishings, the gadgets and the finances, rather than on the community, the home, the relationships, the people. But the Bible has got it right: people matter more than places. Our primary interest is making a home where a community of people live as God intends us to live, and find his presence and grace.

Some Bible teaching on house and home

... the glory of the LORD filled his temple [Hebrew, 'house'] (1 Kgs. 8:11).

> Unless the LORD builds the house,
>   its builders labour in vain (Ps. 127:1).

> ... the house of the righteous stands firm ...
> The wise woman builds her house ...
> Better to live on a corner of the roof
>   than to share a house with a quarrelsome wife
>   (Prov. 12:7; 14:1; 21:9).

... everyone who hears these words of mine and puts them into practice is like a wise man who built his house on the rock ... it did not fall, because it had its foundation on the rock (Matt. 7:24–25).

'I was hungry and you gave me something to eat, I was thirsty and you gave me something to drink, I was a stranger and you invited me in ... "... Whatever you did for one of the least of these brothers of mine, you did for me"' (Matt. 25:35, 40).

'When you enter a house, first say, "Peace to this house." If a man of peace is there, your peace will rest on him; if not, it will return to you' (Luke 10:5–6)

Jesus ... said ... 'Zacchaeus, come down immediately. I must stay at your house today.' So he came down at once and welcomed him gladly ...

Zacchaeus stood up and said to the Lord, 'Look, Lord! Here and now I give half of my possessions to the poor ...'

Jesus said to him, 'Today salvation has come to this house' (Luke 19:5–6, 8–9).

Share with God's people who are in need. Practise hospitality (Rom. 12:13).

They devoted themselves to the apostles' teaching and to the fellowship, to the breaking of bread and to prayer ... All the believers were together and had everything in common. Selling their possessions and goods, they gave to anyone as he had need ... They broke bread in their homes and ate together with glad and sincere hearts, praising God and enjoying the favour of all the people (Acts 2:42, 44–45, 46–47).

... the church that meets at their house ... the church in her house ... the church that meets in your home (Rom. 16:5; 1 Cor. 16:19; Col. 4:15; Philem. 2).

... the overseer must be ... hospitable ... He must manage his own family [Greek, 'house'] well (1 Tim. 3:2, 4).

Command those who are rich in this present world not to be arrogant nor to put their hope in wealth, which is so uncertain, but ... to be generous and willing to share (1 Tim. 6:17–18).

... fix your thoughts on Jesus ... Moses was faithful as a servant in all God's house, testifying to what would be said in the future. But Christ is faithful as a son over God's house. And we are his house, if we hold on to our courage and the hope of which we boast (Heb. 3:1, 5–6).

Offer hospitality to one another without grumbling (1 Pet. 4:9).

What could I do?

The decisions we have to make over house and home are generally complex, and affect many other parts of our lives. For most people, buying a home is the biggest financial commitment they ever make, and involves a real struggle. When my wife and I first started buying a home in the 1980s, almost £300 of our monthly income of £330 went on the mortgage; to get a mortgage at all we had to pay 16% interest. In this section we'll look at some general principles, and then at a few more specific issues.

Dedicate your home to God. Whether you're buying or renting, and whether it's a tiny flat or a mansion, give it over to him. Ask him to fill it with his presence and glory (1 Kgs. 8:11). Go through it room by room, praying that all that is done there will be pleasing to him; you might choose to invite your church leaders to share in this act of dedication with you. Let the Lord know that you're committed to the principle that people matter more than things, and that your home is going to be a place where his kingdom comes and his will is done (Matt. 6:10).

Use your home for the Lord. Since you've given it to him, he has the first say over how it should be used. That will certainly include its use as a place where you can relax and spend time with your family. But it will probably also include making it a haven for others, where they can come and find love and the presence of the living God. 'Hospitality' is a key New Testament virtue. That doesn't have to entail elaborate meals, or having an 'open house' all the time for just anybody. But it does mean responding to Christ when he comes to your house, especially in people in need (Luke 19:5–9; Matt. 25:35, 40). Homes provide marvellous opportunities to show the love and goodness of God, to share the good news and to care for people in need. Don't miss those opportunities.

Keep a careful eye on your motives. To purchase a large house in a leafy suburb because that's supposed to be a sign of having 'arrived' is a poor motive. To buy the same house because God wants you to open it up to those in need is a good one.

Deciding on location. Think through such issues as: 'In what kind of neighbourhood could I make the most impact for the kingdom of God?' 'How far would a given location be from work, church, schools and my wider family?' 'Can I justify commuting the distances involved in terms of time, energy, money and environmental pollution?'

To rent or to buy? It is generally felt that investing in buying a property is a wiser use of money than long-term renting. But, again, many factors need to be thought through. If you're likely to want the property for only a short time before moving on, you need to weigh up the considerable costs involved in buying and then selling. Your income may be such that a mortgage is beyond your means, or you may not feel it wise to take on such a long-term commitment. Though house values generally appreciate, there's always a risk of prices going down, and so of losing money.

Deciding on price. The biblical principle is that debt should be avoided or paid off as soon as possible (Rom. 13:8). But, for most people, taking out a long-term mortgage is the only conceivable way of buying a house. Work out carefully what you can afford, preferably with a margin for emergencies. Adopt the principle that while you're in such debt over the house you'll do your utmost to avoid all other debt.

What about sharing? The concept of sharing fits well with the spirit of the early church (Acts 2:44–45). A sharing arrangement could be short-term, to help a temporarily homeless person, or more long-term, perhaps taking in an elderly relative in order to provide adequate care. It may be motivated largely financially, in order to share the rent or the mortgage repayments. It could be an expression of Christian community, or a specific way of advancing Christ's kingdom. If you do plan to share, be realistic and wise in the arrangements you make. Together, draw up an agreement regarding responsibilities and financial commitments. Build in ways of providing space for those involved. Have procedures in place to deal with any hassles or problems before they become serious. Agree to review the arrangements periodically; where possible, it's generally wise to set a time limit on the sharing arrangements: 'We'll do it for two years, reviewing at the end of eighteen months whether we want to go into a third year.'

Injustice

It happens all the time. Partly because we're human. Maybe because we're particularly vulnerable in some way or another. And sometimes because we're Christians and people know we won't hit back.

They take advantage. They cheat. They tell lies. They bend the rules in their favour. They discriminate against us. It's not fair. We're hurt, angry, and very tempted to hit back.

It may happen at work; someone gets preferential treatment or promotion when we feel it should be ours. We get blamed for something that isn't our fault. Life in general seems to have a down on us. Someone pushes in front in the queue at the supermarket checkout. It's not fair.

As Christians we rightly have a strong sense of what is just and fair. What's more, we're called to fight for justice and righteousness in the world. But we need to make a sharp distinction between fighting for justice for ourselves and fighting for justice for others. And, though there are exceptions (see below), while we're called to do the second, we're strongly encouraged to forgo the first. The example of Jesus makes this clear. As individuals,

God calls Christians to be willing to suffer injustice without fighting back. He calls us to 'turn the other cheek' (Matt. 5:39).

Some Bible teaching for when we are victims of injustice

Do not seek revenge or bear a grudge against one of your people, but love your neighbour as yourself. I am the LORD (Lev. 19:18).

> Do not say, 'I'll pay you back for this wrong!'
>   Wait for the LORD, and he will deliver you ...
> Do not say, 'I'll do to him as he has done to me;
>   I'll pay that man back for what he did'
>   (Prov. 20:22; 24:29).

'You have heard that it was said, "Eye for eye, and tooth for tooth." But I tell you, Do not resist an evil person. If someone strikes you on the right cheek, turn to him the other also. And if someone wants to sue you and take your tunic, let him have your cloak as well. If someone forces you to go one mile, go with him two miles ...'

'Love your enemies and pray for those who persecute you' (Matt. 5:38–41, 44).

Bless those who persecute you; bless and do not curse ...

Do not repay anyone evil for evil. Be careful to do what is right in the eyes of everybody. If it is possible, as far as it depends on you, live at peace with everyone. Do not take revenge, my friends, but leave room for God's wrath, for it is written: 'It is mine to avenge; I will repay,' says the Lord. On the contrary:

> 'If your enemy is hungry, feed him;
>   if he is thirsty, give him something to drink.
> In doing this, you will heap burning coals on his head.'

Do not be overcome by evil, but overcome evil with good (Rom. 12:14, 17–21).

... it is commendable if a man bears up under the pain of unjust suffering because he is conscious of God. But how is it to your credit if you receive a beating for doing wrong and endure it? But if you suffer for doing good and you endure it, this is commendable before God. To this you were called, because Christ suffered for you, leaving you an example, that you should follow in his steps.

> 'He committed no sin,
> and no deceit was found in his mouth.'

When they hurled their insults at him, he did not retaliate; when he suffered, he made no threats. Instead, he entrusted himself to him who judges justly (1 Pet. 2:19–23).

... even if you should suffer for what is right, you are blessed. Do not fear what they fear; do not be frightened. But in your hearts set apart Christ as Lord. Always be prepared to give an answer to everyone who asks you to give the reason for the hope that you have. But do this with gentleness and respect, keeping a clear conscience, so that those who speak maliciously against your good behaviour in Christ may be ashamed of their slander. It is better, if it is God's will, to suffer for doing good than for doing evil. For Christ died for sins once for all, the righteous for the unrighteous, to bring you to God (1 Pet. 3:14–18).

Dear friends, do not be surprised at the painful trial you are suffering, as though something strange were happening to you. But rejoice that you participate in the sufferings of Christ, so that you may be overjoyed when his glory is revealed. If you are insulted because of the name of Christ, you are blessed, for the Spirit of glory and of God rests on you. If you suffer, it should not be as a murderer or thief or any other kind of criminal, or even as a meddler. However, if you suffer as a Christian, do not be ashamed, but praise God that you bear that name ...

So then, those who suffer according to God's will should commit themselves to their faithful Creator and continue to do good (1 Pet. 4:12–16, 19).

What could I do if I'm a victim of injustice?

Resist the temptation to hit back. To refuse to retaliate is something profoundly countercultural. Everyone around us will insist that we ought to fight back, insist on our rights and sort the other person out. Jesus disagrees.

Turn the other cheek. Of course we know it's crazy. Usually it's costly. But there's no getting away from it: this is the way of Jesus. Just how we work it out will vary tremendously in different situations. Sometimes it'll be impossible or totally unpractical to do it. If you've just sold a guy a car and he pays you with a dud cheque, you can hardly go out and get another car to sell him. But sometimes God shows us ways we can specifically follow Jesus' teaching here. If he does, then we've got to do it.

Find ways of off-loading the anger and other emotions you may feel. In part at least, these feelings are a natural and healthy human response to injustice; it is quite right to feel a holy anger against what is evil. The problem with most of us is that our holy anger tends to get overlaid with feelings that are rather less holy: resentment, self-pity, a desire to hit back, even elements of hatred. Bottling up these feelings is rarely a good idea. We need to work them through and get rid of them. Ideally, we should take them to Jesus and talk them through with him, and let him sort us out. If we find that difficult, we may need a wise Christian friend with whom we can be completely open about our feelings, and who will pray with us about them. Some suggest writing an angry letter expressing all our feelings – and then giving it to God and formally destroying it. Or it may be right to channel our emotional energy into helping others who suffer injustice – fighting not for ourselves, but for other victims.

Pray. Pray for yourself, that your response will be Christlike. But pray also for those who have wronged you. From his teaching in Matthew 5 to his prayer on the cross (Luke 23:34), Jesus calls us to channel our emotional energy into prayer for those who do us wrong. It takes some doing; it's a costly sort of prayer to ask God to bless someone when everything in you is longing to hit them. But it's the Jesus way.

Do something positive for the person who has wronged you. Maybe this is the hardest of all. We may be willing to forgo our rights, to turn the other cheek and even to pray for our 'enemies'. But to 'love' them, to 'bless' them, to 'feed' them – that's really costly. But, again, it's the Jesus way. Find some way of showing them love in action, the love of Jesus expressed through you. It may take a fair bit of ingenuity to think of how you could do this; but work at it. Ask God to guide you, to give you a brilliant idea. It may blow their minds. Or it may have no obvious effect. But do it anyway, because Jesus calls you to do it. Don't, by the way, misunderstand Paul's bit about 'burning coals'; he's definitely not saying, 'Do something that looks positive, but with the hidden agenda of making the guy squirm'. When we do something positive we do it out of open-hearted, Christlike love. If it should make them feel guilty, fair enough – that may be a bonus. But that's not why we're doing it.

Anything else? We've said that when we're wronged we must resist our natural inclination to rush to defend ourselves, to sort out the situation or even sort out the person. But what about the times when we feel that it would be wrong simply to forgive and forget because failure to take action will result in more injustice? What if, for example, we are being bullied or racially discriminated against at work, and it's clear that just 'turning the other cheek' and letting the person get away with it will result in further injustice and in others suffering? What could we do then? Here are a few suggestions:

- *Make sure you've taken the five steps listed above before you do anything else.* They are the priority; get them in place, and you'll be well protected against the pitfalls the Bible's teaching warns us about.
- *Talk and pray the matter through with a wise Christian friend.* These situations are always complex. Someone from outside the situation may be able to look at it more objectively than you can, and give wise counsel. Listen to what your friend says, and to what God says as you pray over the issues together.
- *Be specially careful to check your motivation.* Pray about it. It's very hard for us humans ever to have wholly unmixed motives. Additionally, we're all good at kidding ourselves that our motives are pure when they're not. But lay the whole thing before God, and ask him to make your motives as pure as

possible – not your own vindication or a desire for revenge, but a genuine and Christlike concern for others.
- *Check out established procedures and be prepared to follow them.* There may be exceptions, but in many situations the established complaints procedures provide a fair and just way of approaching the issues.
- *Soak the whole thing in prayer.* Give it over to God. Make sure that all the action you take is filled with his grace and goodness. And then leave the outcome with him.

The wider scene

All the Bible passages quoted above are for those who are suffering injustice. They make it very clear that Christian victims of injustice should not hit back, but instead follow the example of Christ. But that's not to say, of course, that the Bible teaches that we should never do anything about injustice. Plenty of passages make it very clear that the opposite is the case: God specifically calls his people to right wrong, to fight unrighteousness and to eradicate injustice. But the call is set in a specific context, or, rather, two specific contexts.

Let's put it this way. If someone treats me unjustly, it is not, as we've been seeing, my task to sort out the person who has wronged me, save in exceptional circumstances. I have to leave that to God. But suppose I'm the one who treats somebody else unjustly. In that case, God most certainly expects me to do everything I can to put right the wrong. I need to sort myself out and to correct the injustice. And it's similar if I'm a 'third party'. When I'm not the person being wronged or the person doing the wrong, but I'm aware of what is happening, I have a responsibility to act to set the situation right. Just what to do will almost certainly need careful thought and prayer. It's rarely wise to rush in with instant action; remember Moses killing the Egyptian (Exod. 2:11–15). In many situations there's a high risk that unthinking action will only make things worse. But that's not an excuse for inaction. In every situation, there's got to be something positive that we can do.

Bible passages about our responsibility to tackle injustice suffered by others

Defend the cause of the weak and fatherless;
  maintain the rights of the poor and oppressed.
rescue the weak and needy;
  deliver them from the hand of the wicked (Ps. 82:3–4).

Seek justice,
  encourage the oppressed.
Defend the cause of the fatherless,
  plead the case of the widow (Is. 1:17).

Do what is just and right. Rescue from the hand of his oppressor the one who has been robbed. Do no wrong or violence to the alien, the fatherless or the widow, and do not shed innocent blood (Jer. 22:3).

  ... what does the LORD require of you?
    To act justly and to love mercy
      and to walk humbly with your God (Mic. 6:8).

This is what the LORD Almighty says: 'Administer true justice; show mercy and compassion to one another. Do not oppress the widow or the fatherless, the alien or the poor. In your hearts do not think evil of each other' (Zech. 7:9–10).

Religion that God our Father accepts as pure and faultless is this: to look after orphans and widows in their distress and to keep oneself from being polluted by the world (Jas. 1:27).

See also the parable of the sheep and the goats in Matthew 25:31–46; the way the disciples dealt with inequality in the distribution of food to widows, recorded in Acts 6:1–4, and James's teaching on prejudice and favouritism in James 2:1–13.

What could I do to help victims of injustice?

Let them know you care. Get alongside them. They may well feel alone, isolated, friendless. Show them that that's not so; express in your attitude the love and concern of God. Encourage them. Give them practical help.

If they are Christians, gently help them to take on board and put into practice the Bible's teaching outlined above.

Talk with others about positive steps you or they might take to put the specific situation right.

Where relevant, put those who have been hurt in touch with appropriate victim support networks. In addition, do what you can to ensure that they are being supported in the community of the church, ideally in a small-group context such as a home group.

See if there is an organization (Christian or otherwise) that is especially concerned with the issues involved. There's an ever-increasing number of such organizations, both local and national. Some deal with very specific issues, such as racial or age discrimination. Others are more generic. Most denominations have a department or resource centre with specialists in a range of areas. It's almost always worth contacting these organizations, though you may find that what they offer is not appropriate in the particular circumstances. It may not be easy to locate specific organizations, but try the following: local ministers or church leaders; Citizens' Advice Bureaux; local *Yellow Pages* or a special section in the phone book; the *UK Christian Handbook*; denominational or diocesan offices; and of course the Internet.

Pray. Pray for the victims and their response. Pray also for their healing, and for the righting of wrongs.

Consider whether God is calling you to take up the matter on a larger scale. In some situations it will be right to join (and encourage others to join) pressure groups that are seeking to bring in legislation or reforms to prevent abuse and injustice. There may even be some situations where you will be the one to start the pressure group.

LAW: KEEPING THE LAW

Christians are not subject to the Old Testament law, since we live 'under grace' (Rom. 6:14). But the New Testament teaches that in normal circumstances our lives should be exemplary in our obedience to the civil and criminal law of the land. There will, of course, be exceptions, such as if we live under a totalitarian regime that, say, forbids telling others about Jesus. But the general principle is that we should show by our submission to the law of the land that we are willing to accept the authority of the state, and are trustworthy and responsible citizens.

This attitude of submission taught by the New Testament runs counter to the spirit of our age, where submission to any form of authority seems to be rejected by most people, and flouting the law is seen as something that everyone does as long as they can get away with it. Underlying this attitude is the belief, championed by the Enlightenment and much postmodern thought, but actually having its roots in Genesis 3:5, that each one of us has the right to be our own lawmaker. I can decide how much I should declare to the tax man, or that it's OK to use the office photocopier for my own copying, or at what speed it's right for me to drive through built-up areas. But, for the New Testament, 'submission' is a key concept (1 Pet. 2:13–17). Lawlessness is something very specifically anti-Christian (2 Thess. 2:1–12); it may be a hallmark of our secular age, but it's an area where we are called to be different.

Paul, himself brought up in the strict Jewish legal tradition, wrote scathingly about the way the unbelievers of his day rejected God because the Jews failed to live consistently with the law they claimed to observe: 'You who preach against stealing, do you steal? … You who brag about the law, do you dishonour God by breaking the law? As it is written: "God's name is blasphemed among the Gentiles because of you"' (Rom. 2:21, 23–24).

Unbelievers will, of course, find something in us to criticize whatever we do, but the New Testament makes it clear that it's better to be criticized for being consistent in our obeying of the law than for following the crowd and obeying it only when it suits us. We who demand that motorists should drive carefully when our children are crossing the street should never fall to breaking the speed limit when driving down other people's streets. Nor should we be anything but scrupulously honest with other people's property, including our employer's.

This does not have to lead to legalism. We can treat others' property at all times with the awareness that the Lord is watching us, without getting trapped in a narrow, joyless slavery to rules. It's perfectly possible to be very careful about the way we live and yet experience real freedom. Indeed, James goes so far as to say that it is the person who is careful to keep free from 'being polluted by the world' who really experiences freedom. In a passage where he's talking about keeping 'a tight rein' on our tongues, but where he also mentions 'all moral filth, and the evil that is so prevalent', he is able to talk about 'the perfect law that gives freedom' (Jas. 1:19–27).

Bible teaching about keeping the law of the land

'Is it right to pay taxes to Caesar or not?' But Jesus ... said to them, 'Give to Caesar what is Caesar's, and to God what is God's' (Matt. 22:17, 21).

Everyone must submit himself to the governing authorities, for there is no authority except that which God has established. The authorities that exist have been established by God. Consequently, he who rebels against the authority is rebelling against what God has instituted ... It is necessary to submit to the authorities, not only because of possible punishment but also because of conscience. This is why you pay taxes, for the authorities are God's servants, who give their full time to governing. Give everyone what you owe him: If you owe taxes, pay taxes; if revenue, then revenue; if respect, then respect; if honour, then honour ... The commandments, 'Do not commit adultery,' 'Do not murder,' 'Do not steal,' 'Do not covet,' and whatever other commandment there may be, are summed up in this one rule: 'Love your neighbour as yourself.' Love does no harm to its neighbour. Therefore love is the fulfilment of the law (Rom. 13:1–2, 5–7, 9–10).

Live such good lives among the pagans that, though they accuse you of doing wrong, they may see your good deeds and glorify God on the day he visits us. Submit yourselves for the Lord's sake to every authority instituted among men: whether to the king, as the supreme authority, or to governors, who are sent by him to punish those who do wrong and to commend those who do right. For it is God's will that by doing good you should silence the ignorant talk of foolish men. Live as free men, but do not use your freedom as a cover-up for evil; live as servants of God (1 Pet. 2:12–16).

When Christians cannot keep the law

There are many aspects of the law of the land that conflict with Christian morality and principles; for example, in regard to abortion or some sexual practices. Though we, as Christians, have the right and responsibility to seek to influence such legislation for the good of the community, these laws do not in fact prevent us from living as Christians; we are free to refuse an abortion or to abstain from those sexual practices. So, though we may not be happy with these laws, we can live under them and continue to live our Christian lives.

But in some countries there are laws that prohibit Christians from performing actions that are essential to our faith, or that require them to act in a way that is directly contrary to it. In these cases we are called to take a firm stand, even if it should mean suffering and martyrdom. In the first century, for example, the Romans demanded worship of the state and of the emperor as a sign of good citizenship. This was something the Christians could not do, and they were persecuted and martyred as a result. In many countries today, telling others about Jesus is prohibited by law, and Christians choose to face imprisonment and even death when they do so.

We are largely free of such laws in the West, but they may come. One possible area of legislation concerns employment discrimination on the grounds of religion; Christian organizations may be required to employ non-Christians in order to demonstrate that they are not practising discrimination.

What could I do – when confronted with a law I cannot keep?

Ensure that you've got a correct understanding of the Bible's teaching on the specific issue. We may smile at the way Jehovah's Witnesses have misinterpreted texts like Leviticus 17:10–12 to prohibit blood transfusions, but, sadly, mainstream Christians have sometimes fought battles in which their case depended upon what we would now think of as doubtful interpretations of one or two bits of Scripture, rather than on the general teaching of the Bible as a whole.

Consult those you can trust. Talk with a Christian legal expert, so that you know all about the law in question and its implications for Christians. Talk with godly Christians about their attitude to the law and what they think should be done. Get in touch with groups such as CARE and the Evangelical Alliance, who have officers specifically concerned with public affairs and legal issues.

Think through how far you are prepared to go in your stand against a bad law. Think seriously about adopting the principle 'If it's not worth dying for, it's not worth fighting for.' Are you ready to pay the price to see the issue through? Are you willing to pay any price? Remember the words of Jesus about counting the cost before embarking on a major enterprise (Luke 14:25–33). If you're willing to pay the price of misunderstanding, suffering, ridicule, even imprisonment and martyrdom, but are worried whether you'll be able to cope, be encouraged by the words of Jesus: 'Whenever you are arrested and brought to trial, do not worry beforehand about what to say. Just say whatever is given you at the time, for it is not you speaking, but the Holy Spirit' (Mark 13:11).

Take all the steps you can to get the law changed. You can do a lot on your own, perhaps by writing to your MP; but you may be most effective if you link up with others and use the resources of Christian organizations that are already experienced in campaigning on these sorts of issues.

Be ready to work alongside non-Christians to fight a bad law. There may be exceptions, but there seems no reason why Christians should not fight for justice alongside others who share their vision and who would benefit from their victory. Baptists stood side by side with Jews in the struggle to gain religious freedom in seventeenth-century England.

Avoid any form of campaigning that is not in the spirit of Jesus. Pressure groups use all sorts of methods to gain attention for their cause, ranging from manipulation of facts to deliberate violence. Most of these are unacceptable for Christians. Remember Jesus in Gethsemane: 'all who draw the sword will die by the sword' (Matt. 26:52). Indeed, our most significant methods are such that secular pressure groups would laugh at them: 'Though we live in the world, we do not wage war as the world does. The weapons we fight with are not the weapons of the world. On the contrary, they have divine power to demolish strongholds' (2 Cor. 10:3–4).

Pray – and get others to pray. Don't just pray, 'Lord, please change this law.' Pray for wisdom in your campaigning against it, your witness to Christ as you campaign, and grace and strength to face ridicule, setbacks and maybe even imprisonment and martyrdom.

LOVE

If every professing Christian really lived the love of God in every situation, the world would be a very different place. What's more, plenty of people would be attracted to becoming Christians. The snag is that, though we all know we should be men and women of love, we somehow manage to forget it when we're put under pressure. We react just like everyone else; we treat others in the way the world treats them. We allow feelings such as anger, hurt or selfishness to swamp our love.

Some of what the Bible says about love

Jesus replied: '"Love the Lord your God with all your heart and with all your soul and with all your mind." This is the first and greatest commandment. And the second is like it: "Love your neighbour as yourself." All the Law and the Prophets hang on these two commandments' (Matt. 22:37–40).

'Love your enemies, do good to those who hate you, bless those who curse you, pray for those who ill-treat you' (Luke 6:27–28).

'A new command I give you: Love one another. As I have loved you, so you must love one another. By this all men will know that you are my disciples, if you love one another' (John 13:34–35).

'As the Father has loved me, so have I loved you. Now remain in my love. If you obey my commands, you will remain in my love, just as I have obeyed my Father's commands and remain in his love. I have told you this so that my joy may be in you and that your joy may be complete. My command is this: Love each other as I have loved you' (John 15:9–12).

I will show you the most excellent way.
   If I speak in the tongues of men and of angels, but have not love, I am only a resounding gong or a clanging cymbal. If I have the gift of prophecy and can fathom all mysteries and all knowledge, and if I have a faith that can move mountains, but have not love, I am nothing ...
   Love is patient, love is kind. It does not envy, it does not boast, it is not proud. It is not rude, it is not self-seeking, it is not easily angered, it keeps no record of wrongs. Love does not delight in evil but rejoices with the truth. It always protects, always trusts, always hopes, always perseveres.
   Love never fails ...
   ... these three remain: faith, hope and love. But the greatest of these is love (1 Cor. 12:31; 13:1–2, 4–8, 13).

... the fruit of the Spirit is love (Gal. 5:22).

... live a life of love, just as Christ loved us (Eph. 5:2).

Therefore, as God's chosen people, holy and dearly loved, clothe yourselves with compassion, kindness, humility, gentleness and patience. Bear with each other and forgive whatever grievances you may have against one another. Forgive as the Lord forgave you. And over all these virtues put on love, which binds them all together in perfect unity (Col. 3:12–14).

Anyone who claims to be in the light but hates his brother is still in the darkness ...

This is the message you heard from the beginning: We should love one another ... We know that we have passed from death to life, because we love our brothers. Anyone who does not love remains in death ...

This is how we know what love is: Jesus Christ laid down his life for us. And we ought to lay down our lives for our brothers. If anyone has material possessions and sees his brother in need but has no pity on him, how can the love of God be in him? Dear children, let us not love with words or tongue but with actions and in truth.

... love comes from God ... This is love, not that we loved God, but that he loved us and sent his Son as an atoning sacrifice for our sins. Dear friends, since God so loved us, we also ought to love one another. No-one has ever seen God; but if we love one another, God lives in us and his love is made complete in us ...

God is love. Whoever lives in love lives in God, and God in him ...

We love because he first loved us (1 John 2:9; 3:11, 14, 16–18; 4:7, 10–12, 16, 19).

What could I do?

Take your standards of love from God, not from those around you. The shattering words of Jesus 'My command is this: Love each other as I have loved you' (John 15:12) make it perfectly plain that he expects us to aim for the very highest.

Ask for God's help. There's no way you can reach this level of love without it. You need Christ to live in you. You need the Holy

Spirit to produce his fruit. At the start of each day, 'clothe your-self' in love (Col. 3:12, 14). Faced with particularly unlovable people, cry out to God for a special dose of his love. Ask him to live and love in you.

Watch out for the special opportunities God sends to show love. It may be something small, such as a word of encouragement to someone who is struggling, or something big, such as an oppor-tunity to respond lovingly to someone who's just done something really rotten to you. Take these as God-given opportunities to put Christian love into practice.

Show your love in practical action. Remember that love is much more than a feeling. In many situations, you will find it desper-ately hard or impossible to *feel* love. But that's no problem. The good Samaritan probably had very few warm emotional feelings towards the wounded Jew, but he expressed love by what he did. Love that is demonstrated in action is much more real than love that just feels a warm emotion. To do something loving for someone we can't stand is a great way of loving. That's why Jesus followed his command to 'Love your enemies' with 'do good to those who hate you' (Luke 6:27).

Remember, Jesus is out there, waiting for your love. When he talked about love in action in the passage about the sheep and the goats, Jesus added the amazing words 'I tell you the truth, what-ever you did for one of the least of these brothers of mine, you did for me' (Matt. 25:40).

Spread love around in your local church. Many churches are full of love, but sometimes bad feeling creeps in, people get into cliques, or they're so busy they don't have time for others. If you find that love is lacking in your church, don't grumble about it, and certainly don't further it by your own unloving reaction. Instead, swamp it with love. Do a few outrageously loving things. Wash a few feet. Show a better way. It's God's purpose that every church should be a hotbed of his love. Make sure yours is.

Pray for – and seize – opportunities to show love in your workplace and community. It's an effective way of showing those who aren't Christians the power and reality of God.

Love God. This is the first and greatest commandment. Again, don't worry if you find it difficult to have warm, loving feelings towards God. Some find this easier than others, and in any case feelings can be unreliable. Rather, build your love for God on the foundation of the teaching of Jesus, when he said, 'If you love me, you will obey what I command ... Whoever has my commands and obeys them, he is the one who loves me ... If anyone loves me, he will obey my teaching. My Father will love him, and we will come to him and make our home with him (John 14:15, 21, 23). Show your love by doing what Jesus says, by following his teaching. If you find this tough and costly, then you have a marvellous opportunity to show much love.

MARRIAGE 1: MARRIAGE AND THE UNMARRIED

However much marriage may be losing favour in our generation, it remains a key feature of God's purpose for humankind, providing, as it does, beautiful and rich human relationships, and a secure and stable atmosphere in which children can be born and brought up.

Some Christians are called by God to remain unmarried. Many anticipate being married, but have problems while waiting for marriage to come their way. Others struggle with decisions over the right time and the right person. In this section we'll be looking at some of the issues that might arise, and also at preparing for marriage.

It is important to remember that, while the Old Testament sees marriage as the normal and the preferred state, since 'It is not good for the man to be alone' (Gen. 2:18), the fact that Jesus was single sheds a new light on being unmarried. Jesus was the perfect representative of the new humanity, and the one we're called to follow. His life was lived in total obedience to the Father, and was complete and perfect in every respect. So singleness is no longer a kind of second best. Indeed, Paul was personally quite convinced that it was marriage that was the second best, although, like Jesus, he accepted that singleness takes a special calling and enabling from God, which not everybody has.

Some relevant Bible teaching

> God created man
>   in his own image,
>   in the image of God
>   he created him;
>   male and female
>   he created them.

God blessed them and said to them, 'Be fruitful' ... God saw all that he had made, and it was very good (Gen. 1:27–28, 31).

> The LORD is my shepherd, I shall not be in want ...
> He guides me in paths of righteousness
>   for his name's sake ...
> Surely goodness and love will follow me
>   all the days of my life (Ps. 23:1, 3, 6).

> Trust in the LORD with all your heart
>   and lean not on your own understanding;
> in all your ways acknowledge him,
>   and he will make your paths straight (Prov. 3:5–6).

'I tell you, do not worry, about your life ... Who of you by worrying can add a single hour to his life?
... 'the pagans run after all these things, and your heavenly Father knows that you need them. But seek first his kingdom and his righteousness, and all these things will be given to you as well. Therefore do not worry about tomorrow, for tomorrow will worry about itself' (Matt. 6:25, 27, 32–34).

The disciples said to him, 'If this is the situation between a husband and wife, it is better not to marry.'
Jesus replied, 'Not everyone can accept this word, but only those to whom it has been given. For some are eunuchs because

they were born that way; others were made that way by men; and others have renounced marriage because of the kingdom of heaven. The one who can accept this should accept it' (Matt. 19:10–12).

... let us put aside the deeds of darkness and put on the armour of light. Let us behave decently, not in orgies and drunkenness, not in sexual immorality and debauchery, not in dissension and jealousy. Rather, clothe yourselves with the Lord Jesus Christ, and do not think about how to gratify the desires of the sinful nature (Rom. 13:12–14).

Flee from sexual immorality. All other sins a man commits are outside his body, but he who sins sexually sins against his own body. Do you not know that your body is a temple of the Holy Spirit, who is in you, whom you have received from God? You are not your own; you were bought at a price. Therefore honour God with your body (1 Cor. 6:18–20).

Now for the matters you wrote about: It is good for a man not to marry. But since there is so much immorality, each man should have his own wife, and each woman her own husband ... I say this as a concession, not as a command. I wish that all men were as I am. But each man has his own gift from God: one has this gift, another has that.

Now to the unmarried and the widows I say: It is good for them to stay unmarried, as I am. But if they cannot control themselves, they should marry, for it is better to marry than to burn with passion ...

Now about virgins: I have no command from the Lord, but I give a judgment as one who by the Lord's mercy is trustworthy. Because of the present crisis, I think that it is good for you to remain as you are ... Are you unmarried? Do not look for a wife. But if you do marry, you have not sinned; and if a virgin marries, she has not sinned. But those who marry will face many troubles in this life, and I want to spare you this ...

I would like you to be free from concern. An unmarried man is concerned about the Lord's affairs – how he can please the

Lord. But a married man is concerned about the affairs of this world – how he can please his wife – and his interests are divided. An unmarried woman or virgin is concerned about the Lord's affairs: Her aim is to be devoted to the Lord in both body and spirit. But a married woman is concerned about the affairs of this world – how she can please her husband. I am saying this for your own good, not to restrict you, but that you may live in a right way in undivided devotion to the Lord (1 Cor. 7:1–2, 6–9, 25–26, 27–28, 32–35).

... whatever you do, do it all for the glory of God (1 Cor. 10:31).

Do not be yoked together with unbelievers. For what do right-eousness and wickedness have in common? Or what fellowship can light have with darkness? ... What does a believer have in common with an unbeliever? What agreement is there between the temple of God and idols? For we are the temple of the living God (2 Cor. 6:14–16).

I tell you this, and insist on it in the Lord, that you must no longer live as the Gentiles do, in the futility of their thinking ... they have given themselves over to sensuality so as to indulge in every kind of impurity, with a continual lust for more ...

But among you there must not be even a hint of sexual immorality, or of any kind of impurity, or of greed, because these are improper for God's holy people. Nor should there be obscenity, foolish talk or coarse joking, which are out of place, but rather thanksgiving (Eph. 4:17, 19; 5:3–4).

Rejoice in the Lord always. I will say it again: Rejoice! ... The Lord is near. Do not be anxious about anything, but in every-thing, by prayer and petition, with thanksgiving, present your requests to God. And the peace of God, which transcends all understanding, will guard your hearts and your minds in Christ Jesus ...

I have learned to be content whatever the circumstances ... I have learned the secret of being content in any and every situation ... I can do everything through him who gives me strength (Phil. 4:4–7, 11–13).

It is God's will that you should be sanctified: that you should avoid sexual immorality; that each of you should learn to control his own body in a way that is holy and honourable, not in passionate lust like the heathen, who do not know God; and that in this matter no-one should wrong his brother or take advantage of him. The Lord will punish men for all such sins, as we have already told you and warned you. For God did not call us to be impure, but to live a holy life (1 Thess. 4:3–7).

Marriage should be honoured by all, and the marriage bed kept pure, for God will judge the adulterer and all the sexually immoral (Heb. 13:4).

What could I do?

Trust God. Of course, there are many uncertainties that you might worry about. No-one knows how they'll cope with singleness or whether their marriage will work out as they hope. But what a crazy waste of emotional energy to spend years worrying whether or not you're going to get married, whether you're marrying the right person, or whether your marriage will work out. Even worse, what a waste of a huge opportunity to develop a deep and trusting relationship with your heavenly Father. For many Christians this aspect of their lives is the main one in which they can learn real trust. After all, in our culture it doesn't take much to trust God to 'give us today our daily bread'; but to trust him with the huge issues of singleness and marriage does mean that we're really putting our lives into his hands, getting out of the boat and walking on the water. So make a deliberate choice. Resolve not to face the issues the 'pagan' way, by getting all worried about them. Rather, face them the Christian way, by trusting your 'heavenly Father' (Matt. 6:32).

Since trust is hard to sustain, try taking the following steps.

1. *Write out the relevant biblical truths that you want to apply to your own life*. You may use some of the Bible verses listed above, or

other Bible passages. For example, you might use Matthew 6:33 to write, 'I will seek first God's kingdom and righteousness, and trust him to sort out all the things I need,' or 1 Corinthians 6:19–20, 'I'm not my own; Jesus has bought me by giving everything he had. So God calls me to use my body to bring glory to him.'

2. *Write out the specific implications of these biblical truths for you.* They might be something like: 'I'll stop worrying about whether or not I'll get married,' or, 'I'll give my sexual and emotional desires and needs over to the Lord.' Decide that you will accept these as your foundational principles and goals.

3. *List the problems that stand in the way of the fulfilment of the goals you've listed.* 'I just panic when I realize life is passing me by and I'm still not married,' or, 'I can't control my feelings.'

4. *Think and pray through the things you've listed as problems.* What does the Bible say about them? What is the Holy Spirit saying to you about them? What wise advice would you give to another Christian who came to you for help over these problems? Write down your answers.

5. *If you can't think of adequate answers to the problems, get help.* Talk them through with a wise Christian leader or counsellor.

6. *Arising from points 2, 4 and 5 list specific steps you will take daily, or whenever you find yourself doing anything that doesn't further your goals.* So, for example, to further the goal 'I'll stop worrying about whether or not I'll get married,' and to cope with the problem 'I just panic when I see one of my friends who is already married,' you might write, 'Whenever I begin to panic, I'll deliberately and specifically go through the seven steps listed in Philippians 4:4–13: (1) Rejoice in the Lord; (2) accept that the Lord is near; (3) pray; (4) thank God; (5) accept the incredible peace of God; (6) commit myself to contentment; (7) receive Christ's strength.'

7. *Make yourself accountable to someone who will pray for you and support you and help you win the spiritual battle you're fighting.*

If you are finding it hard to cope with singleness, get help. Everyone you know has faced the singleness issue! Many of them have struggled with it as you're struggling. Talk and pray issues through with them. Try working through the points suggested in Appendix 2, 'Suggestions about singleness'.

Sort out what the Bible says about your sexuality and how you must live as a sexual being, both before and after marriage. (See **sexual issues**). Be very clear in your own mind what this means for you. Talk all the issues through with God. Give your body and your sexuality over to him daily. When you find yourself slipping, get back to him straight away.

Tell God that you're happy for him to have the final say on whether you'll get married, when, and to whom. Accept that his wisdom is much greater than yours; he isn't going to make any mistakes. Of course, you'll want to tell him your preferences; you'll find him very happy to listen to your ideas. But tell him that's what you'd like, not what you're demanding. If he can suggest to you something better, you're more than happy to go along with his ideas.

Meanwhile, get on with living. Don't be one of those people who are so focused on getting married that they miss out on all the joys and benefits of being single. Make the most of your singleness while you've still got it! Develop lots of good friendships; use to the full the extra time and freedom singleness gives you. Take the opportunity to learn Paul's 'secret of being content in any and every situation' (Phil. 4:12).

Face any special concerns. Think, talk and pray through the particular issues that will arise should you be considering marrying someone very different from you in age, someone from a very different culture, someone who has children and so will bring a ready-made family with them, or someone with very different interests. These features can be tremendously enriching for a marriage, but they do also bring extra pressures and strains. You need to be aware of these, and to have thought and talked through how you will face them and deal with them.

Face the 'spiritual' issue. The marriage relationship is – or should be – a deeply spiritual one, and oneness together in Christ is a key feature of a Christian marriage. So test the depth and reality of your relationship together in Christ as a foundational factor in deciding whether God is leading you and another person towards marriage. If the other person has no Christian faith, then the Bible teaching is clear; you should not marry. If the person's relationship with Christ is much more nominal or considerably weaker than yours, be very cautious. It could, of course, be that you help the other person to develop a much stronger relationship with the Lord; but it could work the other way round, and God is not going to lead you to sacrifice your relationship with him in order to have a relationship with another person.

As you grow closer to the other person and your love deepens, be especially careful to keep every aspect of your relationship under the lordship of Christ. Keep your relationship pure and beautiful. Don't do anything that either of you feels unhappy about, or that you'd be ashamed to talk to Jesus about. Agree together which ways of expressing your love for each other are appropriate and which are wrong, and hold each other to what you've agreed. When your sexual feelings are running high, don't put yourselves in any situation where they could overwhelm you.

Sort out issues of commitment. The deep commitment and covenanting together that are at the heart of Christian marriage are largely alien to our culture. For most people, commitment is always conditional: 'I'll do it if it suits me'; 'I'll stick by my word unless I change my mind.' Christian marriage commitment, like Christian love, is unconditional: 'for better, *for worse*, for richer, *for poorer, in sickness* and in health, till death us do part'. If you find this sort of commitment hard to take on board, go back to Christ and his commitment to us. Seek his grace and strength, and trust that he will keep his word and give you all you need.

Make sure you get the best marriage preparation. You want your marriage to be the best, so tap into all the available resources. Go to weekends for engaged couples. Read books; ideally read them together, so you can talk through the issues that arise. Make sure that you go through a series of marriage preparation classes. And don't just learn about marriage. Learn about yourself and your partner-to-be. Check out strengths and weaknesses and how you can turn potential conflicts and difficulties into growth points. The foundation for a great marriage is laid in those months of preparation before the wedding day.

Get the right focus for the wedding. What matters most, the promises or the food? At most weddings the promises come and go in less than a couple of minutes, while the food takes easily a couple of hours. Find ways of making the promises and the other important elements of the day really central. How about writing your own vows, based on the traditional ones, and finding some way of emphasizing them in the service, rather than just repeating them because the person taking the wedding tells you to? Be especially careful over being pressured into a wedding that serves as a great social occasion, but in which the key issues get swamped. Sometimes this pressure comes from parents, perhaps because they want to express their love, or because they have a need to impress family and friends. But, when all's said and done, it's *your* wedding, hopefully the only one you'll ever have. So make it very specially yours. Decide as a couple what you want, and how you're going to make sure you spend time with God as well as with the hairdresser. Get these matters sorted out well in advance, and graciously and firmly stick to your principles. Resist the pressures from others to change them to suit their ideas. And be warned: a 'big' wedding may benefit some, but it rarely does the bride and groom much good. All too often the story is of hassle and mounting pressure as the Big Day draws near. This takes its toll on everybody, including the couple. With the addition of late-night stag and hen parties, they arrive at the start of their wedding day exhausted, and by the time it finishes they're shattered. The key matters, such as their vows together before God, and the pouring out of the Holy Spirit on the new life they're beginning, have been pushed out of their central place by everything else. That's no way to start a marriage.

MARRIAGE 2: ENRICHING A MARRIAGE

A marriage is a living thing. All living things need feeding; if they aren't fed they'll die. A marriage that is not being continually fed will wither and die. Few marriages die suddenly. But too many marriages die slowly, step by step, month by month, often without the couple's really being aware of what's happening. At almost any stage the marriage could be rescued if some action was taken and the slow starvation was reversed. But nothing is done, and it dies.

Keeping a marriage alive takes effort. All couples need to keep working at their marriage, continually finding ways to deepen and enrich their relationship. Without work and enriching, the marriage will become routine and dull. With them, it will be a continuing journey, a deepening relationship, a living, growing experience that is strong enough to face any situation and use even setbacks and problems as points of growth.

Our culture has changed so much since biblical times that the specific instructions given by Paul and Peter about how wives and husbands should treat each other can seem dated and rather irrelevant. But the principles that underlie them haven't changed, especially the foundational principle that the relationship between wives and husbands should be modelled on Christ.

Some Bible teaching relevant to enriching a marriage

The husband should fulfil his marital duty to his wife, and likewise the wife to her husband. The wife's body does not belong to her alone but also to her husband. In the same way, the husband's body does not belong to him alone but also to his wife. Do not deprive each other except by mutual consent and for a time, so that you may devote yourselves to prayer. Then come together again so that Satan will not tempt you because of your lack of self-control (1 Cor. 7:3–5).

I will show you the most excellent way ...

Love is patient, love is kind. It does not envy, it does not boast, it is not proud. It is not rude, it is not self-seeking, it is not easily angered, it keeps no record of wrongs. Love does not delight in evil but rejoices with the truth. It always protects, always trusts, always perseveres.

Love never fails (1 Cor. 12:31; 13:4–8).

Submit to one another out of reverence for Christ.

Wives, submit to your husbands as to the Lord. For the
husband is the head of the wife as Christ is the head of the
church, his body, of which he is the Saviour. Now, as the church
submits to Christ, so also wives should submit to their husbands
in everything.

Husbands, love your wives, just as Christ loved the church
and gave himself up for her to make her holy, cleansing her by
the washing with water through the word, and to present her to
himself as a radiant church, without stain or wrinkle or any
other blemish, but holy and blameless. In this same way,
husbands ought to love their wives as their own bodies. After all,
no-one ever hated his own body, but he feeds and cares for it,
just as Christ does the church – for we are members of his body.
'For this reason a man will leave his father and mother and be
united to his wife, and the two will become one flesh.' This is a
profound mystery – but I am talking about Christ and the
church. However, each one of you also must love his wife as he
loves himself, and the wife must respect her husband (Eph.
5:21–33).

... clothe yourselves with compassion, kindness, humility, gentleness and patience. Bear with each other and forgive whatever
grievances you may have against one another. Forgive as the
Lord forgave you. And over all these virtues put on love, which
binds them all together in perfect unity ...

And whatever you do, whether in word or deed, do it all in
the name of the Lord Jesus, giving thanks to God the Father
through him.

Wives, submit to your husbands, as is fitting in the Lord.

Husbands, love your wives and do not be harsh with them
(Col. 3:12–14, 17–19).

Wives, in the same way be submissive to your husbands so that,
if any of them do not believe the word, they may be won over
without words by the behaviour of their wives, when they see
the purity and reverence of your lives. Your beauty should not
come from outward adornment, such as braided hair and the
wearing of gold jewellery and fine clothes. Instead, it should be

that of your inner self, the unfading beauty of a gentle and quiet spirit, which is of great worth in God's sight ...

Husbands, in the same way be considerate as you live with your wives, and treat them with respect as the weaker partner and as heirs with you of the gracious gift of life, so that nothing will hinder your prayers (1 Pet. 3:1–4, 7).

What could I do to enrich my marriage?

Be committed to working at your relationship. Don't assume that it will simply take care of itself. It's your responsibility to keep your marriage very much alive, to keep feeding it, enabling your love, joy and oneness, and all the other aspects of your relationship, to keep growing.

Give time to continuing to build your relationship. Many couples are too busy doing so many other things that they neglect this one. Check how much quality time you spend together, and how you use it.

Go to a marriage enrichment weekend. There are several Christian organizations that arrange these; some of them make no charge, simply asking you to make a donation if you feel the weekend has been worth it. Don't assume that these weekends are just for couples who've got problems; they are designed to make good marriages better. Think of them as you would a refresher course or a development training course in your career; going on such a course doesn't mean that there's anything wrong with your job skills – simply that you want to make them even better.

Read books. There's a wealth of Christian books on enriching marriages. Try reading one aloud to each other, and stopping to discuss the points that arise.

Learn from others. Sometimes, sadly, we learn from the mistakes of others, such as from the couple who put all their energies into getting a nice home and equipping it with all the latest gadgets, and have no energy left for each other. But we can also learn in a positive way. You may know, for instance, an older couple whose relationship is a beautiful example of what a Christian marriage should be. Take the opportunity to learn from them and their experiences.

Have regular marriage check-ups. Again, if we're wise, we don't wait until we're seriously ill before getting a medical check-up. There are a number of ways of doing a marriage check-up; a suggested approach is given in Appendix 3. It's also good periodically to recall together the vows you made on your wedding day, maybe each time you go to someone else's wedding and hear them repeated.

Enrich your love. Check that *agapē*, the kind of love that really puts the other person first, is at the heart of your relationship. Some kinds of love can be selfish, as when we love someone for what we can get out of him or her. Selfishness is one of the biggest destroyers of marriages. Keep working, too, at the sexual side of your relationship, continuing to grow in your understanding of each other and in the beauty of your love-making.

Increase the place that Jesus has in your marriage. Some Christian couples start their married lives together consciously putting Christ at the centre, praying together and bringing decisions to the Lord. But as time goes by and pressures increase, the Lord gets pushed to one side. If this has happened to you, bring him right back into the centre. Get back to praying together daily, and consciously acknowledge Jesus' lordship over every part of your life together. Keep working at following Paul's advice to let Jesus be the model for the way you treat each other.

Use everything that happens as an opportunity to enrich your relationship. If you have a row, make sure that, when you've made up, your understanding and love for each other are deeper than before you fell out. Turn setbacks and problems into growth points. With God's help there's no problem that is too hard to solve. Other couples have faced the same problems as you and have come through. God can and will turn them into growth points for you. Again, ensure that the major life-stage changes, such as the arrival of the first child, a change of a job, moving house, major illness, redundancy, children leaving home, and retirement, are used as opportunities for growth, rather than as threats to your relationship.

Keep developing your communication skills. Sadly, some couples who loved talking together when they were courting find that after being married for a few years there seems to be nothing left to say. Don't let that happen to you. Keep finding new things to talk about. Work at making opportunities to talk together. Go for walks, ban the TV, use car journeys. Be honest with each other, and allow each other to be open about your feelings. Make it easy for each to off-load. Listen; don't criticize or rush to your own defence. Learn from non-verbal communication – attitude, tone of voice and body language. Make sure you communicate honestly. Don't say one thing and mean another. Don't use sarcasm or innuendo.

Find ways of keeping your relationship exciting. Getting into a rut and boredom are good ways of killing a marriage. Find new activities you can do together, such as new hobbies or a specific project.

Marriage 3: Marriage Difficulties

Every marriage has difficulties. No two people have identical interests and approaches to life. Everyone has faults and makes mistakes. All marriages are threatened by external pressures and face times of testing.

Difficulties can destroy marriages. But they can also be a great means of enriching them. Every time a couple faces a problem and solves it, their relationship can be strengthened and enriched. So when difficulties arise in my marriage it's not so much a matter of trying to find out what terrible mistake I've made to get myself into such a mess. Rather, what I need to do is find ways of tackling the situation or of responding to the problem that will have a beneficial effect on my marriage relationship.

Bible teaching relevant to marriage difficulties

… through Christ Jesus the law of the Spirit of life set me free from the law of sin and death.

... those who live in accordance with the Spirit have their minds set on what the Spirit desires.

... our present sufferings are not worth comparing with the glory that will be revealed.

... the Spirit helps us in our weaknesses.

... in all things God works for the good of those who love him ...

If God is for us, who can be against us? ... Who shall separate us from the love of Christ? Shall trouble or hardship ...? No, in all these things we are more than conquerors through him who loved us (Rom. 8:2, 5, 18, 26, 28, 31, 35, 37; see the whole chapter).

... since there is so much immorality, each man should have his own wife, and each woman her own husband. The husband should fulfil his marital duty to his wife, and likewise the wife to her husband. The wife's body does not belong to her alone but also to her husband. In the same way, the husband's body does not belong to him alone but also to his wife. Do not deprive each other except by mutual consent and for a time, so that you may devote yourselves to prayer. Then come back together again so that Satan will not tempt you because of your lack of self-control (1 Cor. 7:2–5).

Love [*agapē*] is patient, love is kind. It does not envy, it does not boast, it is not proud. It is not rude, it is not self-seeking, it is not easily angered, it keeps no record of wrongs. Love does not delight in evil but rejoices with the truth. It always protects, always trusts, always perseveres.

Love never fails (1 Cor. 13:4–8).

... he said to me, 'My grace is sufficient for you' ... That is why, for Christ's sake, I delight in ... difficulties. For when I am weak, then I am strong (2 Cor. 12:9–10).

Consider it pure joy, my brothers, whenever you face trials of many kinds, because you know that the testing of your faith develops perseverance. Perseverance must finish its work so that you may be mature and complete, not lacking anything (Jas. 1:2–4).

What could I do?

Resist the temptation to adopt a negative attitude. Deliberately reject any suggestion that the situation is disastrous. This is not the end of the road. Nor is it the beginning of the end. Life is not being unfair. You are not the victim of a conspiracy. Forget about apportioning blame. Give up your self-pity.

Work at building a positive attitude to the issue. All problems can be solved. Every failure and sin can be forgiven and redeemed. God is able to bring good out of any situation. He has allowed this problem into your marriage because he wants to use it for good and for his glory. Work at following James's advice and Paul's example. Accept the problem as an exciting new challenge, an opportunity for growth and the enrichment of your marriage.

Help your partner to view the situation positively. Clearly, tackling the issues together with a shared, positive mindset will go a long way towards solving them. But make sure *you* approach things positively even if your partner finds it hard to do so.

Go back to your marriage vows. In your wedding ceremony you probably made promises to each other based on the Christian marriage service that has been used for centuries, which includes a commitment to each other 'for better for worse, for richer for poorer, in sickness and in health, to love and to cherish, till death us do part'. Even if you didn't actually make these promises in your wedding ceremony, accept that they are foundational elements of a true marriage commitment, and that when you got married this was the underlying commitment you were making. You promised each other that you would not let setbacks and difficulties damage your relationship, that you would 'love' and 'cherish' and 'remain faithful' to each other through them all. Agree together now that this is your commitment to each other in this present situation.

Get back to true love. True love, what the New Testament calls *agapē*, is never deterred by setbacks and difficulties. It's the very opposite of the self-centred attitude that we're tempted to adopt when confronted with problems in a marriage relationship. It's the love expressed continuously by Jesus, both towards his disciples when they consistently got things wrong, and towards his enemies when they deliberately made life hell for him. Self-centred love says, 'I'm not enjoying this situation. What can I do to get out of it?' *Agapē* love says, 'Never mind whether I'm enjoying it or not. What can I do to help my partner in it?' Selfish love says, 'I'm hurt, and I've a right to express that hurt, by being angry, or self-pitying'; *agapē* love says, 'Maybe I've got rights, but I'm prepared to forgo them in order to avoid hurting my partner.' Selfish love says, 'I'm not getting what I want'; *agapē* love asks, 'What can I give?'

Talk together. Don't argue about things, but talk them through together in order to find the best possible solution. Discuss the issue, how you feel about it, ways through it and what God might be saying or doing in it. Be honest with each other. Listen to each other. Take the opportunity to develop your communication skills, and to grow in your understanding of life, of each other and of God's ways. Try thinking together of ways to turn the problems into growth points. For example, shortage of money can help you to learn to live more simply; difficulties in having intercourse can stimulate you to expressing love in other ways; difficult decisions or an uncertain future can teach you to depend far more heavily on God.

Pray together. Be honest with God. Put him in charge of the problem, and of everything else in your marriage. Accept that, though he may choose to solve all your problems straight away, it may be his will to take you on a longer, harder road, so that the outcome will be all the more beautiful.

Talk with a wise friend, a minister or a Christian counsellor. Lots of other people have faced difficulties very similar to yours and found a way through. Use their wisdom as a resource.

If your sex life is unsatisfactory, do everything within your power to improve it. Sexual issues lie at the heart of many marriage difficulties. Problems in other areas can have an adverse effect on love-making. Conversely, many couples find that their disagreements and difficulties can be resolved much more easily if their sexual life together is vibrant and rich. Remember that one of the biggest killers of a satisfactory love life is selfishness: one or both of the partners approaches intercourse primarily to satisfy his or her own needs. The other person becomes an object, and intercourse ceases to express love. True love approaches intercourse primarily concerned to bring joy to the other person, even at the price of not fulfilling one's own needs. Review your sex life. Talk things through together, or, if necessary, get help from a wise friend or counsellor.

Keep a sense of perspective. When you're underneath a thunder-cloud, it fills the sky; but seen from a satellite, it covers only a tiny proportion of the Earth's surface. Make a point of spending more time focusing on the good things in your marriage than on the difficulties. There's wisdom in the old Victorian hymn

> When upon life's billows you are tempest-tossed;
> When you are discouraged, thinking all is lost,
> Count your many blessings, name them one by one,
> And it will surprise you what the Lord has done.

Remind yourselves of the difficult times the Lord has already brought you through. He has promised to stay with you and to bring you through this difficulty too.

Be ready to take significant action. Don't leave the problem and hope it will go away. It may do; but it may not. It may stay and get worse, and become harder to tackle. If the problems are being caused or aggravated by an overstressful job, for example, explore changing it for a less demanding one, even if it means a drop in salary or status. If boredom is at the root of the problems, take up a new hobby together. If communication is dying, do something radical such as getting rid of the TV.

MEDIA AND INFORMATION TECHNOLOGY

There is much that is very good about the media and information technology. They enrich our lives in countless ways, providing information, communication and entertainment. They keep us up to date with what's happening in the world, so that we can pray and act responsibly and put the love of Christ into action where it is most needed. They give us all sorts of opportunities to express the Christian worldview and proclaim the gospel to those who wouldn't otherwise hear it. Regional newspapers and radio stations help to foster local community spirit. Creative media programmes give under-represented groups, such as charities, effective vehicles for publicity. Many religious programmes take Christian preaching and teaching to thousands of people in the comfort of their living rooms. Used rightly they are a great influence for good.

But the sad fact is that for the most part they are not used rightly. They do not operate according to Christian principles. The worldview they present is largely anti-Christian. To a great extent, instead of being a tool for righteousness and truth and the coming of God's kingdom, they've been hijacked by interests and power structures that are in no way submitted to God and his goodness and truth. An article in *The Times* has claimed that 90% of Internet use is pornographic. Films and TV present beliefs, attitudes and lifestyles that are contrary to Christian values. In many cases the criteria used in presenting news have more to do with sensationalism, relativism and vested interests than with an honest desire to offer objective truth. Similarly, the whole philosophy of advertising seems to be to manipulate us into buying the product, rather than giving us facts about it by which we can decide in a responsible way whether or not we want it.

Living in our culture, it's impossible to escape the enormous influence of the media. But because, as Christians, we belong to a counterculture, it is crucial that we avoid being taken in or dragged down by what we see, read and hear. We need to keep the biblical criteria clear in our minds. The worldview, attitudes and material presented by the media are to be assessed and judged by them and, where necessary, rejected. The issue must never become 'How can we revise our principles and practices as Christians to fit in with the culture expressed by the media?' Rather, our task is to stand firm for what is true, good and pure and to expose and reject all that is evil.

Is it possible for Christians to have a positive effect on the values and practices of the media? Most certainly. And if we are to be salt and light in our community, we must exercise every opportunity to do so. God calls us to stand up for truth and goodness, whether, as he said to Ezekiel when he called him to prophesy, 'they listen or fail to listen'. At the very least, as he added, 'they will know that a prophet has been among them' (Ezek. 2:5).

In chapter 18 of the book of Revelation there is a graphic description of Babylon the Great. Babylon is the devil's alternative to the City of God, the new Jerusalem, in which everything is pure and beautiful and full of the the living God. The description of Babylon contains many things that were to be seen in first-century Rome. But it is also a timeless symbol of the world's rejection of God and his purposes, values and truths. It is the devil's alternative to the kingdom of God. There can be little doubt that if John, the writer of Revelation, were alive in the twenty-first century he would see the values and worldview presented by so much of the media as nothing other than the current manifestation of the City of Babylon.

In the first century 'Babylon', with its propaganda and power structures, was all-powerful. The Christian church was tiny, poorly organized, with no voice and having apparently negligible influence. Yet chapter 18 of Revelation is a song of triumph: through the victory of Christ the powers of evil have been smashed; God has declared judgment on all the false values and evil practices; the whole mighty structure has been shattered. In its place has come the glory and beauty of the kingdom of God. That's a vision worth working towards.

Some biblical comment on the worldview presented by the media

'I am the LORD your God. You must not do as they do in Egypt, where you used to live, and you must not do as they do in the land of Canaan, where I am bringing you. Do not follow their practices. You must obey my laws and be careful to follow my decrees. I am the LORD your God' (Lev. 18:2–4).

'You are the salt of the earth. But if the salt loses its saltiness, how can it be made salty again?' (Matt. 5:13).

[Jesus prayed] 'I am not praying for the world, but for those you have given me, for they are yours. All I have is yours, and all you have is mine. And glory has come to me through them ...

My prayer is not that you take them out of the world but that you protect them from the evil one. They are not of the world, even as I am not of it. Sanctify them by the truth; your word is truth. As you sent me into the world, I have sent them into the world (John 17:9–10, 15–18).

Jesus answered, '... for this reason I was born, and for this I came into the world, to testify to the truth. Everyone on the side of truth listens to me' (John 18:37).

Do not conform any longer to the pattern of this world, but be transformed by the renewing of your mind. Then you will be able to test and approve what God's will is – his good, pleasing and perfect will (Rom. 12:2).

I tell you this, and insist on it in the Lord, that you must no longer live as the Gentiles do, in the futility of their thinking ... they have given themselves over to sensuality so as to indulge in every kind of impurity, with a continual lust for more ...

But among you there must not be even a hint of sexual immorality, or of any kind of impurity, or of greed, because

these are improper for God's holy people. Nor should there
be obscenity, foolish talk or coarse joking, which are out
of place, but rather thanksgiving. For of this you can be
sure: No immoral, impure or greedy person – such a man
is an idolater – has any inheritance in the kingdom of
Christ and of God. Let no-one deceive you with empty
words, for because of such things God's wrath comes on
those who are disobedient. Therefore do not be partners
with them.

For you were once darkness, but now you are light in
the Lord. Live as children of light ... Have nothing to do
with the fruitless deeds of darkness, but rather expose
them ... Be very careful, then, how you live – not as unwise,
but as wise, making the most of every opportunity, because
the days are evil. Therefore do not be foolish, but understand what the Lord's will is (Eph. 4:17, 19; 5:3–8, 11,
15–17).

See to it that no-one takes you captive through hollow
and deceptive philosophy, which depends on human tradition and the basic principles of this world rather than on
Christ.

... you died with Christ to the basic principles of this
world ...

Since, then, you have been raised with Christ, set your
hearts on things above ... Set your minds on things above
(Col. 2:8, 20; 3:1–2).

... don't you know that friendship with the world is hatred
towards God? Anyone who chooses to be a friend of the world
becomes an enemy of God (Jas. 4:4).

... do not conform to the evil desires you had when you lived
in ignorance (1 Pet. 1:14).

Do not love the world or anything in the world. If anyone
loves the world, the love of the Father is not in him. For
everything in the world – the cravings of sinful man, the

lust of his eyes and the boasting of what he has and does –
comes not from the Father but from the world. The world
and its desires pass away, but the man who does the will of
God lives for ever (1 John 2:15–17).

Dear friends, do not believe every spirit, but test the spirits
to see whether they are from God ... every spirit that does not
acknowledge Jesus is not from God. This is the spirit of the
antichrist, which you have heard is coming and even now is
already in the world.

    You, dear children, are from God and have overcome
them, because the one who is in you is greater than the one
who is in the world. They are from the world and therefore
speak from the viewpoint of the world, and the world listens
to them. We are from God, and whoever knows God listens to
us; but whoever is not from God does not listen to us (1 John
4:1, 3–6).

> 'Fallen! Fallen is Babylon the Great!
> ... all the nations have drunk
>   the maddening wine of her adulteries.
> Come out of her, my people,
>   so that you will not share in her sins,
>   so that you will not receive any of her plagues;
> for her sins are piled up to heaven,
>   and God has remembered her crimes'
> (Rev. 18:2–3, 4–5; see the whole chapter).

What could I do?

Make a choice. Choose to be totally committed to God and to his
values, truths and way of living, and to take all your principles and
practices from him. This will mean that you refuse to be shaped
by the enormous pressures exerted by the anti-God worldview
that lies behind so much of the material presented to us by the
media.

    Be vigilant. Much of the influence exerted by the media is
very subtle; we're not aware what it's doing to us. We all know

of instances where watching violent films has led to violence; frequent portrayal of sexual acts provokes lust and indoctrinates people with the belief that anything is acceptable. You may feel you are too strong a Christian to be influenced in those ways, but the tragic fact is that strong Christians have, despite themselves, been influenced and eventually led into sin, sometimes with disastrous consequences. Even if you are strong in these respects, still be vigilant in other areas. Constant repetition of ideas, beliefs and values can subtly indoctrinate us. Adverts, and the way some programmes are presented, can pander to our greed – something the New Testament warns us against very specifically.

Be critical. People see a clever advert, and go out and buy the product. But what's really happening? Is the advert giving a good reason for buying the product? Or is it playing on our emotions, manipulating our greed, telling us lies or whatever? Listen to and watch news items critically. What values lie behind the way the news is presented, the pictures shown, the comments made?

Add up your TV viewing hours. The statistics are alarming. At an average of four hours per person per day, the total hours of TV viewing for the whole population well outnumber the total hours spent at work. Your average will probably be lower than that; but how does it compare with time spent with God, or with your family? Could you free up more time to serve the Lord if you cut down your TV viewing hours?

Scrutinize what you watch or listen to for entertainment. How does it measure up to Paul's words to the Ephesians 'But among you there must not be even a hint of sexual immorality, or of any kind of impurity, or ... obscenity, foolish talk or coarse joking' (Eph. 5:3–4)? Granted, this would appear to cut out a huge amount of contemporary entertainment programmes, but it has got to be possible to find means of entertainment where you'd be happy to have Jesus sitting in the seat next to you.

Examine your motives. It is possible to have excellent motives in choosing to watch a TV programme or a film that expresses anti-Christian values or, say, uses sex to entertain or titillate. You may feel it important, for instance, to know what sort of material other people are watching. Or you may wish to protest. But excellent motives can be swamped by less good ones. You rather enjoy the programme, and want to see the next episode. You like being sexually titillated. The worldview portrayed attracts you, so you watch some more ...

If you use the Internet, use it for God's glory. The powers of evil have wasted no time in exploiting it to the full. God's people have been rather slower, but there are many possibilities for doing so, such as keeping in close touch with God's work in remote places, or developing effective evangelistic or caring websites.

When appropriate, protest or praise. Audience reaction is important, and can have an effect. Phone, write or email; programmers do take notice.

Where you can, use the media for God. Get involved from the inside. Consider a career in the media. Find out if you could take a 'Thought for the Day' slot on your local radio station. If you have something to say, ring in to a phone-in programme and give a positive Christian viewpoint on a topical issue. Alternatively, write a letter to a newspaper, or send a report (with pictures) of one of your church activities to the local paper. Why should the devil get all the attention? Give them some good news for a change.

Pray. Pray for Christians involved in the media; they have a tough job, and often have to make hard decisions. Pray against the evil influences in and through the media. Pray for the impact of Christian TV and radio. Pray for the fall of Babylon the Great, and pray that God's kingdom will come and his will be done on earth as it is in heaven.

MENTORING

In the body of Christ we need each other. We need the community of the church, where we can find encouragement, example and support. We need to pray and worship with others; we need to learn and serve together and to share what we have with each other.

Alongside the mutual support and fellowship we experience with the community of believers, we can often develop a one-to-one relationship in which we help a specific individual to grow as a Christian, or we ourselves are helped, or each helps the other. Such a relationship has a number of names, including spiritual direction, discipling and mentoring. We can see examples of it in the Bible in the relationships between Moses and Joshua, and Elijah and Elisha, and in Paul's relationships with Silas, Timothy and Titus. Doubtless Jesus, too, was in such a relationship with his disciples as individuals; an example would be his conversation with Peter in John 21:15–22.

The relationship can take a number of forms. It can be a strongly one-sided arrangement, in which a wise and mature Christian takes responsibility for directing and encouraging the personal growth of another, who chooses to submit to the leadership and direction offered. Perhaps one person chooses to be accountable to another in a specific area; someone struggling with a certain weakness asks a friend or church leader to supervise his or her attempts to deal with the problem, on the understanding that he or she will be totally open and give an honest account of successes and failures. It can be a formal or informal arrangement between two Christians who meet on an equal footing; rather than one being the supervisor and the other the learner, they mentor each other and each is discipled by the other.

Some biblical material relevant to mentoring

> Two are better than one,
>   because they have a good return for their work:
> If one falls down,
>   his friend can help him up.
> But pity the man who falls
>   and has no-one to help him up! (Eccles. 4:9–10).

Each of us should please his neighbour for his good, to build him up ...

    I myself am convinced, my brothers, that you yourselves are full of goodness, complete in knowledge and competent to instruct one another (Rom. 15:2, 14).

... in Christ Jesus I became your father through the gospel. Therefore I urge you to imitate me (1 Cor. 4:15–16).

Follow my example, as I follow the example of Christ (1 Cor. 11:1).

Do not let any unwholesome talk come out of your mouths, but only what is helpful for building others up according to their needs, that it may benefit those who listen (Eph. 4:29)

Join with others in following my example ...

    Whatever you have learned or received or heard from me, or seen in me – put it into practice (Phil. 3:17; 4:9).

Let the word of Christ dwell in you richly as you teach and admonish one another with all wisdom (Col. 3:16).

... encourage one another and build each other up, just as in fact you are doing (1 Thess. 5:11).

We did this ... in order to make ourselves a model for you to follow (2 Thess. 3:9).

... encourage one another daily (Heb. 3:13).

... let us consider how we may spur one another on towards love and good deeds (Heb. 10:24).

... confess your sins to each other and pray for each other so that you may be healed. The prayer of a righteous man is powerful and effective (Jas. 5:16).

What could I do to mentor someone?

Decide upon the relationship you will have. Will it be that of teacher and pupil? Or one of equality, in which you help each other? Or one of accountability in a specific area? Or a special one to suit the situation? Make sure both are happy with the arrangement.

Take time to develop a deep relationship of openness and trust. Make sure that you think of the person you are mentoring as a friend, not as a pupil or counsellee.

Minister Christ. Give yourself in the relationship; but, even more importantly, give Christ-in-you. It's good that the person should follow you, but it's essential that he or she follows Christ.

Agree on a main goal. It could be a fairly general one, though you'll need to make sure it isn't so general that you'll never be able to tell whether you've reached it or not. Or it could be specific. General goals could be to teach Mike (a new Christian) the basics of Christian living; or to enable Suzie to enrich and develop her prayer life. More specific goals might be to enable Jeanette to witness to her faith at work; to prepare Jon (who's getting married next spring) to be a Christian husband; to break Paul's habit of viewing Internet porn.

Follow a structure. Without some sort of structure, it's all too easy to let things slide or to miss out on the benefits. If at all possible, have a regular meeting-time and place, perhaps weekly or monthly. Fix a period of time, say an hour, when you will concentrate on the mentoring issues; coffee and social chat can come before or after, but that hour is reserved for the real business. It's generally a help to follow a regular structure in that hour. As an example, you could start with prayer for God's presence and leading. Then you could spend a short time on a general review of what has happened since you last met. After that you could go on to a brief review of any specific points for action that you agreed at the last meeting, and of the progress made. This could be followed by comment and committing them to the Lord in prayer. You could then move on to the main issue for that meeting. This could be something agreed between you, perhaps at your last meeting, or something you as mentor feel needs to be raised, or perhaps a significant point that has come up in the opening part of your time together. Arising out of that may be points for action in the coming days and maybe some agreed 'homework'. Then have a time of prayer ministry; since it's important not to squeeze this out or to have to rush it, you'll need to keep a careful eye on the time. Soon after your session together, make a few notes of what has happened and of any thoughts or suggestions for progress.

Maintain confidentiality. Resist the temptation to talk to others about matters that come up between you. If an issue arises where you feel you need to consult with someone wiser than you, either get the person's permission to do so, or raise the issue in such a way as to avoid revealing who you're talking about.

Beware of developing a dependent relationship. Sometimes the mentor or the person being mentored has a need in this area, and encourages a relationship of dependency. But your aim is to help the person you are mentoring to grow and become strong as a Christian; dependency is likely to hinder this in the long run, and should be avoided.

Put a time limit on the relationship, at least in this form. It may be right for some mentoring relationships to be open-ended, but it's often helpful to work within a specific time-frame, which could then be extended if necessary. 'Let's meet once a week up to the summer holidays,' or 'on the last Thursday of each month for one year'. This helps to focus the task of the relationship and avoids the danger of letting it drift once it has achieved its main usefulness.

MONEY

The part played by money in our culture is far greater than in biblical times. But there are sufficient principles set out in the New Testament to lay a foundation for our approach today. Though Jesus did not appear to have any money, the possession of money in itself is not condemned. What is condemned is a wrong attitude to money, and in particular to riches.

Some New Testament teaching about money and wealth

'Do not store up for yourselves treasures on earth, where moth and rust destroy, and where thieves break in and steal. But store up for yourselves treasures in heaven, where moth and rust do not destroy, and where thieves do not break in and steal. For where your treasure is, there your heart will be also ...

'No-one can serve two masters. Either he will hate the one and love the other, or he will be devoted to the one and despise the other. You cannot serve both God and Money.

'Therefore I tell you, do not worry about your life, what you will eat or drink; or about your body, what you will wear. Is not life more important than food, and the body more important than clothes?

'... the pagans run after all these things, and your heavenly Father knows that you need them. But seek first his kingdom and his righteousness, and all these things will be given to you as well' (Matt. 6:19–21, 24–25, 32–33).

'... the worries of this life, the deceitfulness of wealth and the desires for other things come in and choke the word' (Mark 4:19).

'Give to Caesar what is Caesar's and to God what is God's' (Mark 12:17).

'Give to everyone who asks you, and if anyone takes what belongs to you, do not demand it back. Do to others as you would have them do to you.

... if you lend to those from whom you expect repayment, what credit is that to you? Even "sinners" lend to "sinners", expecting to be repaid in full. But love your enemies, do good to them, and lend to them without expecting to get anything back. Then your reward will be great, and you will be sons of the

Most High, because he is kind to the ungrateful and wicked. Be merciful, just as your Father is merciful ...

'Give, and it will be given to you. A good measure, pressed down, shaken together and running over, will be poured into your lap. For with the measure you use, it will be measured to you' (Luke 6:30–31, 34–36, 38).

'... the worker deserves his wages' (Luke 10:7).

'Watch out! Be on your guard against all kinds of greed; a man's life does not consist in the abundance of his possessions' (Luke 12:15).

'Do not be afraid, little flock, for your Father has been pleased to give you the kingdom. Sell your possessions and give to the poor. Provide purses for yourselves that will not wear out, a treasure in heaven that will not be exhausted, where no thief comes near and no moth destroys. For where your treasure is, there your heart will be also' (Luke 12:32–34).

All the believers were one in heart and mind. No-one claimed that any of his possessions was his own, but they shared everything they had ... There were no needy persons among them (Acts 4:32, 34).

Let no debt remain outstanding, except the continuing debt to love one another (Rom. 13:8).

Remember this: Whoever sows sparingly will also reap sparingly, and whoever sows generously will also reap generously ... he who supplies seed to the sower and bread for food will also supply and increase your store of seed and will enlarge the harvest of your righteousness. You will be made rich in every way so that you can be generous on every occasion (2 Cor. 9:6, 10–11).

I know what it is to be in need, and I know what it is to have plenty. I have learned the secret of being content in any and every situation, whether well fed or hungry, whether living in plenty or in want. I can do everything through him who gives me strength ...

And my God will meet all your needs according to his glorious riches in Christ Jesus (Phil. 4:12–13, 19).

... the overseer must be ... not a lover of money ... not pursuing dishonest gain ... not greedy for money (1 Tim. 3:2–3; Titus 1:7; 1 Pet. 5:2).

... godliness with contentment is great gain. For we brought nothing into the world, and we can take nothing out of it. But if we have food and clothing, we will be content with that. People who want to get rich fall into temptation and a trap and into many foolish and harmful desires that plunge men into ruin and destruction. For the love of money is a root of all kinds of evil. Some people, eager for money, have wandered from the faith and pierced themselves with many griefs.

But you, man of God, flee from all this (1 Tim. 6:6–11).

Keep your lives free from the love of money and be content with what you have, because God has said,

'Never will I leave you;
  never will I forsake you,'

So we say with confidence,

'The Lord is my helper; I will not be afraid' (Heb. 13:5–6).

... do not forget to do good and to share with others, for with such sacrifices God is pleased (Heb. 13:16).

If anyone has material possessions and sees his brother in need but has no pity on him, how can the love of God be in him? (1 John 3:17).

See also the story of the rich young man in Matthew 19:16–30, and the parable of the talents in Matthew 25:14–30.

What could I do?

Acknowledge the lordship of Christ over your finances. Thank him for all he has provided so far. Trust him for what's to come. Ask him to direct your earning and spending, and to use all your money and possessions for his glory. Commit yourself to developing an attitude to money that is pleasing to him; ask him to protect you from 'the deceitfulness of wealth' (Mark 4:19).

Make sure you love Jesus more than money. 'You cannot serve both God and Money' (Matt. 6:24); 'though your riches increase, do not set your heart on them' (Ps. 62:10).

Learn to be content in all circumstances. Paul had experienced poverty and plenty. And he'd learnt to be content in both (Phil. 4:12–13). The secret of contentment is the knowledge that God is with us in each situation and will bring good out of it for his glory (Heb. 13:5–6).

Cultivate a simple lifestyle. Extravagant spending and ostentatious wealth are out of place for Christians in a world where so many struggle with poverty. Decide which items are essential and which are luxuries, and be content with the first (1 Tim. 6:8).

Periodically make sure you're not being sucked into the self-centred and greedy mindset of the age (Luke 12:15). Be on your guard against the insidiousness of advertisers and the social and cultural pressures that attack us from all directions. Don't believe the lies; you can live a great life without a high income and all those 'must-have' possessions.

Think through principles of responsible stewardship. You want all your money to be used for God's glory. There are several ways this could be done. You could give it all away to the poor. You could invest it and use the income to take early retirement and go as a missionary to some distant land. You could use it to make more money so that you'll be able to give more to the Lord's work. Think and pray through the policies you are going to follow, and make sure Christ stays at the centre of them.

Be careful about debt. The biblical principle is to avoid it, or to pay it off as soon as you can (Rom. 13:8). In today's society it's hard to avoid it completely, whether in the form of student loans or home mortgages. Don't go for any loan without thinking through how you're going to repay it. Be especially careful about impulse buying on 'credit'. If you do find yourself facing a debt you can't cope with:

- *Get help.* Talk through with a wise counsellor where you've gone wrong, and how you might set about sorting things out.
- *Stop spending, as far as is humanly possible.* Far too many people expect to be able to carry on an extravagant lifestyle, even when they're badly in debt. Do everything you can to cut down your outgoings.
- *Resolve that, once you're out of debt, you'll never get back in.* Work out plans to make sure this is so.

Invest responsibly. Many Christians feel that the practice of getting something for nothing is unacceptable, and so are unwilling to invest their money in the stock market. Others argue that we should get the best return we can from our money, and perhaps find some justification for such investments in the parable of the talents (Matt. 25:14–30). Most Christians would be unhappy investing their money in certain activities, such as arms manufacture. But even in seemingly acceptable sectors, such as food manufacture, some of the profits may be generated by practices that are unacceptable to Christians. It's not always possible to get the whole picture on every issue (though you do have a right to ask questions at shareholders meetings), but do your best to keep clear of what the New International Version translates as 'dishonest gain' (Titus 1:7) but what is simply a sordid way of making a profit. Again, pray over this whole issue, that God will lead you to methods of using your money creatively for his glory.

Make reasonable provision for the future. This would normally be through a pension scheme. It may well have to include provision for those who are dependent upon you. But take seriously the New Testament warning against piling up savings for the sake of it (Matt. 6:19–32). The two key concepts here are 'store up treasures in heaven' (that is, use your money for Christ's kingdom rather than saving it up for your own indulgence) and 'where your treasure is, there your heart will be also'. Always make sure your heart belongs to the Lord, not to your savings.

Be generous. Plan to give a proportion of all your income specifically for God's work (1 Cor. 16:2). The amount is up to you; many Christians see the Old Testament principle of a tenth as a minimum guideline. Give it cheerfully, wisely and prayerfully, keeping an eye on your motives (Matt. 6:1–4). Be generous in other ways. Use your home and possessions for God's glory. Be prepared to share what you have (Acts 4:32). Be ready to lend even when there's a high risk of losing your money (Luke 6:35). But in all this, use your money responsibly; confronted with so many good causes and needs, it would be foolish simply to scatter it around without careful thought. Check through the details of organizations and individuals to ensure you are making the best use of your money. Giving a lump sum to a Christian centre for the homeless, for example, would seem to be a wiser use of your money than giving indiscriminately to those begging on the street, who may well spend it on drink or drugs. Choose the missionaries or Christian organizations that you give to with care; follow up your giving with continuing interest, support and prayer. (See also the section on **giving.**)

NATIONALISM, PATRIOTISM AND THE WORLD

There's no biblical reason why we should not love our own country, whether that love is expressed in an attachment to the land, the culture, the scenery or the national team playing in a World Cup competition. What would seem unacceptable for Christians, according to biblical teaching, is any form of rejection of another country, and particularly of its people. All expressions of prejudice or racism, all criticizing or looking down on people because they belong to a different nation or culture, are totally alien to the spirit of Jesus. So it's vitally important to demonstrate any nationalism and patriotism we may feel in such a way as to show God's love and commitment to every person and nation he has made.

Though Israel is seen in the Old Testament as a nation specially chosen by God, it's evident right from the beginning of the story of salvation that God's purpose in calling Israel was to bring salvation and blessing to 'all peoples on earth' (Gen. 12:3). And though the nations round about Israel came under the judgment of God for their sinful ways (as Israel itself did), it is also clear that God's love and grace reached out to them, both in his commands to the Israelites to care for 'aliens' and in his desire that all nations might find salvation (Acts 10:34–35; 1 Tim. 2:3).

The breaking down of all barriers between Jew and Gentile (and so between all national groupings) through the work of Christ is a central theme of the New Testament. Though we do not cease to be citizens of our earthly country, and thus have to live within its structures (Rom. 13:1), the primary status of Christians is citizenship of heaven (Phil. 3:20). We are united in an eternally unbreakable bond with all Christians of every nation and culture.

Bible passages relevant to nationalism and patriotism

The LORD had said to Abram, 'Leave your country, your people and your father's household and go to the land I will show you.

> 'I will make you into a great nation
>   and I will bless you;
> I will make your name great,
>   and you will be a blessing.
> I will bless those who bless you,
>   and whoever curses you I will curse;
> and all peoples on earth
>   will be blessed through you' (Gen. 12:1–3).

... the LORD your God is God of gods and Lord of lords, the great God, mighty and awesome, who shows no partiality and accepts no bribes. He defends the cause of the fatherless and the widow, and loves the alien, giving him food and clothing. And you are to love those who are aliens, for you yourselves were aliens in Egypt (Deut. 10:17–19).

'Give to Caesar what is Caesar's and to God what is God's' (Mark 12:17).

The story of the good Samaritan (Luke 10:25–37).

'Love each other as I have loved you' (John 15:12).

'God does not show favouritism but accepts men from every nation who fear him and do what is right' (Acts 10:34–35).

... my heart's desire and prayer to God for the Israelites is that they may be saved (Rom. 10:1).

... there is no difference between Jew and Gentile – the same Lord is Lord of all and richly blesses all who call on him (Rom. 10:12).

Accept one another ... just as Christ accepted you, in order to bring praise to God (Rom. 15:7).

To the Jews I became like a Jew, to win the Jews ... To those not having the law I became like one not having the law ... To the weak I became weak, to win the weak. I have become all things to all men so that by all possible means I might save some. I do all this for the sake of the gospel (1 Cor. 9:20–23).

... our citizenship is in heaven (Phil. 3:20).

[In Christ] there is no Greek or Jew, circumcised or uncircumcised, barbarian, Scythian, slave or free, but Christ is all, and is in all (Col. 3:11).

... you are a chosen people, a royal priesthood, a holy nation, a people belonging to God, that you may declare the praises of him who called you out of darkness into his wonderful light ...

Submit yourselves for the Lord's sake to every authority instituted among men: whether to the king, as the supreme authority, or to governors, who are sent by him to punish those who do wrong and to commend those who do right. For it is God's will that by doing good you should silence the ignorant talk of foolish men. Live as free men, but do not use your freedom as a cover-up for evil; live as servants of God (1 Pet. 2:9, 13–16).

What could I do?

Be a world citizen. View the world as God views it. No discrimination. No prejudice. Enjoy a foretaste now of heaven, where there will be people 'from every nation, tribe, people and language' (Rev. 7:9).

Show a special concern for the underprivileged of the world. In the past, the more privileged nations have tended to look down on what were seen as 'underdeveloped' countries, and have regarded their own way of doing things as superior. Fight that tendency; God doesn't look on the outward appearance of fine homes, lots of motorways and a surfeit of mobile phones, but rather on the heart (1 Sam. 16:7). His assessment of other nations may well be very different from the one we've picked up from our culture, but it's the one that matters.

Fight racial prejudice wherever you find it. Oppose it in yourself and in others, in the workplace and social structures, in the church and in the media, when it's overt and when it's very subtle. (See the section on **prejudice**.)

Work at building up your awareness of belonging to the worldwide church. Again, we've not been very good at this. Sometimes we've even found it difficult to recognize that our church and the one down the road actually belong together. Get to know Christians from different nations and cultures. Read about the worldwide church. When you travel, look out local congregations and worship with them, even if you don't understand the language.

Show the love of Jesus to immigrants and asylum seekers. Pray for those who have to make the incredibly difficult decisions on whom to admit and whom to turn away. Even if you think they're making a bad job of it, as Christians we must care for the individuals in every way we can. Many of these people have lost everything; they have nothing, and we have so much. Seek to follow John the Baptist's principle in Luke 3:11.

Pray for your country. God calls us to pray for the world and for leaders of all nations (1 Tim. 2:2), but we have a special responsibility to pray for our own land and our rulers. Follow Paul's example, and pray fervently for the salvation of your people (Rom. 10:1).

Be a good national citizen. Peter says there's a sense in which we as Christians don't really belong to this world or to our own nation: we are 'aliens and strangers'. But there's also a sense in which we do belong to them. So he goes on to urge that as far as we can we should be exemplary citizens, so that those around us who aren't Christians will see the reality of God in us (1 Pet. 2:11–17. (See the section on **politics and citizenship**.)

Express your nationalism in love. Find ways of extolling the virtues of your land or supporting your national teams that don't cause any offence to others.

PEOPLE WE CAN'T GET ON WITH

If everybody else was like me, life would be great. I'd get on with everybody.

But they aren't. Everybody's different. That's part of the rich and complex world that God has made. And some people are particularly difficult to get on with – at any rate as far as we're concerned. Maybe it's who they are, their character and personality, that grates on us. Maybe it's what they do that annoys and upsets us. Maybe it's the attitude they take or the beliefs they hold.

There's the guy next door who plays his thumping music in the middle of the night. There's Aunt Matilda, who's so incredibly fussy. There's the woman at work who's always got her nose into everyone's business. There's the motorcyclist who roars at 60 through the street where kids are playing. Then there's the boss, and the guy at church who seems to love to stir things.

Some Bible teaching about relating to difficult people

... love your neighbour as yourself (Lev. 19:18).

'Blessed are those who are persecuted because of righteousness
    for theirs is the kingdom of heaven.

'Blessed are you when people insult you, persecute you and falsely say all kinds of evil against you because of me. Rejoice and be glad, because great is your reward in heaven, for in the same way they persecuted the prophets who were before you (Matt. 5:10–12).

'... if you are offering your gift at the altar and there remember that your brother has something against you, leave your gift there in front of the altar. First go and be reconciled to your brother; then come and offer your gift.

'Settle matters quickly with your adversary who is taking you to court. Do it while you are still with him on the way, or he may hand you over to the judge, and the judge may hand you over to the officer, and you may be thrown into prison. I tell you the truth, you will not get out until you have paid the last penny' (Matt. 5:23–26).

'You have heard that it was said, "Eye for eye, and tooth for tooth." But I tell you, Do not resist an evil person. If someone strikes you on the right cheek, turn to him the other also. And if someone wants to sue you and take your tunic, let him have your cloak as well. If someone forces you to go one mile, go with him two miles ...

'You have heard that it was said, "Love your neighbour and hate your enemy." But I tell you: Love your enemies and pray for those who persecute you, that you may be sons of your Father in heaven. He causes his sun to rise on the evil and the good, and sends rain on the righteous and the unrighteous. if you love those who love you, what reward will you get? Are not even the tax collectors doing that? And if you greet only your brothers, what are you doing more than others? Do not even pagans do that? Be perfect, therefore, as your heavenly Father is perfect' (Matt. 5:38–41, 43–48).

> '"Forgive us our debts,
> as we also have forgiven our debtors ..."

'For if you forgive men when they sin against you, your heavenly Father will also forgive you. But if you do not forgive men their sins, your Father will not forgive your sins' (Matt. 6:12, 14–15).

'All men will hate you because of me, but he who stands firm to the end will be saved' (Matt. 10:22).

'Lord, how many times shall I forgive my brother when he sins against me? Up to seven times?'

Jesus answered, 'I tell you, not seven times, but seventy-seven times' (Matt. 18:21–22).

One of the teachers of the law ... asked him, 'Of all the commandments, which is the most important?'

'The most important one,' answered Jesus, 'is this: "Hear, O Israel, the Lord our God, the Lord is one. Love the Lord your God with all your heart and with all your soul and with all your mind and with all your strength." The second is this: "Love your neighbour as yourself." There is no commandment greater than these' (Mark 12:28–31).

Who shall separate us from the love of Christ? Shall trouble or hardship or persecution ...? No, in all these things we are more than conquerors through him who loved us (Rom. 8:35, 37).

Bless those who persecute you; bless and do not curse (Rom. 12:14).

Do not repay anyone evil for evil. Be careful to do what is right in the eyes of everybody. If it is possible, as far as it depends on you, live at peace with everyone. Do not take revenge, my friends, but leave room for God's wrath, for it is written: 'It is mine to avenge; I will repay,' says the Lord. On the contrary:

> 'If your enemy is hungry, feed him;
>   if he is thirsty, give him something to drink.
> In doing this, you will heap burning coals on his head.'

Do not be overcome by evil, but overcome evil with good (Rom. 12:17–21).

We who are strong ought to bear with the failings of the weak and not to please ourselves. Each of us should please his neighbour for his good, to build him up. For even Christ did not please himself (Rom. 15:1–3).

When we are cursed, we bless; when we are persecuted, we endure it; when we are slandered, we answer kindly (1 Cor. 4:12–13).

Love ... keeps no record of wrongs ...
   Love never fails (1 Cor. 13:4–5, 8).

The entire law is summed up in a single command: 'Love your neighbour as yourself' (Gal. 5:14)

'In your anger do not sin': Do not let the sun go down while you are still angry, and do not give the devil a foothold ...
   And do not grieve the Holy Spirit of God, with whom you were sealed for the day of redemption. Get rid of all bitterness,

rage and anger, brawling and slander, along with every form of malice. Be kind and compassionate to one another, forgiving each other, just as in Christ God forgave you.

Be imitators of God, therefore, as dearly loved children (Eph. 4:26, 30–32; 5:1).

... clothe yourselves with compassion, kindness, humility, gentleness and patience. Bear with one another and forgive whatever grievances you may have against one another. Forgive as the Lord forgave you (Col. 3:12–13).

Consider it pure joy, my brothers, whenever you face trials of many kinds, because you know that the testing of your faith develops perseverance. Perseverance must finish its work so that you may be mature and complete, not lacking anything ...

Blessed is the man who perseveres under trial, because when he has stood the test, he will receive the crown of life that God has promised to those who love him (Jas. 1:2–4, 12).

Christ suffered for you, leaving you an example, that you should follow in his steps ... When they hurled their insults at him, he did not retaliate; when he suffered, he made no threats. Instead, he entrusted himself to him who judges justly (1 Pet. 2:21, 23).

What could I do?

Let's take three scenarios.

The first is when someone deliberately and expressly wrongs us. Someone tells malicious lies about us, defrauds us of a large sum, or deliberately harms us in some way. In this case any of the suggestions below may be relevant. See also the suggestions in the section on **injustice**.

The second is when someone wrongs us probably without realizing it. It may just be carelessness or thoughtlessness. She or he may not even be aware that we've been hurt or are upset. Here suggestions 2–8 may be helpful.

The third is when we haven't been wronged, but we still find the person difficult to cope with. In that case, suggestions 4–8 may be particularly relevant.

1. *Stop the fighting.* The New Testament teaching leaves us no option. However much we want to hit back, to score points and to sort the other person out, the way of Christ is to refuse to retaliate, to turn the other cheek. So, by God's grace, bite your tongue when you think of that stinging reply, ditch those plans to get your own back, refuse to grumble about what the person has done. For this you'll need Jesus, his grace and goodness in you, breaking the cycle of evil.

2. *Clear the inner ground.* It's one thing to stop the external fighting. But often it's quite a different matter to deal with our inner feelings of anger, resentment, hurt and the desire to get our own back. But the New Testament is quite straight. We have to get rid, it says, of all un-Christlike feelings and attitudes towards the other person. That takes some doing! It may well take time, and may need to be repeated again and again. But it's got to be done. Discipline yourself to take these feelings to the Lord at the start of each day and whenever they arise. With his help, reject them: 'Lord, I don't want to go on feeling that way.' You'll probably find that it's comparatively easy to feel gracious and Christlike towards the person when, say, you're in the middle of a Sunday morning service, but it's a very different story at two o'clock on Monday morning when his or her loud music is ruining your sleep. In that case you'll have to tell the Lord that it's the Sunday and not the Monday morning you that is the real you, or at least that you want your Sunday self to be the real you. 'Lord, I love my neighbour; help me during those times when I wish he'd drop dead.' (See Appendix 4, 'Ten steps to changing thought patterns'.)

3. *Forgive.* As with dealing with our inner feelings, forgiving is something we often have to keep working at. In our more spiritual moments we may feel that we have followed Christ's teaching and example and have forgiven our enemy; but a few hours later the old attitude comes back and we feel anything but forgiving. But keep on forgiving. The more often you do it, the more expert at it you'll become. And, since forgiving is such a Godlike thing, the nearer to God you'll get. Where necessary, try another adapta-

tion of the prayer of the father in Mark 9:24: 'I do forgive; help me overcome my unforgiveness!'

4. *Take the opportunity for self-analysis*. There's an outside chance that part of the problem may lie in you. Could it be that somehow you've upset the other person, or that something in you rubs her or him up the wrong way? Ask for the Spirit's help in checking this out; it might be a good idea to consult a wise friend who knows you both. If you do find something, get to work to put it right.

5. *Start doing good to your enemy*. When the Bible tells us to love our neighbours even if they're our 'enemies', it doesn't primarily mean that we have to feel a warm, emotional glow towards them. The story of the good Samaritan (Luke 10:25–37) shows that it's perfectly possible to think someone repulsive and yet to express Christian love to him or her at the same time. So, as far as you can, do something that expresses Christlike love towards the person. It may be something very simple, like a word of encouragement or a card; or something a bit more complex, like going the 'second mile' or inconveniencing yourself to do a good deed. And don't forget that Jesus added, 'pray for those who persecute you' (Matt. 5:44).

6. *Try to find ways of building a good relationship with the person.* The New Testament talks about 'being reconciled' (Matt. 5:24), and seeking to 'living at peace with everyone' (Rom. 12:18). It may not always be possible to do this, or it may take time to build a good relationship. But that's got to be our aim. If the person concerned is a Christian, this may well mean following the procedure Jesus outlines in Matthew 18:15–17. Doing it this way isn't always necessary or appropriate, however; particularly when the person is not a Christian, it's likely be counterproductive to go to someone and tell them we can't stand them! Take it as a principle that with God's help, you can reach the point where you can get on with anybody; you can win any enemy over to being a friend. Of course, it'll take time, effort, quite a bit of ingenuity and lots of prayer. But accept it as a challenge, a God-given opportunity to do the impossible, the miracle he's already done with you, turning an enemy into a friend.

7. *Have a go at rejoicing*. Try following the mind-blowing advice of Jesus in Matthew 5:12, or of James in James 1:2. Remember,

neither Jesus nor James lived in an ivory tower. They both had far tougher lives than you, with lots of very unpleasant people around them, who said and did nasty things. So take their advice seriously. After all, getting down and miserable isn't going to help the situation, and self-pity is a killer. Granted, you may not be able to say, 'Praise the Lord for rotten neighbours,' or 'Yippee, the boss is in a bad mood again.' But you're walking the way Jesus walked, and sharing in his suffering; and that's a great way of getting closer to him, and of learning all sorts of great lessons you'd never learn if everything was easy all the time.

8. *Find ways of learning and growing through the experience.* God can use any situation for good in our lives. So make the most of all the potential good that this experience sets before you. Learn all you can about human behaviour, what makes people tick and how they react in difficult circumstances. Learn about yourself, and about God and his ways. And grow – as a person, in grace and forgiveness, patience and love, and in dependence on Christ.

See also the sections on **conflict** and **injustice**.

PLURALISM: DECLARING CHRISTIAN TRUTH IN A PLURALISTIC AGE

Religious pluralism is nothing new. Other religions have always existed alongside Christianity. What is new in these days is a spirit of relativism, which refuses to allow that one religion may be right and another wrong; all religions are to be accepted as equally valid. As a result, many Christians are reticent about making dogmatic claims for Christianity, for fear of seeming to be intolerant of those who follow other religions.

The first century AD was a time of unprecedented religious

pluralism. The Christians of the New Testament were surrounded by a bewildering array of alternative religions. The Roman Empire opened up communication and travel in a way the world had never known before. People were being brought into contact with ancient religions, such as the Druidism of the remote Britons, or the Buddhism and Confucianism from the East. New religions were springing up, some full of sex and orgies, some declaring secret mysteries and esoteric knowledge. Then there were the more respectable religions, such as Stoicism and Epicureanism, and the developments of traditional Greek and Roman religion. On top of it all came the religion of the Roman state, Roma as a goddess and the emperor as a god.

So pluralism was nothing new to Paul and the New Testament writers. But that didn't deter them from making very dogmatic claims about the truth of the gospel. They were utterly convinced that what they were saying was true; and, if it was true, to the extent that other religions and philosophies disagreed with it, they must be false.

Some New Testament passages about the gospel

'All authority in heaven and on earth has been given to me. Therefore go and make disciples of all nations, baptising them in the name of the Father and of the Son and of the Holy Spirit, and teaching them to obey everything I have commanded you. And surely I am with you always, to the very end of the age' (Matt. 28:18–20).

'God so loved the world that he gave his one and only Son, that whoever believes in him shall not perish but have eternal life. For God did not send his Son into the world to condemn the world, but to save the world through him. Whoever believes in him is not condemned, but whoever does not believe stands condemned already because he has not believed in the name of God's one and only Son. This is the verdict: Light has come into the world, but men loved darkness instead of light because their deeds were evil ...

'Whoever believes in the Son has eternal life, but whoever

rejects the Son will not see life, for God's wrath remains on him'
(John 3:16–19, 36).

'... how can we know the way?'
   Jesus answered, 'I am the way and the truth and the life. No-
one comes to the Father except through me' (John 14:5–6).

'Jesus Christ of Nazareth ... Salvation is found in no-one else, for
there is no other name under heaven given to men by which we
must be saved.
   '... we cannot help speaking about what we have seen and
heard' (Acts 4:10, 12, 20).

'You know the message God sent to the people of Israel, telling
the good news of peace through Jesus Christ, who is Lord of
all ...
   'We are witnesses of everything he did ... God raised him
from the dead ... He commanded us to preach to the people and
to testify that he is the one whom God appointed as judge of the
living and the dead ... everyone who believes in him receives
forgiveness of sins through his name' (Acts 10:36, 39–40,
42–43).

I am not ashamed of the gospel, because it is the power of God
for the salvation of everyone who believes (Rom. 1:16).

'Everyone who calls on the name of the Lord will be saved.'
   How, then, can they call on the one they have not believed in?
And how can they believe in the one of whom they have not
heard? And how can they hear without someone preaching to
them? (Rom. 10:13–14).

... the message of the cross is foolishness to those who are
perishing, but to us who are being saved it is the power of God.
   ... we preach Christ crucified: a stumbling-block to Jews and
foolishness to Gentiles, but to those whom God has called, both
Jews and Greeks, Christ the power of God and the wisdom of
God (1 Cor. 1:18, 23–24).

... we have renounced secret and shameful ways; we do not use deception, nor do we distort the word of God. On the contrary, by setting forth the truth plainly we commend ourselves to every man's conscience in the sight of God. And even if our gospel is veiled, it is veiled to those who are perishing. The god of this age has blinded the minds of unbelievers, so that they cannot see the light of the gospel of the glory of Christ, who is the image of God. For we do not preach ourselves, but Jesus Christ as Lord, and ourselves as your servants for Jesus' sake. For God, who said, 'Let light shine out of darkness,' made his light shine in our hearts to give us the light of the knowledge of the glory of God in the face of Christ (2 Cor. 4:2–6).

Christ's love compels us, because we are convinced that one died for all, and therefore all died. And he died for all, that those who live should no longer live for themselves but for him who died for them and was raised again ...

God ... reconciled us to himself through Christ and gave us the ministry of reconciliation ... We are therefore Christ's ambassadors, as though God were making his appeal through us. We implore you on Christ's behalf: Be reconciled to God.

... now is the time of God's favour, now is the day of salvation (2 Cor. 5:14–15, 18, 20; 6:2).

Paul, an apostle – sent not from men nor by man, but by Jesus Christ and God the Father, who raised him from the dead (Gal. 1:1).

... the word of truth, the gospel that has come to you. All over the world this gospel is bearing fruit and growing, just as it has been doing among you since the day you heard it and understood God's grace in all its truth (Col. 1:5–6).

... the commission God gave me to present to you the word of God in its fulness – the mystery that has been kept hidden for ages and generations, but is now disclosed to the saints. To them God has chosen to make known among the Gentiles the glorious riches of this mystery, which is Christ in you, the hope of glory.

We proclaim him (Col. 1:25–28).

... our gospel came to you not simply with words, but also with power, with the Holy Spirit and with deep conviction (1 Thess. 1:5).

God our Saviour ... wants all men to be saved and to come to a knowledge of the truth. For there is one God and one mediator between God and men, the man Christ Jesus, who gave himself as a ransom for all men – the testimony given in its proper time. And for this purpose I was appointed a herald and an apostle – I am telling the truth, I am not lying – and a teacher of the true faith to the Gentiles (1 Tim. 2:3–7).

God's household ... is the church of the living God, the pillar and foundation of the truth. Beyond all question, the mystery of godliness is great:

> He appeared in a body,
>   was vindicated by the Spirit,
> was seen by angels,
>   was preached among the nations,
> was believed on in the world,
>   was taken up in glory (1 Tim. 3:15–16).

... do not be ashamed to testify about our Lord, or ashamed of me his prisoner. But join with me in suffering for the gospel, by the power of God ... of this gospel I was appointed a herald and an apostle and a teacher. That is why I am suffering as I am. Yet I am not ashamed, because I know whom I have believed, and am convinced that he is able to guard what I have entrusted to him for that day (2 Tim. 1:8, 11–12).

... test the spirits to see whether they are from God ... This is how you can recognise the Spirit of God: Every spirit that acknowledges that Jesus Christ has come in the flesh is from

God, but every spirit that does not acknowledge Jesus is not from God (1 John 4:1–2).

... another angel ... had the eternal gospel to proclaim to those who live on the earth – to every nation, tribe, language and people (Rev. 14:6).

What could I do to declare God's truth in the face of religious pluralism?

Accept that the Christian gospel, like every religion, is unique. Of course, there's lots that Christianity shares with other religions. But that's not to say that all religions are the same. Every religion has its distinctive points. Where two religions conflict, one of them must be wrong, or, at any rate, less right.

Recognize that the most distinctive point about Christianity is Jesus. He's the key to everything else. 'Acknowledging Jesus' (1 John 4:2–3), who he is and what he has done, is what makes Christianity unique. The message proclaimed by the first-century Christians in the face of religious pluralism was Jesus, God come to us in his Son.

Accept that the command of God has not been withdrawn. God hasn't admitted that, since the twenty-first century is a pluralistic age, we should go soft on the uniqueness of Jesus. The very fact that this is a pluralistic age means that we should explain Christianity's distinctive points more clearly.

Be gracious and tactful. 'All other religions are wrong and only Christianity's right' is not likely to be a helpful approach. Think out a way of expressing your case that will win you a hearing. It might be something like 'I accept there's a lot in all religions; they all express the way we human beings reach out and try to find God, and practically all of them have helpful insights into the profound questions of life and wise advice on how to live. But, if I may, I'd like to explain to you what's so special about Christianity.'

Seize the great opportunity the postmodern mindset offers. Many people today aren't really interested in concepts and ideas. What matters is being, living, relating and personal experience. All of that can be found in Jesus. He's not a set of philosophical ideas; he's a person. Some might be persuaded to become Christians by debating doctrines, but far more in our contemporary society will be won over by the reality and beauty of the life of Jesus. Of course, there's a place for doctrine, but remember the approach of the Gospels. They don't set out primarily to expound doctrine; rather, they present Jesus, a real person living a real life, and expressing all the reality and truth of God in who he was and what he did. Doctrinal formulations and clarifications came after the events the Gospels record. It was Jesus, the real person, who was the foundation for these later developments.

Stress the historical reality of Jesus. Compared with most religions, we have a huge amount of utterly dependable material about his life. Forget the sceptical debates of liberal scholars. The bottom line is that we have far better evidence for the real existence of Jesus Christ than we have for Julius Caesar; and no-one doubts that Caesar existed. You could try taking the line: 'What we decide to do about Jesus is up to each individual. But in all honesty we need to face the historical facts before deciding to accept or reject him.'

Remember that many people who won't accept the Bible will be prepared to listen to Jesus. If someone can accept the authority of statements beginning 'The Bible says ...', well and good. But if they can't, try 'The life of Jesus shows ...' or perhaps 'Jesus taught ...'

Express Jesus in who you are even more than in what you say. Both saying and being are important, but, in the current climate, being is often what makes most impact. Make sure they see his love, beauty and goodness in you. To do this you'll need the filling of the Holy Spirit. Being Christlike in our own strength is an impossible task. Expressing Christ when we're full to overflowing with him is much easier.

Don't pressurize. There are at least two good reasons for this. First, if people do decide to become Christians, we want it to be because of the work of the Holy Spirit in them, not as a result of our persuasiveness or pressure. And the second reason is that pressure will usually be counterproductive. Despite the fact that people generally accept the hard-sell techniques of advertisers without a murmur, they almost always react negatively when they feel under pressure in a religious discussion. Maybe we're reaping the harvest of the techniques of Jehovah's Witnesses on the doorsteps. Instead of pressure, give people space. Win the battle by prayer and love, not by techniques.

Encourage people to express their own beliefs and to ask questions. Again, we've all had religious salespersons on the doorstep who are only interested in pushing their line, and don't let us get a word in edgeways. That's not the way of love. Be a good listener as well as a good witness.

If they ask questions you can't answer, offer to find them the answer. This both shows that you value the question and gives you the opportunity of consulting wiser Christian friends or literature to find the answer. Remember, over the past 2,000 years just about every question that could be asked about Christianity has been raised and answered, so you're not likely to get one that's totally unanswerable.

Avoid making dogmatic statements. In a relativistic age, if you make such a statement – such as 'God is love' – you're likely to get the response 'That may well be true for you, but it's not true for me.' Rather, let Jesus make the claims. They're much more likely to have an impact than statements that would be seen as just your opinion. 'Jesus claimed to be showing us how much God loves us, and I think you have to agree that he showed it clearly.' Remember, it's not ourselves and our beliefs we're putting forward, but Jesus.

Don't argue. That is, don't aggressively present your way of seeing things over against the other person's way; there may be appropriate times when you can graciously present the credentials of the Christian case, just as Paul 'reasoned', 'explained' and 'proved' his case at Thessalonica (Acts 17:2–3). But remember Jesus. 'He will not quarrel or cry out; no-one will hear his voice in the streets. A bruised reed he will not break, and a smouldering wick he will not snuff out' (Matt. 12:19–20). If you argue, you risk pushing people into defensive positions and causing them to move further away from you as they find new ways of standing up for their position.

Don't reject. Even if you disagree quite strongly with them, accept and affirm them, whatever they say. If they start talking about flower fairies (yes, someone did with me the other day), don't, either in your words or in your attitude, show that you think the idea is rubbish. Instead, continue to express acceptance and affirmation, and lead the conversation on to something rather more helpful. 'Hey, that's a new idea. Christians certainly believe there's much more to the world than what the scientists can examine in a test tube. But I can't think of anything Jesus said about flower fairies. What he did say was that God cares about us even more than he cares about the flowers.' This is true 'tolerance': not abandoning our beliefs because someone happens to disagree, but accepting the people who disagree with us, whatever they may believe.

Don't be ashamed of the gospel. Paul's words in Romans 1:16 and 2 Timothy 1:8 seem to accept that for many of us there's a basic diffidence or even shame in sharing the good news of the gospel. But Paul had an answer, even though he often suffered as a result of telling people about Jesus. It was that the gospel is 'the power of God'. Though at times he may have spoken with fear and trembling, he knew that the good news of Jesus wasn't just another set of religious ideas, but rather the means through which he had repeatedly seen the Holy Spirit of God breaking through into people's lives.

Pray. Soak everything in prayer. You're in a spiritual battle, and spiritual battles are won with spiritual weapons (Eph. 6:12, 18). Pray specifically that people will come face to face with Jesus, and accept his salvation.

Get on with the task of telling everyone the good news. There's still a long way to go, but God still 'wants all men to be saved and to come to a knowledge of the truth' (1 Tim. 2:4), and he has promised to be with us and to build his church through us.

POLITICS AND CITIZENSHIP

The Old Testament's instructions on the organization of the state and on the responsibilities of individual citizens were set in a unique context: Israel was God's covenant people. Indeed, there's more than a hint in the Old Testament that in an ideal world there would be no human government as such; rather, God would be directly acknowledged as King and would rule the affairs of nations. When Gideon was invited to become king of Israel, he replied, 'I will not rule over you, nor will my son rule over you. The LORD will rule over you' (Judg. 8:23). The eventual establishment of the monarchy was very much a second best (1 Sam. 8:4–22).

By the time of the New Testament the context was very different, and much closer to ours today. The early Christians were called to be citizens in a state that rejected God and that followed and imposed values that were often alien to Christianity. This sometimes meant that Christians had to take a firm stand against policies and practices, with all the resulting conflict and persecution.

However, for the most part, the New Testament calls Christians to live as good citizens, accepting the rule of government as God's way of regulating society, and living within its framework and structures as far as possible. As a small and weak minority group living under a totalitarian government, the early Christians had no opportunity to exercise any direct influence on the politics of their day. Nevertheless, they were called to do at least four things. First, they were to pray, especially for their rulers and leaders. Secondly, they were called to be exemplary citizens, to 'give to Caesar what is Caesar's, and to God what is God's' (Matt. 22:21), to 'live at peace with everyone' (Rom. 12:18), and to commend the gospel in every aspect of their living in their local community (1 Pet. 2:12–17). Thirdly, they were to proclaim the good news of Jesus and allow his kingdom to come, spreading like yeast through individuals, families and communities (Matt. 13:33). Fourthly, they were to hold on, with the anticipation that the day would soon come when the Lord would return and 'the kingdom of the world' would become 'the kingdom of our Lord and of his Christ, and he will reign for ever and ever' (Rev. 11:15).

In later centuries the church ceased to be a weak minority group and used its considerable power to influence the affairs of governments. This undoubtedly brought benefits at times, though it is open to debate whether the imposition of Christian values and policies from a position of power is ever truly in keeping with the spirit and approach of Jesus, who rejected such a policy in favour of the way of weakness (Luke 4:1–13; Matt. 12:15–21) and taught his disciples to follow his example (Matt. 20:25–28; 26:52).

Most Christian writers today take it for granted that the church should be involved in politics. But it's not always clear what they mean by 'the church'. Some might argue for the special privileges and powers of a state church in the affairs of the nation; but others regard this as running counter to the principle that a minority should not force its views and policies on the majority. Some would say that denominational leaders or assemblies should speak out on political issues; but in the event there are comparatively few political issues over which Christians are fully agreed and can speak incisively with one voice. Maybe it would be better to substitute 'Christians' for 'the church'; each of us as individual followers of Jesus needs to take action, rather than some institution or power structure. This avoids the danger of shifting the responsibility on to others ('They ought to do something about it'). It also avoids the temptation to engage in a power game in which the church as an institution engages with the state, something that seems alien to the way of Jesus.

To say that Christians should be involved in politics, then, means that, so far from pushing the responsibility on to others or an institution, we accept that responsibility ourselves; every Christian should be involved in politics. How we fulfil this responsibility will, of course, vary. We'll all follow the example of the New Testament Christians by praying for our rulers, being good citizens and seeking to bring the kingdom of God into our community and nation through sharing the good news. Additionally, in a democratic state, we'll fulfil our responsibility to vote thoughtfully and prayerfully, and to let those who represent us know our views so that they can take them into consideration when making decisions.

Furthermore, we all have opportunities to be involved more directly in formulating policies and making decisions that affect our community at various levels. Most local communities have

Residents Associations or similar groups, where Christians can become involved, attend meetings and serve as street wardens or in other capacities. Then there are local school governing bodies, and committees and boards responsible for a whole range of community, social, sports and leisure activities. There are trades unions, chambers of commerce, parish councils, city councils, district councils and county councils, with all their various committees. All of this local involvement is open to most Christians and can be undertaken in their spare time. Getting further involved, in national organizations and politics, is a possibility for some who have the necessary abilities and time.

Then there are Christian organizations that seek to feed Christian values and concepts into the social and political processes. Again, the level of involvement in them will vary according to the individual's situation, ranging from prayer and concern to full-time voluntary or paid employment.

In all of this we're seeking to live out Christ's statement that we are salt and light (Matt. 5:13–16), not by exploiting a privileged position, or by exercising power or using manipulative methods (2 Cor. 4:2), but by being Christ-filled and Spirit-led people creatively involved in the life of our community and nation.

New Testament teaching on politics and citizenship

'You are the salt of the earth. But if the salt loses its saltiness, can it be made salty again? It is no longer good for anything, except to be thrown out and trampled by men.

'You are the light of the world. A city on a hill cannot be hidden. Neither do people light a lamp and put it under a bowl. Instead they put it on its stand, and it gives light to everyone in the house. In the same way, let your light shine before men, that they may see your good deeds and praise your Father in heaven' (Matt. 5:13–16).

'The kingdom of heaven is like yeast that a woman took and mixed into a large amount of flour until it worked all through the dough' (Matt. 13:33).

'Is it right to pay taxes to Caesar or not?' [Jesus] said to them, 'Give to Caesar what is Caesar's, and to God what is God's' (Matt. 22:17, 21).

'... we cannot help speaking about what we have seen and heard' (Acts 4:20).

'We must obey God rather than men!' (Acts 5:29).

... my heart's desire and prayer to God for the Israelites is that they may be saved (Rom. 10:1).

Be careful to do what is right in the eyes of everybody. If it is possible, as far as it depends on you, live at peace with everyone (Rom. 12:17–18).

Everyone must submit himself to the governing authorities, for there is no authority except that which God has established. The authorities that exist have been established by God. Consequently, he who rebels against the authority is rebelling against what God has instituted, and those who do so will bring judgment on themselves. For rulers hold no terror for those who do right, but for those who do wrong. Do you want to be free from fear of the one in authority? Then do what is right and he will commend you. For he is God's servant to do you good. But if you do wrong, be afraid, for he does not bear the sword for nothing. He is God's servant, an agent of wrath to bring punish-ment on the wrongdoer. Therefore, it is necessary to submit to the authorities, not only because of possible punishment but also because of conscience.

This is why you pay taxes, for the authorities are God's servants, who give their full time to governing. Give everyone what you owe him: If you owe taxes, pay taxes; if revenue, then revenue; if respect, then respect; if honour, then honour ...

The commandments, 'Do not commit adultery,' 'Do not murder,' 'Do not steal,' 'Do not covet,' and whatever other commandment there may be, are summed up in this one rule: 'Love your neighbour as yourself.' Love does no harm to its neighbour. Therefore love is the fulfilment of the law (Rom. 13:1–7, 9–10).

… we have renounced secret and shameful ways; we do not use deception, nor do we distort the word of God. On the contrary, by setting forth the truth plainly we commend ourselves to every man's conscience in the sight of God … For we do not preach ourselves, but Jesus Christ as Lord, and ourselves as your servants for Jesus' sake (2 Cor. 4:2, 5).

… our citizenship is in heaven (Phil. 3:20).

You are a chosen people, a royal priesthood, a holy nation, a people belonging to God, that you may declare the praises of him who called you out of darkness into his wonderful light …
Live such good lives among the pagans that, though they accuse you of doing wrong, they may see your good deeds and glorify God on the day he visits us.
Submit yourselves for the Lord's sake to every authority instituted among men: whether to the king, as the supreme authority, or to governors, who are sent by him to punish those who do wrong and to commend those who do right. For it is God's will that by doing good you should silence the ignorant talk of foolish men. Live as free men, but do not use your freedom as a cover-up for evil; live as servants of God (1 Pet. 2:9, 12–16).

What could I do as an ordinary citizen?

Be a good citizen. Keep the law of the land, unless it directly conflicts with foundational Christian principles. Be concerned for others. Let your light shine. Accept the authority of the state. Obey police officers, traffic wardens and local bye-laws. Non-Christians may well find something to criticize in us whatever we do, but the New Testament makes it clear that it's better to be criticized for doing right than for doing wrong. And there's always the hope that our witness will have a positive effect.

Pray. Pray for those who do take on responsibilities in local and national affairs. Pray especially for any you know personally, and for those who seek to speak up for Christian values and policies. Pray for the coming of God's kingdom in your nation.

Take on board Paul's call to 'respect' and 'honour' those in authority (Rom. 13:7). This goes right against the stream of our culture. Not only is the mood of the age anti-authority, but the very concepts of respecting and honouring are foreign to most people. Instead, we criticize and grumble about our leaders and those in authority and take delight in scandal and gossip. But these are biblical commands; we are to respect and honour those who, for all their faults, are part of the God-given structures of our community and nation. Think through appropriate ways of obeying these commands today.

Use your vote. Voting representatives on to local committees may be fairly straightforward. Deciding how to vote in national general elections certainly isn't. The issues tend to be complex, and each candidate probably represents some policies that you can accept and others that you reject. Even so, after studying and praying through the issues, you need to make a responsible choice.

Use other legitimate ways of influencing those who represent you. Apart from personal face-to-face contact, writing letters and emails is probably still the most effective way. Keep them short and to the point. Present arguments clearly, without exaggeration. Make the letter or email attractive and easy to read. Don't forget to encourage your representatives, to thank them for what they are doing, and to assure them that you're supporting them and praying for them.

What could I do to be involved in local or national political affairs?

Start somewhere. The most obvious place may well be a local committee, though if you have a special skill or interest you could try for a place in a regional or national structure, as a volunteer, or possibly in a paid capacity. You'll probably find it's easier to get on to committees than you might imagine; widespread apathy and a general disillusionment with politics mean that comparatively few people are willing to be involved. CARE operates a programme of short-term internship enabling people to work alongside MPs at Westminster. Talk with those who have a good knowledge of what might be possible; pray; and follow God's guidance and provision.

Show Jesus in all you are and do. The world of politics and community involvement can be a place where tough battles are fought, and in some cases this brings out the worst in those involved. Let it bring out the best in you. Show Christlike grace and love whatever the situation, and however others are behaving. Constantly ask God to fill you with his Spirit and to give you the grace and wisdom you need.

Pray for those you're involved with. Pray for fellow committee members, councillors and governors. Pray for those who oppose your policies. Pray for righteousness, justice, truth and the coming of God's kingdom. Pray for those you're seeking to serve. Follow Paul's example, and pray fervently for their salvation (Rom. 10:1). Pray for all involved in local and national politics (1 Tim. 2:2).

Pray for yourself. Get others to pray for you. If you're a local councillor, you need as much prayer support as a minister or a missionary. Soak everything in prayer. You're in a spiritual battle, and spiritual battles are won with spiritual weapons (Eph. 6:12, 18). Pray specifically that, through what you are doing, people will come face to face with Jesus and accept his salvation.

Keep telling everyone the good news. The old debate over whether Christians should spend their time evangelizing or being involved in social and political affairs is mercifully all but over. No division needs to be made between them; both are ways of presenting the kingdom of God. But just as it was a mistake to focus on evangelism to the exclusion of social involvement, so, save perhaps in countries where direct witness to the gospel is impossible, it's a mistake to spend all our energies in social and political activity and never to tell people the good news of Jesus.

Use all the help you can get. Talk with others who have been involved in similar situations. Your denominational offices, or interdenominational organizations such as the Evangelical Alliance and CARE, will be able to give you details of helpful literature and organizations that can offer valuable information on how to proceed.

Accept that you will face opposition, setbacks and disappointments.

Keep in mind the words of Jesus when he said that the world would hate his followers: 'Remember the words I spoke to you: "No servant is greater than his master." If they persecuted me, they will persecute you also. If they obeyed my teaching, they will obey yours also. They will treat you this way because of my name' (John 15:20–21). Be willing to walk the way of the cross. Expect misunderstanding, false accusations, frustration, and all the other hassles Jesus had to face. By his grace, take them in your stride and keep going.

Avoid engaging in any form of political activity that is not in accordance with Christian values and principles. Others may choose to use lies, manipulation or bribery. Keep your hands clean; show that there are other, and better, ways of achieving your aims. 'For though we live in the world, we do not wage war as the world does. The weapons we fight with are not the weapons of the world. On the contrary, they have divine power to demolish strongholds' (2 Cor. 10:3–4). Don't exaggerate or overstate your case. Steer clear of belligerence and partisanship. (See the sections on **promises** and **truth: telling the truth**.

Never attack people. Only ever oppose ideas, policies and practices; never make your attack personal. Instead, show grace, kindness and Christian love towards those with whom you disagree. If they attack you, use it as an opportunity to follow Christ's example and teaching. (See the section on **conflict**.)

Be especially careful over any hint of corruption. Christians will come to you because you are a Christian and ask you to use the influence of your position to further their interests or those of some worthy cause. Of course you want to help, but stop and think. If, say, the Freemasons worked this way, would you be able to accept it as totally fair and above board? Granted, 'everybody' does it, and sometimes, after careful thought, you may feel it right to do it yourself. But be very careful. It's one of the ways of the world, and it's the source of a huge amount of injustice. If you should decide to do it, be sure to be open about it.

Show a specific concern for the underprivileged. They have a special place in the heart of God. Remember the instructions of Jesus to his host at the society dinner in Luke 14:12–14. When he throws a party, Jesus told him, instead of inviting those who are able to invite him back in return, he should invite 'the poor, the crippled, the lame, the blind' – those who can never do anything for him in return.

Try to influence legislation without unfairly imposing your Christian views. Remember, your task is to offer your fellow committee members and other colleagues the opportunity of following Christian values and principles, not to force these values and principles on them or on anyone. Present your case as attractively as possible. While few may accept an approach that starts with 'The Bible says ...', most people will listen to a well-argued case demonstrating that a specific Christian value or principle would be of benefit to the community if applied in a certain way. In presenting your case, Jesus said, 'Be as shrewd as snakes and as innocent as doves' (Matt. 10:16).

See also the section on **nationalism, patriotism and the world**.

PRAYER

We all pray. It's a foundational element of being a Christian. Christianity is a relationship with the living God; relationships entail communication, and prayer is communication. It is, of course, communication that operates in all sorts of ways and at all sorts of levels. It most certainly is not just asking for things, though it definitely includes that. It's talking matters over with God, listening to his voice, loving him, worshipping him, expressing our feelings to him, rejoicing, submitting, hungering, opening our minds and hearts and bodies to him, and much more. It can include silent communication, just sitting in the presence of the Lord and enjoying his company. It can be offered in tongues. It can be gloriously simple, or wonderfully profound, lasting a few seconds or going on all day.

All of us are dissatisfied with our prayer life. There are two reasons for that, one good and one bad. The bad one is that we let other activities push prayer out of its central place. We're so busy; the TV is more attractive than the prayer room; we haven't learnt the art and discipline of praying. The good one is that the more we pray the more we realize there's so much more to prayer – so much more to learn and experience. We're on the edge of an ocean, just paddling, and we want to go in deeper.

Hopefully all of us want to improve our praying. But we find it hard to do so. We buy books on prayer. We use other people's prayers. We try the latest fashion: Celtic prayer, or medieval prayer, or how they pray in South Korea. Some of it helps, and some of it doesn't.

In a sense, the issue is simple. It's not 'How good am I at praying?' or 'How satisfied am I with my prayer life?' The answer to those questions will always be rather negative, until we get to glory. The issue isn't really prayer at all. Prayer is only a means to an end. The end, of course, is the Lord. So the issue is God; what place does he have in my life? Get that right, and prayer will follow.

Some Bible passages on prayer

> The LORD is my light and my salvation ...
> One thing I ask of the LORD,
>   this is what I seek:
> that I may dwell in the house of the LORD
>   all the days of my life,
> to gaze upon the beauty of the LORD
>   and to seek him in his temple ...
> Hear my voice when I call, O LORD;
>   be merciful to me and answer me.
> My heart says of you, 'Seek his face!'
>   Your face, LORD, I will seek (Ps. 27:1, 4, 7–8).

> As the deer pants for streams of water,
>   so my soul pants for you, O God.
> My soul thirsts for God, for the living God.
>   When can I go and meet with God? (Ps. 42:1–2).

> O God, you are my God,
>   earnestly I seek you;
> my soul thirsts for you,

my body longs for you,
in a dry and weary land
   where there is no water.
I have seen you in the sanctuary
   and beheld your power and your glory.
Because your love is better than life,
   my lips will glorify you.
I will praise you as long as I live,
   and in your name I will lift up my hands.
My soul will be satisfied as with the richest of foods;
   with singing lips my mouth will praise you.
On my bed I remember you;
   I think of you through the watches of the night
   (Ps. 63:1–6).

'... when you pray, do not be like the hypocrites, for they love
to pray standing in the synagogues and on the street corners to
be seen by men. I tell you the truth, they have received their
reward in full. But when you pray, go into your room, close the
door and pray to your Father, who is unseen. Then your Father,
who sees what is done in secret, will reward you. And when you
pray, do not keep on babbling like pagans, for they think they
will be heard because of their many words. Do not be like
them, for your Father knows what you need before you
ask him.
   'This, then, is how you should pray:

         '"Our Father in heaven,
         hallowed be your name,
         your kingdom come,
         your will be done
            on earth as it is in heaven.
         Give us today our daily bread.
         Forgive us our debts,
            as we also have forgiven our debtors.
         And lead us not into temptation,
         but deliver us from the evil one."

'For if you forgive men when they sin against you, your heavenly Father will also forgive you. But if you do not forgive men their sins, your Father will not forgive your sins' (Matt. 6:5–15).

'Ask and it will be given to you; seek and you will find; knock and the door will be opened to you. For everyone who asks receives; he who seeks finds; and to him who knocks, the door will be opened.

　'Which of you, if his son asks for bread, will give him a stone? Or if he asks for a fish, will give him a snake? If you, then, though you are evil, know how to give good gifts to your children, how much more will your Father in heaven give good gifts to those who ask him!' (Matt. 7:7–11).

'... if two of you on earth agree about anything you ask for, it will be done for you by my Father in heaven. For where two or three come together in my name, there I am with them' (Matt. 18:19–20).

Very early in the morning, while it was still dark, Jesus got up, left the house and went off to a solitary place, where he prayed (Mark 1:35).

Jesus told his disciples a parable to show that they should always pray and not give up (Luke 18:1).

'Remain in me, and I will remain in you ...

　'If you remain in me and my words remain in you, ask whatever you wish, and it will be given you. This is to my Father's glory, that you bear much fruit, showing yourselves to be my disciples' (John 15:4, 7–8).

Pray in the Spirit on all occasions with all kinds of prayers and requests (Eph. 6:18).

... pray continually; give thanks in all circumstances, for this is God's will for you in Christ Jesus (1 Thess. 5:17–18).

See also the great prayers of the New Testament: Matthew 26: 36–42; John 17:1–26; Ephesians 1:15–23; 3:14–21; Philippians 1:9–11; Colossians 1:9–14; 2 Thessalonians 1:11–2.

What could I do to improve my praying?

Be hungry for God. Seek him. Put him first; don't worry about the forms, patterns and problems of prayer; go for God, and he'll look after everything else (Matt. 6:33).

Use a wide range of types of prayer. Asking is important, but so are praising, worshipping, thanking, loving, listening, confessing, enjoying, trusting, off-loading, laughing, crying, hurting and relaxing. After all, you're a child with your Father. Jesus, before he says, 'Ask whatever you wish', invites us to make him our home, and our lives his home (John 15:4, 7).

Try all sorts of ways of praying. There's no one right way of praying, any more than there's one right way for a child to address his or her father. Learn from the experience and approaches of others, but if you find that their practice doesn't suit you, try something else.

Train yourself to live in a continual spirit of prayer. Praying 'continually' (1 Thess. 5:17) is probably beyond the reach of all of us if it means we should always be consciously praying. But that's probably not what Paul meant; after all, he was writing to comparatively new Christians, not super-saints. Part of his meaning may be that we should consciously or unconsciously keep in touch with the Lord whatever else we're doing, keeping the lines open and staying in tune with him. From time to time this will surface in verbalized prayer, or an attitude of thankfulness or the virtually unconscious shifting of a burden from our shoulders to his. After all, he is with us always (Matt. 28:20). When we live in a spirit of prayer, we're responding, 'Yes, and I'm with you always.'

Set aside specific times for prayer. Besides living in a spirit of prayer, we need to set aside times to focus specifically on prayer. Again, these will incorporate many elements of prayer, but we may want to focus on some specific aspect, such as worship, seeking guidance, or intercession. Fixing these regular times of prayer – and sticking to them – may require considerable effort and self-discipline; the powers of darkness seem determined to prevent them happening. Find a time each day that is right for you. If you can, occasionally plan a longer period of prayer: an evening when you're on your own, a couple of hours while you're walking in the country or sitting quietly in a church, or a day at a retreat centre.

Pray with others. Spending a time of prayer with someone else or with a small group helps to solve many of the problems we encounter in praying on our own. It discourages wandering thoughts and getting into a rut; another person's perspective enriches our approach. The New Testament teaches that such prayer can be particularly effective (Matt. 18:19–20). Having a prayer partner with whom you share regular times of prayer, and especially intercession, can be invaluable, both for yourselves and for the kingdom. Pray, too, with larger groups, in evenings, days or nights of prayer. Do all you can to ensure that the prayer in Sunday services is real prayer, and not just going through the motions.

Pray for others. Again, there are many ways of doing this. Some find it helpful to pray graphically, using their imaginations to picture the person or the issue and then lifting them up and putting them into Christ's hands. Others will talk to the Lord about the person or the situation. Others prefer a more stylized format, listing requests rather in the way we'd expect in a public 'church' prayer. God accepts all these approaches, welcoming our prayers as the expression of our love and of our concern for the coming of his kingdom.

Above all, trust God. Prayer is a mystery. Though, in a sense, it's so simple and straightforward that a child has no problem with it, nevertheless, in that it carries us into the heart of God and his purposes, it inevitably takes us out of our depth. But why should that worry us? God is not out of his depth. The intellectual problems and questions that trouble us don't trouble him. He can cope. And if he can, we've got nothing to worry about. We trust him, and keep praying.

PREGNANCY: UNWANTED PREGNANCY

There are no accidents with God. Nothing catches him unawares; nothing is beyond his grace and his power to redeem it and work it into his loving purposes.

The standard response of our culture to an unwanted pregnancy is to propose abortion. The 1968 Abortion Act in Britain was intended to permit abortion in a carefully limited range of situations. But in practice the fact that a pregnancy is unwanted is widely accepted as a sufficient reason for terminating it.

Christians are committed to the principle of the sanctity of life and the protection of the weak and vulnerable. This has generally meant that they have been opposed to abortion on principle, although many Christians would accept that abortion is permissible in very special circumstances, such as rape or when the mother's life is seriously threatened by the pregnancy.

Quite apart from the moral issue, any decision whether or not to have an abortion is a serious one because of its possible repercussions. Though an abortion rarely has adverse affects on the mother physically, it frequently does so psychologically; some women carry the pain of it for years. Equally, bringing a child into the world is a grave responsibility, especially if that child has particular needs, or the support structures for the child are unlikely to be in place. Christians have rightly accepted that if we campaign against abortions we must be prepared to help to provide the needed care and support for the mother and for the child.

An unwanted pregnancy may be within or outside marriage. When it's within marriage, the necessary support structures should already be in place. Many couples, once they've recovered from the shock of an unexpected pregnancy, have been able to adapt to it and provide all the love and care that is needed. When it's outside marriage, the situation is frequently much more complex: the mother may be very young and unready or unwilling to take on the responsibilities of motherhood; the mother may be married but may have become pregnant by an extramarital affair;

the pregnancy may be the result of rape or incest. In these situations the pressure to solve the problems by having an abortion becomes great.

An alternative to abortion or keeping the baby is adoption. This raises a whole range of issues of its own, but it can be an excellent way of securing a good home and upbringing for a child when the parents are unable to provide it.

Some background Bible passages

'You shall not murder' (Exod. 20:13).

> ... you created my inmost being;
>   you knit me together in my mother's womb.
> I praise you because I am fearfully and wonderfully made;
>   your works are wonderful,
>   I know that full well.
> My frame was not hidden from you
>   when I was made in the secret place.
> When I was woven together in the depths of the earth,
>   your eyes saw my unformed body (Ps. 139:13–16).

The word of the LORD came to me, saying,

> 'Before I formed you in the womb I knew you' (Jer. 1:4–5).

... we know that in all things God works for the good of those who love him, who have been called according to his purpose (Rom. 8:28).

You are not your own; you were bought at a price. Therefore honour God with your body (1 Cor. 6:19–20).

What could I do when confronted with an unwanted pregnancy within marriage?

Take a deep breath. Give yourself space for a day or two. It's quite a shock to the system.

As soon as you can, turn your initial rejection into acceptance. Despite all your misgivings, accept that God, in his wisdom, is entrusting you with a new life. Lay aside your own feelings. Trust his wisdom, even though you don't understand it. Thank him for the privilege and high calling of this unexpected parenthood. Accept that when he calls us to a task he also provides what we need to do it. Changing early on to a positive attitude towards the pregnancy is important not just for you, but for the child.

Avoid telling others that the pregnancy is unwanted. Talking about your feelings with a discreet friend could be a great help, but making your initial reaction public could cause deep feelings of insecurity and rejection when it gets back to the growing child. If you have to say anything to your friends, wait until you've adjusted to the pregnancy and have been able to accept it, and then tell them it's a delightful surprise and privilege.

What could I do when confronted with an unwanted pregnancy outside marriage?

Put the whole matter into God's hands. This is something much too big for you to cope with alone. Only he can sort out all the complexities; only his wisdom is great enough for all the decisions. If you should feel that your guilt and shame stop you putting everything into God's hands, remember that the point of the gospel is that God longs to accept and welcome those who are full of guilt and shame, and to sort out their problems in his own beautiful way.

Ask for and receive God's forgiveness. If you have broken his principles for sexual behaviour, admit your sin and ask him to forgive you. Perhaps the most suitable way of doing this is in a time of prayer ministry with a small group of wise Christian friends. Remember that no sin is too great for him to forgive (1 John 1:9); but also remember Jesus' words to the woman who had been caught committing sexual sin: 'Neither do I condemn you ... Go now and leave your life of sin' (John 8:11).

Give your body to God for him to cleanse and make pure. If your pregnancy is the result of rape, you will almost certainly feel that your body has been defiled, and wonder if you'll ever feel clean again. But the gospel is absolutely clear. Through what Christ has done, all of us – our bodies and our minds – can be washed and purified (Heb. 10:22; 1 John 1:9). In a time of unhurried prayer ministry, ask the Holy Spirit to cleanse every part of your body through the power of the blood of Christ. 'Offer the parts of your body ... to God' (Rom. 6:13). Let the Holy Spirit fill every part, dealing with any defilement and replacing it with his purity. Pray the same for the baby who is being formed within you.

Face the issue of having an abortion. As a Christian, you may feel that this is not an option for you. Or you may reluctantly feel that in the particular circumstances an abortion is the best option. Here are some suggestions to follow in facing this issue.

- *Give yourself time to think things through.* Since, if you are going to have an abortion, it is best to do so early in the pregnancy, you may feel pressurized to make a quick decision. While you certainly shouldn't put off making a decision unnecessarily, don't rush into it in a panic. Remember that in the early weeks of pregnancy many women are emotionally volatile; an important decision like this must not be unduly affected by your emotions.
- *Talk to others.* Talk to your doctor, the baby's father, your family, your minister and friends you can trust. Listen without feeling you have to agree. If you talk to someone from a pregnancy clinic or from a pro-life organization, be aware that their advice will be coloured by their views on abortion.
- *Talk to God.* He knows and understands all the issues. Don't feel that you have forfeited the right to ask God for help at this time. He longs to help you. He's even more concerned than you are that you should make the right decision.
- *Weigh up the alternatives to an abortion.* If your health or well-being is at risk, how big is the risk? If the child is likely to be born with a disability, could you cope with being the parent of a disabled child? If you keep the baby, how will you cope with the practical and financial demands? Adoption could be a very creative and positive outcome for the baby and for a childless couple. There are many would-be parents who are ready and waiting to give a child a loving home. Is this something you could consider?

- *Make up your mind on the moral issues.* There is a lot of debate over the rights and wrongs of abortion. None of us is really capable of following through all the arguments. But think it through as far as you can, and ask God to direct you as you make up your mind and do what you are convinced is right for you and your baby, whatever others may say.
- *Be aware of the possible effects of an abortion.* Medical or physical complications are rare, but psychological symptoms, such as depression or feelings of loss and guilt, are fairly common.
- *Make your choice.* You may do this together with the baby's father, but in the last analysis it is you who have the right and the responsibility to choose to have an abortion or to have your baby. Though they may advise and even pressurize you, no-one else can make this choice for you.

If you do have an abortion:

- *Allow yourself to grieve.* You have suffered a bereavement, and should allow yourself to go through the normal grieving process. (See the section on **death**.)
- *Accept the finality of the abortion.* You will almost certainly question from time to time whether your decision was right or wrong. But focusing on 'if only' will not do you any good. Accept that you made the decision, and trust that, even if it was not the best one, you are going to be able to live with it, with help, if necessary. Again, place it in God's hands, and seek his forgiveness if you know you did wrong. Don't allow the abortion to spoil the rest of your life.
- *Find someone you can talk to.* You need someone you can be honest with, such as your minister or a close friend, or a counsellor, who will listen and understand. If you have feelings of remorse or guilt, talk about them rather than bottling them up.
- *Ask God for his healing.* If appropriate, ask your church elders or other Christian friends to have a time of prayer ministry with you in which you take to God all the issues that have arisen from the abortion, including, perhaps, sorrow, guilt, bad memories, anger, depression or fear. God can set you free from these things; you don't have to keep carrying them.

- *As with any loss, allow yourself time to get over the abortion.* If you feel you are making no progress, however, it is important that you make the time to seek help from a specialist Christian counsellor.

If you do decide to go ahead with the pregnancy, bring yourself, with God's help, to the point where you can accept it. Once you've made the decision to go through with it, it's important for you and for the baby that you feel positive towards the pregnancy. Given the circumstances, this may be far from easy. But remember that God is big enough to redeem any situation. Whatever the background to the pregnancy, he can turn it into something beautiful. Remember Joseph's initial negative reaction to Mary's pregnancy (Matt. 1:19), and the beautiful outcome of that. Accept God's wisdom and grace, and believe that he has entrusted you with a precious life to nurture and care for. When feelings of remorse, regret and guilt return, take them back to the cross of Jesus Christ and leave them there.

If marrying the father of the child is an option, give it careful thought. Don't be pressurized or rush into marriage just to solve the problem of the pregnancy. Weigh up the issues as you would do if the pregnancy hadn't occurred. If you do decide to go ahead with marriage, be sure to undertake a full process of marriage preparation together.

If you're considering the possibility of adoption, contact an adoption agency early. Talk things through with them, make the decision, and follow their advice on preparing yourself to part with the baby.

If you're facing the prospect of being a single parent, do all you can to prepare yourself for the task. There's no reason why you shouldn't be an excellent parent, and give your child a marvellous start in life; be determined that this will be so. Make sure that you get all the help that is available to you. Read books on parenting and single parenting. Tap into the wisdom and experience of others. Allow family and friends to help you. Ideally, there will be people in your church who will be a special help to you: an older person who'll gladly become an adopted granny or granddad, two or three 'uncles' and 'aunties', your house group as an extended family. Get the church to pray for the baby and for you, during the pregnancy, and for the years that follow.

PREJUDICE

Prejudice takes many forms and has many objects: motorcyclists, state schools, private schools, women, some ethnic groups, evangelical Christians, single mums, the poor, the rich, the elderly, the young, and lots more. But, for Christians, any form of prejudice would seem unacceptable, on at least two grounds. In the first place, prejudice involves rejection, and, if we follow the example of our God, we will not wish to reject anyone. Secondly, prejudice involves making sweeping judgments that are often false or only partly true, breaking the important principle Jesus gives us in Matthew 7:1.

The story of Jesus and the woman at the well in John 4:1–42 makes a particularly strong statement about Jesus' attitude to the prejudice he would have been expected to show; she was a woman, a Samaritan and living in sexual sin. Jesus broke through all the prejudices.

Though it's easy to see prejudice in others, it is harder to admit it in ourselves; most of us are very good at justifying our attitudes. But, as with sexual immorality or greed, we should do everything we can to make sure that there isn't 'even a hint' (Eph. 5:3) of prejudice in our attitude or living. Maybe we need to make a special point of stating (and believing) that some motorcyclists are excellent and thoughtful drivers.

To be opposed to prejudice doesn't mean we can't have preferences. Preferring English Coxes to French Golden Delicious could be prejudice if we also go for English Golden Delicious in preference to French Coxes. But if our preference is based on the taste of the apple rather than on a bias against all things French, there's no element of prejudice in it. And we're quite justified in feeling unhappy about noisy machines that exceed the speed limit, as long as we show the same unhappiness about noisy, speeding cars as we do about noisy, speeding motorbikes.

Fighting prejudice in our society needs to be done on two levels. We need to oppose it wherever it occurs, in ourselves or others; and we need to demonstrate clearly in our lives Christ's love and acceptance for everyone, whoever they are.

Some Bible passages relevant to prejudice

'When an alien lives with you in your land, do not ill-treat him. The alien living with you must be treated as one of your native-born. Love him as yourself, for you were aliens in Egypt. I am the LORD your God' (Lev. 19:33–34).

'Do not judge or you too will be judged. For in the same way as you judge others, you will be judged, and with the measure you use, it will be measured to you.

'Why do you look at the speck ... in your brother's eye and pay no attention to the plank in your own eye?' (Matt. 7:1–3).

'The Son of Man ... "... a friend of tax collectors and 'sinners'"' (Matt. 11:19).

The story of the good Samaritan (Luke 10:25–37).

'Love each other as I have loved you' (John 15:12).

'God does not show favouritism but accepts men from every nation who fear him and do what is right' (Acts 10:34–35).

Accept one another, just as Christ accepted you, in order to bring praise to God (Rom. 15:7).

To the Jews I became like a Jew, to win the Jews ... To those not having the law I became like one not having the law ... To the weak I became weak, to win the weak. I have become all things to all men so that by all possible means I might save some. I do all this for the sake of the gospel (1 Cor. 9:20–23).

[In Christ] there is no Greek or Jew, circumcised or uncircumcised, barbarian, Scythian, slave or free, but Christ is all, and is in all.

Therefore, as God's chosen people, holy and dearly loved, clothe yourselves with compassion, kindness, humility, gentleness and patience. Bear with each other and forgive whatever grievances you may have against one another. Forgive as the Lord forgave you. And over all these virtues put on love, which binds them all together in perfect unity (Col. 3:11–14).

My brothers, as believers in our glorious Lord Jesus Christ, don't show favouritism. Suppose a man comes into your meeting wearing a gold ring and fine clothes, and a poor man in shabby clothes also comes in. If you show special attention to the man wearing fine clothes and say, 'Here's a good seat for you,' but say to the poor man, 'You stand there' or 'Sit on the floor by my feet,' have you not discriminated among yourselves and become judges with evil thoughts? ...

Speak and act as those who are going to be judged by the law that gives freedom, because judgment without mercy will be shown to anyone who has not been merciful. Mercy triumphs over judgment (Jas. 2:1–4, 12–13).

What could I do?

Commit yourself to fighting prejudice wherever it occurs, in yourself, your church, the community around you or the wider world.

Stand up for the rights of persecuted and minority groups, and all who face prejudice and discrimination. Some 600 million Christians worldwide suffer from discrimination and legal impediments. Every country and culture has its oppressed minorities. Gather information and support pressure groups that are campaigning for justice.

Set an example in your local community. Show love to the homeless and asylum seekers. Treat the 'rejects' of our society as Jesus would treat them. Be full of his grace (John 1:14).

Dispel myths. Prejudice flourishes on myths or generalized beliefs that are at least partially false. Seek to show the falsehood and unjustness of such beliefs.

'*Hate the sin, love the sinner.*' Even where the criticisms that are levelled are justified, still work at distinguishing between rejection of people's actions and rejection of them as persons. Disapprove of the speeding, but accept and show love to the motorcyclist. Here's a great opportunity to exercise one of the highest forms of love, love towards an 'enemy' (Matt. 5:43–6).

Be particularly sensitive if your Christian convictions may be seen by others as expressing prejudice. You may, for example, disapprove of divorce, or of sexual activity between people of the same sex. Be sure to demonstrate a fully Christlike attitude to individual divorcees or homosexuals, showing them acceptance, grace and love, while still exercising your freedom to disagree with their actions.

PROMISES

'We are truth speakers, we men of Gondor,' said Faramir in *The Lord of the Rings.* 'Even though I knew not clearly what this thing was when I spoke, still I should take those words as a vow, and be held by them.' For most of us, that attitude is a glimpse into a world very different from our own, where people speak truth and keep their word, even if costs them much to do so. Promises are real promises; commitments are genuine commitments. And surely Faramir's world, in this respect at least, is much nearer to the vision of the kingdom of God that Jesus taught and lived.

Scripture has a great deal to say about the faithfulness of God. He is utterly trustworthy. If he says something, we can accept it as true. If he promises something, he will keep his word. And it is trustworthiness that makes trust possible. Because God is trustworthy, we can trust him; because he is faithful, we can have faith in him.

By contrast, trust and faith are rare commodities in our culture. Perhaps it's partly because we have forgotten how to trust one another that we find it hard to trust God. 'I'll do the job on Thursday,' says the washing-machine repairer. 'Hospital waiting-lists will be halved,' say the politicians. 'For better for worse, for richer for poorer, in sickness and in health, to love and to cherish, till death us do part ... and thereto I plight thee my troth,' say the happy couple. Maybe we believe them when they say it. But all too often the promises are broken; by bitter experience we learn to be cynical, not to trust and not to believe; and another brick in the structure of strong and beautiful human relationships falls out of place.

'I needed someone to sort out my garden,' said a friend of mine. 'So I tried the *Yellow Pages*. Every time I contacted someone they said they'd come, but although I waited in for them they never turned up. Then I found this man who actually came when he said he'd come. And it turned out he was a Christian.'

As Christians we have at least four good reasons why we should keep our promises. First, we belong to a God who is utterly trust-worthy. Secondly, we follow a Saviour who taught that we should keep our word. Thirdly, if trustworthiness and trust continue to evaporate, the whole of society will ultimately collapse. Finally, as in so many other areas, here is an issue where we can offer those around us a distinctive alternative, something that will show the difference that being a Christian makes.

Of course, it's not easy. The easy way is to follow the crowd and break our word if it suits us. To keep a promise can be costly, and in some circumstances we may have to accept that we can't do it. But the basic principle has to remain: we are truth speakers, we followers of Jesus. As we can trust him, others can trust us.

There's a significant passage in the Sermon on the Mount, re-iterated by James (Matt. 5:33–37; Jas. 5:12). It arose from the culture of the first century, in which it was socially acceptable to break a straight promise, but if you promised with an oath, you were expected to keep your word. Jesus' condemnation of this double standard was total. Every word of a Christian should be totally trustworthy; an oath should never be necessary; to count-enance its use is to admit that our straight promise is hollow.

Bible passages relevant to promises

Know therefore that the LORD your God is God; he is the faithful God, keeping his covenant of love to a thousand

generations of those who love him and keep his commands
(Deut. 7:9).

'Praise be to the LORD, who has given rest to his people Israel
just as he promised. Not one word has failed of all the good
promises he gave through his servant Moses' (1 Kgs. 8:56).

> Your word, O LORD, is eternal;
>   it stands firm in the heavens.
> Your faithfulness continues through all generations
> (Ps. 119:89–90).

'Again, you have heard that it was said to the people long ago,
"Do not break your oath, but keep the oaths you have made to
the Lord." But I tell you, Do not swear at all: either by heaven,
for it is God's throne; or by the earth, for it is his footstool; or
by Jerusalem, for it is the city of the Great King. And do not
swear by your head, for you cannot make even one hair white
or black. Simply let your 'Yes' be 'Yes' and your 'No', 'No';
anything beyond this comes from the evil one' (Matt.
5:33–37).

... this is our boast: Our conscience testifies that we have
conducted ourselves in the world, and especially in our relations
with you, in the holiness and sincerity that are from God ...

I planned to visit you ... When I planned this, did I do it
lightly? Or do I make my plans in a worldly manner so that in
the same breath I say, 'Yes, yes' and 'No, no'?

But as surely as God is faithful, our message to you is not 'Yes'
and 'No'. For the Son of God, Jesus Christ, who was preached
among you by me and Silas and Timothy, was not 'Yes' and
'No', but in him it has always been 'Yes'. For no matter how
many promises God has made, they are 'Yes' in Christ. And so
through him the 'Amen' is spoken by us to the glory of God (2
Cor. 1:12, 15–20).

Let us hold unswervingly to the hope we profess, for he who
promised is faithful (Heb. 10:23).

My dear brothers, take note of this: Everyone should be quick to listen, slow to speak and slow to become angry (Jas. 1:19).

Now listen, you who say, 'Today or tomorrow we will go to this or that city, spend a year there, carry on business and make money. Why, you do not even know what will happen tomorrow ... Instead you ought to say, 'If it is the Lord's will, we will live and do this or that.' As it is, you boast and brag. All such boasting is evil (Jas. 4:13–14, 15–16).

Above all, my brothers, do not swear – not by heaven or by earth or by anything else. Let your 'Yes' be yes, and your 'No', no, or you will be condemned (Jas. 5:12).

What could I do?

Follow God's character. Be determined to be trustworthy and faithful. Ask the Holy Spirit to deal with any elements in you that make you untrustworthy, such as a tendency to put yourself and your convenience before others, or to make promises you can't keep, out of a desire to impress.

Follow Jesus' teaching. There's no need for oaths; everything you say should be trustworthy. Simply let your 'Yes' be yes. Your word is your bond.

Follow James's advice. Be slow to promise. Think before you commit yourself. It's easy to say 'Yes, I'll do it' without thinking through the implications. People even stand at the front of a church and make solemn marriage vows without really having thought through the depth of commitment they say they are making. Think it through; count the cost; know what you're committing yourself to. Then, and not till then, make your promise.

Follow Paul's example. Of course there will be times when, for all our caution, promises made in all sincerity turn out to be unkeepable, or we realize, in the light of subsequent developments, that keeping them would not be the wisest course. This seems to have happened to Paul. He had told the Christians at Corinth that he would visit them. But then problems arose in their relationship with him, and Paul decided that it would be pastorally insensitive to go to Corinth at that time. So he changed his mind. This certainly is not a rerun of my friend's unreliable gardeners. Paul didn't cancel the trip to suit his own convenience; rather, it was because he realized that it was in the best interests of the Corinthians to do so. Nor did he leave them waiting and wondering what was happening; he sent them a careful explanation of why he had changed his mind (see 2 Cor. 1:23 – 2:1). There are two principles to follow, then: make sure that your motivation in changing course is Christlike love for others, not your own self-interest; and give a full and honest explanation to those you disappoint.

Include James's proviso. I don't think that James's teaching means that we have to add 'If the Lord wills' to everything we say. But the principle is an excellent one and well worth following. Forget boasting and bragging; show a bit of humility and caution. Not 'I'll do it on Thursday,' but, 'I'm definitely planning to get it done on Thursday, and I'll let you know immediately if there are any problems.'

RELAXING AND HOLIDAYS

Though the Bible doesn't specifically advocate two weeks in the sun every year, it is absolutely clear that God does not want us to work all the time without a break. The observance of the Sabbath was a key part of the Old Testament law. Its purpose was not to diminish life, but to enrich it. In particular, it was to provide an opportunity for rest and refreshment. Other holidays and festivals were built into the year, such as the Feast of Tabernacles, when God specifically instructed his people to have a thoroughly good time of holiday and celebration after all the work of gathering in the harvest.

Despite the huge pressures of his ministry, Jesus made time to withdraw, and encouraged his disciples to do the same. Paul may strike us as an incurable workaholic, but the Lord managed to arrange things so that periodically he had spells in prison, where, apart from writing letters, he was compelled to take a break.

Quite apart from the many pressures of contemporary living, most of us miss out on the natural rhythms of life that the majority of people in biblical times enjoyed: summer and winter, sowing and reaping, day and night. We work as hard in the winter as in the summer; we think nothing of working after dark; our jobs go on and on, without the climax and joy of a harvest and subsequent time of rest. This makes it all the more important that we build breaks and times of relaxation into our lives.

Some relevant Bible passages

'Six days you shall labour and do all your work, but the seventh day is a Sabbath to the LORD your God. On it you shall not do any work ...

'Six days do your work, but on the seventh day do not work, so that your ox and your donkey may rest and the slave born in your household, and the alien as well, may be refreshed ...

'Six days you shall labour, but on the seventh you shall rest; even during the ploughing season and harvest you must rest' (Exod. 20:9–10; 23:12; 34:21).

'... the LORD's Feast of Tabernacles ...

'... after you have gathered the crops of the land, celebrate the festival to the LORD for seven days; the first day is a day of rest, and the eighth also is a day of rest. On the first day you are to take choice fruit from the trees, and palm fronds, leafy branches and poplars, and rejoice before the LORD your God for seven days. Celebrate this as a festival to the LORD for seven days each year (Lev. 23:34, 39–41).

'The Sabbath was made for man, not man for the Sabbath. So the Son of Man is Lord even of the Sabbath' (Mark 2:27–28).

The apostles gathered round Jesus and reported to him all they had done and taught. Then, because so many people were coming and going that they did not even have a chance to eat, he said to them, 'Come with me by yourselves to a quiet place and get some rest.'

So they went away by themselves in a boat to a solitary place (Mark 6:30–32).

Jesus often withdrew to lonely places and prayed (Luke 5:16).

'I'm going out to fish,' Simon Peter told them, and they said, 'We'll go with you' (John 21:3).

What could I do?

Make sure that at least a substantial proportion of your holiday really is holiday. Maybe the kitchen does need redecorating, and you ought to spend a few days on that, but the essential feature of a real holiday is that it provides both relaxation and a complete change.

If you can't afford to fly to the sun, find a way of getting a cheap holiday. House-sit for a friend or family member in another part of the country. Camp. Go out for day trips. Join a group of volunteers repairing countryside footpaths or restoring wildlife habitats. If you're on your own, join one of the many group holidays that are available.

When you go on holiday, leave your mobile phone and laptop behind. A staggering 63% of executives maintain contact with the office while on holiday. That's an excellent way to destroy the value of the holiday. Don't tell yourself they can't manage without you. You're not indispensable. Nor do you need to impress your family and the other people on the beach that you are that important. Leave your work behind. Switch off completely. That's what a holiday's about.

Quite apart from holidays, build a range of other ways of relaxing into your life. Remember, your work shouldn't occupy much more than about 40 hours a week on average throughout the year. That means you've got about 80 hours a week on average to spend on other things, quite apart from sleeping. Granted, some of that time is taken up with other responsibilities, many of which are far from relaxing. But it should be possible to think of ways of relaxing that can be fitted in. Don't just say, 'I must take up painting some time'; you could go on saying that for years. Make specific space for it; mark off every Thursday night in your diary as your painting night. Here are a few suggestions; use your imagination to think of some things that would be just right for you.

- Read or write detective stories, or historical novels, or science fiction.
- Spend time with friends.
- Play a musical instrument.
- Get interested in some aspect of the natural world: study the stars, become an amateur meteorologist, entomologist, ornithologist or botanist.
- Get involved in a sport – playing, not watching it on TV.
- Find a new hobby, something you've never done before.
- Revive an old hobby; resurrect that stamp collection.
- Get exercise: swimming, cycling, walking, running.
- Find a project that excites you and that you enjoy, and get stuck into it. It could be anything from campaigning to save the red squirrel to building a house.

There is, of course, the risk that what you hope will be relaxing will turn out rather different. Your trumpet-playing meets with a hostile reception; all hell is let loose at the committee meetings of the Red Squirrel Society; you keep dropping stitches. In that case, pull out. The last thing you want is that your source of relaxation should become a source of stress.

Don't be put off by the apparent cost of these activities. Granted, skiing or building a house will set you back a bit. But you can find ways of doing many leisure activities cheaply. Of course, the leisure industry will tell you you can't go for a country walk or a bike ride unless you've got all the latest gear, but they're only interested in getting your money, not in helping you to relax. Find ways of showing that they're wrong; take a plastic mac on your walk; use the old bike that's sitting in the garden shed.

Find ways of unwinding at night before going to bed. God has made us so that up to a third of our day is total relaxation in sleep.

We spoil this by going to bed stressed and tense, and fail to relax even while sleeping. Find ways that are right for you, so that you go to bed relaxed: a warm bath, a book, a nightcap or a time of prayer off-loading all the events of the day.

Relax regularly. Don't wait for the weekend or the annual holiday. Practise the art of relaxation at those odd times of the day when you've got a few free minutes. Refuse to be driven all the time. Switch off. Stand and stare. Practise relaxation techniques.

SELF-DISCIPLINE

Self-discipline is an unpopular concept in our culture. But, for the Christian, the word 'discipline', linked directly as it is to 'disciple', is a key feature of our commitment to follow and obey the Lord Jesus. The New Testament leaves us in no doubt: throughout our lives, however experienced and mature we may be as Christians, we'll constantly be confronted with situations where it'll be easier to disobey than to obey, to sin than to stay holy, to follow the way of the world than to follow the teaching of the Bible. And though we have the promise of God to give us the strength to follow his way, and the presence of the Holy Spirit to fulfil that promise, we still have to exercise self-control or self-discipline. Even standard elements of the Christian life, such as prayer and loving our neighbour, though they may come naturally at times, still frequently require effort and self-discipline on our part.

It's important to be absolutely clear that the exercise of self-discipline should never be something we do in order to win God's favour or to secure his salvation. Far too many people fall into the trap of thinking that being disciplined is the way to catch God's attention and attract his goodwill; he sees how hard we're trying, and, because he's pleased with us, he accepts us and blesses us. Such a concept goes right against the clear teaching of the New Testament that God's love and salvation are a matter of grace, not of our earning them: 'it is by grace you have been saved, through faith – and this is not from yourselves, it is the gift of God – not by works, so that no-one can boast' (Eph. 2:8–9). We discipline ourselves to live holy and godly lives, not to *win* God's favour, but *in response* to it. Since he has done so much for us, we want to live lives that please him. We want to make time to pray; we want our thoughts to be pure and pleasing to him; we want to work to bring in his kingdom.

Self-discipline operates in all aspects of life. Perhaps there are two main classifications. There are those aspects in which we exercise discipline to avoid sin; faced with temptation to tell a lie or to be selfish or lustful, we make the effort to resist and to remain holy. And then there are the aspects in which we choose to be disciplined out of love for God and a desire to share in the coming of his kingdom. We save a proportion of our income and give it to him. We set time aside to pray. We fast. We give up a good job to to be involved in full-time Christian work. We go out of our way to befriend in the name of Christ someone we wouldn't normally get on with.

Some New testament teaching on self-discipline

'If anyone would come after me, he must deny himself and take up his cross and follow me' (Mark 8:34).

Run in such a way as to get the prize. Everyone who competes in the games goes into strict training ... I do not run like a man running aimlessly; I do not fight like a man beating the air. No, I beat my body and make it my slave (1 Cor. 9:24–27).

The weapons that we fight with are not the weapons of the world. On the contrary, they have divine power to demolish strongholds ... we take captive every thought to make it obedient to Christ (2 Cor. 10:4–5).

... live by the Spirit, and you will not gratify the desires of the sinful nature. For the sinful nature desires what is contrary to the Spirit, and the Spirit what is contrary to the sinful nature. They are in conflict with each other, so that you do not do what you want ...

But the fruit of the Spirit is ... self-control ... Those who belong to Christ Jesus have crucified the sinful nature with its passions and desires. Since we live by the Spirit, let us keep in step with the Spirit (Gal. 5:16–17, 22, 24–25).

Be strong in the Lord and in his mighty power. Put on the full armour of God so that you can take your stand against the devil's schemes ... Stand firm then ... be alert and always keep on praying (Eph. 6:10–11, 14, 18).

Not that I have already obtained all this, or have already been made perfect, but I press on to take hold of that for which Christ Jesus took hold of me. Brothers, I do not consider myself yet to have taken hold of it. But one thing I do: Forgetting what lies behind and straining towards what lies ahead, I press on towards the goal to win the prize for which God has called me heavenwards in Christ Jesus.

All of us who are mature should take such a view of things (Phil. 3:12–15).

... we instructed you how to live in order to please God, as in fact you are living. Now we ask you and urge you in the Lord Jesus to do this more and more ...

It is God's will that you should be sanctified: that you should avoid sexual immorality; that each of you should learn to control his own body in a way that is holy and honourable ... For God did not call us to be impure, but to live a holy life (1 Thess. 4:1, 3–4, 7).

We do not belong to the night or to the darkness. So then, let us not be like others, who are asleep, but let us be alert and self-controlled ... since we belong to the day, let us be self-controlled, putting on faith and love as a breastplate, and the hope of salvation as a helmet (1 Thess. 5:5–8).

... prepare your minds for action; be self-controlled ... As obedient children, do not conform to the evil desires you had when you lived in ignorance. But just as he who called you is holy, so be holy in all you do; for it is written: 'Be holy, because I am holy' (1 Pet. 1:13–16).

The end of all things is near. Therefore be clear minded and self-controlled so that you can pray (1 Pet. 4:7).

Be self-controlled and alert. Your enemy the devil prowls around like a roaring lion looking for someone to devour. Resist him, standing firm in the faith (1 Pet. 5:8–9).

What could I do?

Recognize that this is an area of your Christian life you need to work at. Self-discipline may be out of fashion in our society, but it's a key part of following Christ, who 'did not please himself' (Rom. 15:3). There may be one or two specific issues where you know you have failed to control your thoughts or actions; you need to repent, seek God's forgiveness and make a new start in his strength. Or perhaps you're aware that an aspect of your Christian life, such as your study of God's Word or your practical service, has been getting very slack and you need to take action to reinvigorate it.

Be hungry for God. However important you may feel it is to practise self-discipline in this or that part of your life, never look on the discipline as an end in itself. It isn't the discipline that matters. It's God and your relationship with him. Being more disciplined in your study of the Bible, praiseworthy though it is, is only worth all the effort if it brings you closer to the Lord. So let your hunger for God be the basis and driving force behind everything you do.

Ask for God's guidance over the steps you should take. Generally speaking, it is wise not to set yourself too ambitious a programme at the start. If you've never fasted, a forty-day total fast is not the best way to begin. If you've become hooked on lust, it's hardly realistic to say, 'I'll never think a lustful thought again.' Better to start with a short fast, or with a decision to get help over your lust problem.

Acknowledge your need of the Spirit. Though the Bible talks about 'self-control', we know all too well that on our own we simply don't have what it takes to control ourselves. Paul described this graphically in the famous passage in Romans 7: 'I am unspiritual, sold as a slave to sin ... For what I want to do I do not do, but what I hate I do ... It is no longer I myself who do it, but it is sin living in me. I know that nothing good lives in me, that is, in my sinful nature. For I have the desire to do what is good, but I cannot carry it out. For what I do is not the good I want to do; no, the evil I do not want to do – this I keep on doing.' No wonder he cries out, 'What a wretched man I am! Who will rescue me from this body of death?' But then the answer comes immediately: 'Thanks be to God – through Jesus Christ our Lord!' (Rom. 7:14–15, 17–19, 24–25). The secret of self-discipline is the power of the Holy Spirit at work in us, 'The fruit of the Spirit is ... self-control' (Gal. 5:22–23). Perhaps in the context of a time of prayer ministry, invite the Spirit to fill you afresh, and to empower and control you. Repeat this as often as you feel you need to.

Get others to help you. Don't fight a lonely battle. Ask others to pray for you. Better still, have someone to whom you can be accountable, who will support and encourage you, but will also help to keep you up to scratch and rebuke you if you slip back.

Where appropriate, use the suggestions under 'Ten steps to changing thought patterns' and 'Twelve steps to break free from sexual sin' (Appendixes 4 and 5).

SEXUAL ISSUES

We live in a sex-obsessed age. But that's nothing new. The world of the New Testament and of certain parts of the Old Testament was just the same. As a result, there is rich and clear teaching on most sexual issues for us to study and follow.

Some of the Bible's teaching on sexual issues

> God created man
> > in his own image,
> in the image of God
> > he created him;
> male and female
> > he created them.

God blessed them and said to them, 'Be fruitful' ... God saw all that he had made, and it was very good (Gen. 1:27–28, 31).

... a man will leave his father and mother and be united with his wife, and they will become one flesh (Gen. 2:24).

'I am the LORD your God. You must not do as they do in Egypt, where you used to live, and you must not do as they do in the land of Canaan, where I am bringing you. Do not follow their practices ...

'No-one is to approach any close relative to have sexual relations. I am the LORD.

'Do not have sexual relations with your neighbour's wife and defile yourself with her ...

'Do not lie with a man as one lies with a woman; that is detestable.

'Do not have sexual relationships with an animal and defile yourself with it. A woman must not present herself to an animal to have sexual relations with it; that is a perversion.

'Do not defile yourselves in any of these ways' (Lev. 18:2–3, 6, 20, 22–24).

> Drink water from your own cistern,
> > running water from your own well.
> Should your springs overflow in the streets,
> > your streams of water in the public squares? ...
> May your fountain be blessed
> > and may you rejoice in the wife of your youth.
> A loving doe, a graceful deer –

> may her breasts satisfy you always,
> may you always be captivated by her love.
> Why be captivated, my son, by an adulteress?
> Why embrace the bosom of another man's wife?
> (Prov. 5:15–16, 18–20).

'You have heard that it was said, "Do not commit adultery." But I tell you that anyone who looks at a woman lustfully has already committed adultery with her in his heart. If your right eye causes you to sin, gouge it out and throw it away. It is better for you to lose one part of your body than for your whole body to be thrown into hell. And if your right hand causes you to sin, cut it off and throw it away. It is better for you to lose one part of your body than for your whole body to go into hell' (Matt. 5:27–30).

The teachers of the law and the Pharisees brought in a woman caught in adultery … But Jesus … said to them, 'If any one of you is without sin, let him be the first to throw a stone at her.'

… those who heard began to go away one at a time, the older ones first, until only Jesus was left, with the woman still standing there. Jesus … asked her, 'Woman, where are they? Has no-one condemned you?'

'No-one, sir,' she said.

'Then neither do I condemn you,' Jesus declared. 'Go now and leave your life of sin' (John 8:3, 6–7, 9–11).

… let us put aside the deeds of darkness and put on the armour of light. Let us behave decently, not in orgies and drunkenness, not in sexual immorality and debauchery, not in dissension and jealousy. Rather, clothe yourselves with the Lord Jesus Christ, and do not think about how to gratify the desires of the sinful nature (Rom. 13:12–14).

Do not be deceived: Neither the sexually immoral nor idolaters nor adulterers nor male prostitutes nor homosexual offenders nor thieves nor the greedy nor drunkards nor slanderers nor swindlers will inherit the kingdom of God. And that is what some of you were. But you were washed, you were sanctified, you were justified in the name of the Lord Jesus Christ and by the Spirit of our God.

'Everything is permissible for me' – but not everything is beneficial. 'Everything is permissible for me' – but I will not be mastered by anything ... The body is not meant for sexual immorality, but for the Lord, and the Lord for the body ... Do you not know that your bodies are members of Christ himself? Shall I then take the members of Christ and unite them with a prostitute? Never! Do you not know that he who unites himself with a prostitute is one with her in body? ... But he who unites himself with the Lord is one with him in spirit.

Flee from sexual immorality. All other sins a man commits are outside his body, but he who sins sexually sins against his own body. Do you not know that your body is a temple of the Holy Spirit, who is in you, whom you have received from God? You are not your own; you were bought at a price. Therefore honour God with your body (1 Cor. 6:9–13, 15–20).

... whatever you do, do it all for the glory of God (1 Cor. 10:31).

I tell you this, and insist on it in the Lord, that you must no longer live as the Gentiles do, in the futility of their thinking ... they have given themselves over to sensuality so as to indulge in every kind of impurity, with a continual lust for more.

... live a life of love ...

But among you there must not be even a hint of sexual immorality, or any kind of impurity, or of greed, because these are improper for God's holy people. Nor should there be obscenity, foolish talk or coarse joking, which are out of place, but rather thanksgiving. For of this you can be sure: No immoral, impure or greedy person – such a man is an idolater – has any inheritance in the kingdom of Christ and of God. Let no-one deceive you with empty words, for because of such things God's wrath comes on those who are disobedient. Therefore do not be partners with them.

For you were once darkness, but now you are light in the

Lord. Live as children of light (Eph. 4:17, 19; 5:1, 3–8).

Since, then, you have been raised with Christ, set your hearts on
things above ... Set your minds on things above ...
   Put to death, therefore, whatever belongs to your earthly
nature: sexual immorality, impurity, lust (Col. 3:1–2, 5).

It is God's will that you should be sanctified: that you should
avoid sexual immorality; that each of you should learn to
control his own body in a way that is holy and honourable,
not in passionate lust like the heathen, who do not know God;
and that in this matter no-one should wrong his brother or
take advantage of him. The Lord will punish men for all such
sins, as we have already told you and warned you. For God did
not call us to be impure, but to live a holy life (1 Thess.
4:3–7).

Marriage should be honoured by all, and the marriage bed kept
pure, for God will judge the adulterer and all the sexually
immoral (Heb. 13:4).

What could I do?

Take your sexual principles from the teaching of the Bible. Don't pick
them up from the world around us, whether that's the remnants
of Victorian prudery or the 'Do what you like as long as you enjoy
it' approach of our age. Foundational biblical principles include:

* God has made us sexual beings. Sexuality is his gift and is very
  good. That is, our masculinity or femininity, our sexual feelings,
  and the outworking of our sexuality in our bodies, emotions
  and relationships are all parts of the good and wholesome power
  of sex that God has put in us.
* Everything that we have, including our bodies and our sexuality, is to be used for the good of others, not for our own selfish
  ends. This principle goes right against the self-centred, pleasure-
  seeking attitude of our culture that uses the bodies of others for
  self-indulging titillation and sexual gratification.

- We can choose to express our sexuality in wholesome or unwholesome ways. We express it in ways that give glory to God when we develop a truly loving marriage relationship, or a beautiful friendship (like that between David and Jonathan) in which we relate as male or female beings without the issue of sexual intercourse arising. We express it in ways that are not pleasing to God when we practise lust or engage in intercourse outside marriage.
- Sexual intercourse is God's gift for the marriage relationship.
- Sexual intercourse outside marriage is sinful.
- Sexuality can be used sinfully in situations where no physical intercourse takes place.
- The sinless life of Jesus, as a fully sexual being, and his relationships with both women and men, give us an example to follow, and demonstrate the falsehood of the contemporary notion that the only way to satisfy our sexual feelings is to engage in intercourse.
- God calls us to control our bodies and our feelings, not to be controlled by them.

Give God your body. Don't do this just once; we're all experienced in taking back what we've given over to him. Do it as often as you need to, at the start of each day, or when you are faced with sexual pressures or temptations. Ask him to show you how you can direct the sexual energy in your body in ways that are pure and pleasing to him. In particular, give God your sex organs. It may have been significant that for males in the Old Testament the mark of belonging to God was made on the penis. Paul states that baptism has replaced circumcision for Christians as the expression of our belonging to God; in baptism all parts of our body, including our sex organs, are washed clean and baptized into the name of the triune God (see Rom. 6:3–4, 11–14). He puts his name on them; they belong to him.

Give God your feelings. He already knows about them, so there's no point in trying to hide them from him. Tell him about your temptations, your lustful thoughts, your guilt over past failures, your fears about staying pure and your struggles with sexual orientation. Be honest with him about them. Admit that you can't manage them on your own. Ask him to give you what you need to cope with them. Again, ask him to channel them in ways that are pure and beautiful.

Be filled with the Spirit. Ask the Spirit of holiness to fill your body, thoughts and feelings. Remember the teaching of Jesus about the seven wicked spirits (Matt. 12:43–45). Again, being filled with the Spirit is something to be experienced often, not just once.

Ask for his forgiveness for sexual sin in the past. Remember that, though the Bible takes sexual sin seriously, in God's eyes many other sins, such as pride and selfishness, are just as serious. God, through the work of Christ on the cross, is ready to cleanse us from every sin we bring to him for forgiveness. Remember Jesus and the woman caught committing adultery (John 8:1–11).

If you fall again, go straight to him for cleansing and renewal. The continuous and insidious emphasis on sex in our society, and the sexual pressures we feel in our own bodies, make it very hard to stay pure. But the amazing grace of God means that we can go back to him again and again and find forgiveness for our sin. Remember the promise of forgiveness and purification from all unrighteousness in 1 John 1:9, and Jesus' reply to Peter about how many times we should forgive each other (Matt. 18:21–22).

Where necessary, take very specific, even drastic, action. If you're in a sexual relationship that is sinful, break it off. If you're using pornography, burn it. If you're into Internet porn and can't resist logging on, cancel your Internet subscription. 'If your right eye causes you to sin, gouge it out and throw it away ... If your right hand causes you to sin, cut it off and throw it away' (Matt. 5:29–30).

Watch your language. Take seriously Paul's teaching about obscenity, foolish talk and coarse joking (Eph. 5:4). This may have a serious effect on the comedy programmes you choose to watch or listen to on TV and radio.

If you are struggling with sexual issues, get help. Talk with a trusted Christian friend or counsellor. Where appropriate, make yourself accountable to someone.

Be the sexual being God has made you, without falling into sin. If you are single, find ways of expressing your sexuality that are holy, pure and right for you; have lots of loves without having inter-course; channel your sexual energy into creativity and service. If you are married, keep your marriage relationship beautiful and pleasing to God, and obey the biblical commands to avoid any form of immorality.

Be a great lover, without losing your purity. Jesus, who was a fully sexual being, loved people deeply, both male and female, and expressed that love fully without falling into sin. The sexual aspect of our loving is not something to be afraid of or to be isolated from other aspects of our loving, such as *agapē*, but something to open up to the Holy Spirit, and to use, along with those other aspects, to form positive and beautiful loving relationships.

Fill your mind so full of pure and beautiful thoughts that there's no space left for lust. Try following the advice of Paul in Philippians 4:8 and getting your mind into the habit of focusing on good, wholesome, Christ-centred things, so that there's no room for sexual sin to enter. A mind filled with the Spirit can't be filled with impure or immoral thoughts at the same time. Follow Paul's call to 'clothe yourselves with the Lord Jesus Christ', so that you won't even think about 'how to gratify the desires of the sinful nature' (Rom. 13:14).

Live a full and rich life. Leave a narrow obsession with sex to others. Have lots of interests. Take plenty of exercise. Give your mind and body plenty of outlets for their creative energy.

Train yourself to say no to the devil. Fight all sinful ways of expressing your sexuality. Practise self-control. With the Spirit's help you can be different from those around. Set them an example of Christian purity, rather than letting their lifestyle control you.

Avoid situations in which you are particularly vulnerable to sexual temptation. Switch off the TV; keep away from relationships and places where you know the pressure will be high.

If masturbation is an issue, give it to the Lord. The Bible doesn't give direct teaching on masturbation. Compulsive masturbation certainly seems wrong, since you've effectively lost control over your body, which is unacceptable for Christians, who choose not to be 'mastered by anything' (1 Cor. 6:12). But, given careful safe-guards, the occasional use of masturbation may not be sinful in itself; it is one way of expressing and enjoying our sexuality and of dealing with the build-up of sexual pressure in our bodies. If you feel this might be the case for you, take special note of 1 Corinthians 6:20 and 10:31: 'honour God with your body'; 'whatever you do, do it all for the glory of God'. Practise masturbation only if you can do so for God's glory, free from impure motives or sinful fantasizing.

If you believe that your sexual orientation is homosexual, give that, too, to the Lord. He knows all about you. He has watched over you from the time you were conceived. He knows all the factors that have influenced your personality and sexual development, both good and not so good. He loves you as you are. He doesn't say, 'Get that sex thing sorted out and then I'll love you'; he loves you now, exactly as you are. What's more, he's got a great purpose that he's going to bring about through your sexuality. He wouldn't have allowed you to be as you are if he wasn't able to bring something really beautiful out of it. In giving your sexual orientation over to the Lord, you may find these ideas helpful:

- *As far as you can, thank him for your body.* There may be aspects of it you wish were different, but God, in his wisdom and love, has given it to you as you are. So accept it, acknowledge that it is his gift, and thank him for it.
- *Give it back to him for him to do what he chooses.* He may choose to change your feelings. He may choose to let them remain, and show you ways of using them for his glory. The vital thing is to put him in charge. You may choose to follow Paul's example, when he cried to God to remove the 'thorn' in his flesh, and found that God's answer was to leave it there, and to turn it into a blessing (2 Cor. 12:7–10).
- *Declare his lordship over every part of your body, including your sex organs, your eyes and your thoughts.* This is something that you will have to repeat again and again. Make the declaration of the early Christians your motto: 'Jesus is Lord!'
- *Stop any sexual practices that are contrary to God's directions.*
- *Ask the Holy Spirit to fill and protect your mind.* Find ways of following Paul's instruction in Philippians 4:8. Remember, having homosexual feelings isn't sinful in itself, any more than having heterosexual feelings is sinful. Sin comes in when we use

our sexual feelings, whether homosexual of heterosexual, to engage in lust, fantasizing in the mind what would be sinful to practise with the body.

- *Remember, being sexually attracted to people of your own sex doesn't make you a homosexual.* There are two important points here. The first is that it's perfectly possible for a person at different stages of development, or even at the same time, to feel sexual attraction to people of both sexes. Many, if not most, adolescents go through a period of same-sex attraction; some take longer than others to come out of it. So the fact that you have homosexual feelings doesn't mean that your orientation will be exclusively that way for life. The second, even more important, point is that, just as wishing somebody dead doesn't make you a murderer, so being attracted to someone of the same sex doesn't make you a homosexual. Leave the label 'homosexual' for those who adopt a gay lifestyle, complete with homosexual practices; someone who has homosexual feelings but does not express them in intercourse is not a homosexual.

- *Remember, you are not alone.* You may feel you are fighting a lonely battle to stay pure. But you're not alone, for two reasons. First, almost all Christians have to fight battles to live sexually pure lives. The exact form may vary: one person struggles with homosexual temptation; another battles with heterosexual lust; someone else has a weakness for pornography; a married person falls for someone else and struggles with the temptation to commit adultery. But in essence the battle is the same: to be a sexual being and to stay pure and holy. A second reason you're not alone is that Jesus is with you. The writer to the Hebrews tells us that he was 'tempted in every way, just as we are – yet was without sin' (Heb. 4:15). You may find it helpful to remember that Jesus was a fully sexual being, who had a deep relationship with John, 'the disciple whom Jesus loved' (John 21:20), and yet he remained sexually pure.

- *Get all the help you can.* Make yourself accountable to someone you can trust. Get help from a wise church leader or counsellor.

- *Develop a range of friendships, both same-sex and other-sex.* Use your power to love to form wholesome and pure relationships.

If you have a particular battle over pornography, try the following:

- *Acknowledge before God that using porn is sinful.* There's no way we could imagine Jesus using it. It's sinful for several reasons. It stimulates lust, and lust is sinful. The people it pictures are committing sin. It debases God's beautiful gift of human sexuality and uses people as objects for cheap selfish gratification. Moreover, it is hugely addictive and has a subtle but profound effect on those who use it. However much our culture claims that it is a harmless diversion, studies show that it has far-reaching effects, sometimes physiological, and certainly psychological and sexual. For Christians it is unacceptable that anything other than the Lord should control them. 'I will not be mastered by anything' (1 Cor. 6:12).
- *Specifically repent and confess your sin to God and receive his forgiveness.* The best way to do this is in a prayer-ministry setting with two or three trusted church leaders. Renounce your use of porn and seek God's infilling of your mind and the power of his Holy Spirit to conquer this sin. Since the power of evil that porn exercises over our minds is very strong and often deeply engrained, ongoing prayer ministry may well be necessary for a long period.
- *Destroy all pornographic material you have.* Take radical steps to avoid using the Internet for porn. Be drastic. Remember the words of Jesus about gouging out your eye if it causes you to sin (Matt. 5:29).
- *If necessary, get the help of a specialist Christian counsellor.*
- *If appropriate, find someone to whom you can be accountable regarding this aspect of your life.*
- *Remember that occasional lapses don't mean you're a failure.* Seek God's forgiveness and cleansing, and keep fighting.
- *Take the parable of the driven-out spirit seriously* (Luke 11:24–26). Find ways of filling the role pornography has played in your life with thoughts and activities that are good and pleasing to God.

If you are indulging in lust:

- *Accept God's verdict on it, that it is wrong.* To commit adultery in the heart, as Jesus described it (Matt. 5:28), is against God's commandments. Our culture, of course, disagrees, and encourages lust in all sorts of ways. Here's an opportunity to stand against the flow, and to show that being a Christian makes a big difference.
- *Remember that feeling sexually attracted to someone isn't lust.* Jesus had sexual feelings, and he remained pure. Sexual attraction becomes lust when we play around with our thoughts and feelings to the point that we are imagining in our minds actions that would be sinful for us to do with our bodies.
- *Talk with God honestly about your lust.* Confess your sin, and ask him to forgive you and make you clean. Tell him that you want to break the habit.
- *In a solemn act of commitment, preferably in a time of prayer ministry with one or more mature Christian friends, give yourself, body and mind, over to God.* You may like to use Romans 12:1–2 in doing so, since Paul there links body and mind together. Ask God to fill every part of your body, and especially your mind, with his Holy Spirit.
- *Be prepared for a long battle.* Lust gets a real grip on our minds and it doesn't disappear overnight. Keep giving yourself to God; keep asking the Spirit to control your mind. When temptation comes, have ways of resisting (1 Cor. 10:13), such as praying for the person, instead of lusting.
- *Take specific steps to avoid lust.* Stop watching provocative films. Censor your reading material. Control what you do with your eyes. If you stop feeding your lust, it will eventually wither and die.
- *Get help.* If you're not winning the battle, talk things through with a Christian leader or counsellor. Consider the possibility of making yourself accountable to someone.

If appropriate, use the 'Twelve steps to break free from sexual sin" (Appendix 5).

SHOPPING

Many aspects of shopping in our culture are very far removed from the world of the Bible. This doesn't make them wrong, but it's important to check them against such biblical principles as there are, and to adjust our practice accordingly.

Originally a relatively straightforward transaction between two people, shopping today has become big business. Designers, advertisers, producers, and those who plan shopping centres and display the goods, all are highly trained professionals who are experts at persuading us to part with our money in exchange for their product. The pressures they bring to bear are often subtle, so that we do not realize how much we are being manipulated. The rules of the game appear to pay little attention to principles of honesty and justice, or to the buyer's best interest. So successful is the game that much of the money we spend shopping is on items we do not really need, and, in many cases, actually had no intention of buying.

For a Christian, shopping raises issues of integrity, honesty and justice, the wise use of money, and how we in a rich 'consumer' society can help those in poor countries, many of whom are being exploited by the big businesses that feed our consumer society. It also raises the issue of greed, or what the Ten Commandments calls covetousness, the key human weakness to which almost all advertising and sales techniques pander.

Bible passages relevant to shopping

'You shall not covet' (Exod. 20:17).

'Do not use dishonest standards when measuring length, weight or quantity. Use honest scales and honest weights ... I am the LORD your God (Lev. 19:35–36).

'If you sell land to one of your countrymen or buy any from him, do not take advantage of each other (Lev. 25:14).

The LORD God detests ... anyone who deals dishonestly (Deut. 25:16).

> The LORD abhors dishonest scales
> but accurate weights are his delight (Prov. 11:1).

> Honest scales and balances are from the LORD;
> all the weights in the bag are of his making (Prov.16:11).

'Give us today our daily bread'(Matt. 6:11).

'Do not store up for yourselves treasures on earth, where moth and rust destroy, and where thieves break in and steal. But store up for yourselves treasures in heaven, where moth and rust do not destroy, and where thieves do not break in and steal. For where your treasure is, there your heart will be also ...
    'You cannot serve both God and Money.
    'Therefore I tell you, do not worry about your life, what you will eat or drink; or about your body, what you will wear. Is not life more important than food, and the body more important than clothes?...
    'So do not worry, saying, "What shall we eat?" or "What shall we drink?" or "What shall we wear?" For the pagans run after all these things, and your heavenly Father knows that you need them. But seek first his kingdom and his righteousness, and all these things will be given to you as well' (Matt. 6:19–21, 24–25, 31–33).

'Watch out! Be on your guard against all kinds of greed; a man's life does not consist in the abundance of his possessions' (Luke 12:15).

[Jesus] entered the temple area and began driving out those who were selling. 'It is written,' he said to them, '"My house will be a house of prayer"; but you have made it "a den of robbers"' (Luke 19:45–46).

... among you there must not be even a hint of sexual

immorality, or of any kind of impurity, or of greed, because these are improper for God's holy people ... of this you can be sure: no immoral, impure or greedy person – such a man is an idolater – has any inheritance in the kingdom of Christ and of God. Let no-one deceive you with empty words, for because of such things God's wrath comes on those who are disobedient. Therefore do not be partners with them (Eph. 5:3, 5–6).

Put to death, therefore, whatever belongs to your earthly nature ... greed, which is idolatry (Col. 3:5).

... godliness with contentment is great gain. For we brought nothing into the world, and we can take nothing out of it. But if we have food and clothing, we will be content with that (1 Tim. 6:6–8).

Do not love the world or anything in the world. If anyone loves the world, the love of the Father is not in him. For everything in the world – the cravings of sinful man, the lust of his eyes and the boasting of what he has and does – comes not from the Father but from the world. The world and its desires pass away, but the man who does the will of God lives for ever (1 John 2:15–17).

What could I do?

Work out a truly Christian approach to shopping. How should you view it as a Christian? Should you simply think about it in the same way as non-Christians do? What sort of difference should being a Christian make to your attitude towards it? What about issues such as greed, justice, integrity and fair trade? Try to reshape your thinking into a truly biblical attitude towards shopping.

Keep God at the centre. Keep him at the centre of your whole understanding of shopping. Remember that everything comes from him, whether it's food or the raw materials from which anything is made. Let others look on the world and its goods as something that humankind is free to exploit, or view their money as theirs to do what they like with. As a Christian, you know that both the world and your money are God's, to be used wisely and responsibly. Keep God with you, too, as you do your shopping. He'll help you with the hassle, and give you wise advice on your spending.

Watch out for any signs of covetousness and greed in your attitude. So enticing are today's advertising and sales techniques that it's almost impossible to avoid them. But spot them when they arise, and get the Lord to deal with them.

Do what you can to discourage bad business practices. The Old Testament states several times that God detests them. Object. Complain. Boycott. Refuse to be taken in. Warn others. Take back shoddy goods. As far as possible, avoid shopping on Sundays.

Put the advertisers in their place. Advertising has a role to play in giving us true information about specific products. But most advertising simply fails to provide accurate information about anything. It may pander to our greed, or use images and concepts to attract our attention, even though they have little or nothing to do with the product. Learn to call the advertisers' bluff; after all, we all know they're saying what they say only because they're paid to say it, not because it's true or helpful for us. Complain about adverts that use innuendo or other dishonest methods.

Shop thoughtfully. There are many factors besides getting the best bargain that may influence you, such as supporting the small, local trader over against big business and supermarkets, supporting 'fairly traded' initiatives, and refusing goods produced in unacceptable ways.

Plan your spending. Make a list of what you need, and stick to it. Decide how much you're prepared to spend on those larger items, and exceed it only if there's a very good reason.

Be careful about impulse buying. Displays are there to entice you. Bargains aren't always what they seem. It looks attractive, but you don't have to give in. Check yourself. Is it actually something you need? Is it really a bargain? Or are you just being sucked in – your covetousness falling to clever sales techniques?

Remember others. Spare a thought for the thousands of millions who have no access to shops, either because they're too poor, or because shops simply don't exist where they live. Work for the poor and for fair trade. Support and pray for organizations such as Tearfund and Christian Aid. Campaign for meas-

ures that will bring about a fairer distribution of wealth and the
world's goods.

STRESS

We live in an age of stress. This may seem strange, since so much
energy in our contemporary society is spent on making life easier
and more pleasant. We have innumerable gadgets that make it
easy to do anything from beating an egg to mowing the lawn.
Compared with former generations, we suffer minimal pain and
illness; even death has, for most of us, been removed to a comfort-
able distance and surrounded with cotton wool. We have endless
resources for relaxation and leisure activities that were unheard of
a century or so ago, and that are still unavailable to many
throughout the world. And yet, we are told, high levels of stress
are endemic in our society.

There are doubtless many reasons why this is so. Personally, I
can't help feeling that a major one is the very sophistication of our
culture, which has made it tragically artificial and has taken away
from us much of the balance and rhythm of life as God made it.
To a large extent, for example, we've lost the basic rhythms of day
and night and the seasons of the year. Former generations went to
bed when it got dark; we don't need to, because we've 'conquered'
the dark. We've also 'conquered' the cold of winter, and removed
the need for seasons. No longer, for most people, is food grown in
fields or in gardens; it's provided by supermarkets. No longer do
we walk; we ride in cars. Even exercise is something we do in the
artificial surroundings of a gym.

Each of these changes increases stress. We stay up late watching
TV, with its overload of hype, bad news and debased values. We're
out of gear with the rhythm of nature. Supermarket shopping is
the polar opposite of picking home-grown runner beans. Driving
to and from the gym isn't a patch on an evening wander through
the fields.

Much stress, then, can be traced back to our lifestyle. But there's another major feature. We've all watched two people going though the same stressful experience, one becoming very stressed and the other coping without becoming stressed at all. It isn't just external factors that produce stress; there's an internal factor too: our response to the external factors. Few of us can escape stressful situations, though it is possible to work at excluding unnecessary stress from our lives. But we can all discipline ourselves to cope positively with those stressful situations and experiences, and to change our response from a negative and destructive one to a creative and helpful one.

Bible teaching relevant to stress

The LORD is my shepherd, I shall not be in want.
    He makes me lie down in green pastures,
he leads me beside still waters,
    he restores my soul ...
Even though I walk
    through the valley of the shadow of death,
I will fear no evil,
    for you are with me;
your rod and your staff,
    they comfort me (Ps. 23:1–3, 4).

The LORD is my light and my salvation –
    whom shall I fear?
The LORD is the stronghold of my life –
    of whom shall I be afraid? ...
One thing I ask of the LORD,
    this is what I seek:
that I may dwell in the house of the LORD
    all the days of my life,
to gaze upon the beauty of the LORD
    and to seek him in his temple.
For in the day of trouble
    he will keep me safe in his dwelling
    (Ps. 27:1, 4–5).

You will keep in perfect peace
　　him whose mind is steadfast,
　　because he trusts in you.
Trust in the LORD for ever,
　　for the LORD, the LORD, is the Rock eternal
　　(Is. 26:3–4).

　　... this is what the LORD says –
　　　he who created you ...
'Fear not, for I have redeemed you;
　　I have summoned you by name; you are mine.
When you pass through the waters
　　I will be with you ...
For I am the LORD, your God,
　　the Holy One of Israel, your Saviour ...
　　... you are precious and honoured in my sight ...
　　　... I love you ...
Do not be afraid, for I am with you' (Is. 43:1–5).

'I tell you, do not worry about your life, what you will eat or
drink; or about your body, what you will wear. Is not life more
important than food, and the body more important than
clothes? Look at the birds of the air; they do not sow or reap or
store away in barns, and yet your heavenly Father feeds them.
Are you not much more valuable than they? Who of you by
worrying can add a single hour to his life?

'And why do you worry about clothes? See how the lilies of
the field grow. They do not labour or spin. Yet I tell you that not
even Solomon in all his splendour was dressed like one of these.
If that is how God clothes the grass of the field, which is here
today and tomorrow is thrown into the fire, will he not much
more clothe you, O you of little faith? So do not worry, saying,
"What shall we eat?" or "What shall we drink?" or "What shall
we wear?" For the pagans run after all these things, and your
heavenly Father knows that you need them. But seek first his
kingdom and his righteousness, and all these things will be given
to you as well' (Matt. 6:25–33).

'Come to me, all you who are weary and burdened, and I will give you rest. Take my yoke upon you and learn from me, for I am gentle and humble in heart, and you will find rest for your souls. For my yoke is easy and my burden is light' (Matt. 11:28–30).

'Peace I leave with you; my peace I give you. I do not give to you as the world gives. Do not let your hearts be troubled and do not be afraid' (John 14:27).

Rejoice in the Lord always ... The Lord is near. Do not be anxious about anything, but in everything, by prayer and petition, with thanksgiving, present your requests to God. And the peace of God, which transcends all understanding, will guard your hearts and your minds in Christ Jesus.

Finally, brothers, whatever is true, whatever is noble, whatever is right, whatever is pure, whatever is lovely, whatever is admirable – if anything is excellent or praiseworthy – think about such things. Whatever you have learned or received or heard from me, or seen in me – put it into practice. And the God of peace will be with you (Phil. 4:4–9).

Cast all your anxiety upon him because he cares for you (1 Pet. 5:7).

What could I do?

Take an inventory of your lifestyle. Which activities occupy most of your time and attention? It may be a worthwhile exercise keeping a detailed diary of a standard week, working out the comparative time spent in various activities such as work, leisure, commuting, family, TV, exercise and time for God. (See the section on **time**.)

Analyse the values expressed by your lifestyle. What values does it express? What are you living for? What really matters to you? What significant elements are missing?

Test these values by the values taught by Jesus and the New Testament. Work out where you've got your priorities wrong and how you need to change them. Decide on specific steps you are going to take to make these changes.

Take the opportunity to reassess the purpose of life. Spend time thinking and praying. Ask God to guide you and to show you his purposes for you.

Find ways of reducing the number of stressful factors you have to deal with. None of us can get rid of them completely, nor would we want to; but some we can do without. Try drawing up a list of all the pressures you face. Classify them as 'unavoidable', 'possibly avoidable' and 'avoidable'. Select some from the last two categories and take positive steps to remove them from your life.

Find creative ways of relaxing. Try a new hobby. Substitute an unhurried walk in the park or in the country for a hectic workout in the gym. Get in touch with nature. Spend time with plants and wildlife. Get in tune with the rhythm of the seasons. Gaze at the glory of the Milky Way. Stop and look at things. Grow plants in the garden. Talk to the trees.

Train yourself to reject stressed responses to situations. In every situation we can choose to make a stressed response or a non-stressed response. We miss the bus; we can get upset, or tell ourselves the walk will do us good. The boss shouts at us; we can take it out on our junior, or we can spend time praying for the boss. We're facing an exam; we can get uptight, or we can use it as a perfect opportunity to experience the truth of John 14:27. The choice is always ours, though often we'll have to ask for extra grace from the Holy Spirit to be able to choose the right way.

Keep control over your thought patterns. When we're under pressure, our minds keep going back to stressful issues and churning them over. When this happens, learn to take positive steps to divert your thoughts to something else. Find ways of switching off that work for you. Plan a holiday or a new project. Read a book. Go through past experiences that recall happy memories. Pray.

Live more simply. Opt out of the consumer rat race. Ignore the adverts. Throw away the junk mail. Let the trendsetters do what they like. Forget the mobile phone.

Keep your job in its rightful place. Don't let it dominate you or your family. It has a right to about 2,000 hours of your life per year; that's well under a quarter of your total annual hours or a third of your waking hours. Don't let it swallow more.

Be thankful. Thank God for each new day, and for all the good things in life. Appreciate the world. Make a point of thanking other people.

Spend more time with Jesus. He's the Prince of Peace. Train yourself to see life as he does, to see your tasks from his perspective and to have his peace.

Stop carrying weights. Get into the habit of handing issues and problems over to God and letting him deal with them. There's something in us all that likes to keep things to ourselves, including problems and hassles. But he doesn't just invite us to let him carry them for us; he commands us to hand them over.

When you have to face unavoidable pressure, meet it as a positive challenge. Pressure is not stress. Stress comes in only if you make a stressful response. Commit yourself to respond without getting stressed. Let the pressure stretch you, excite you, bring out the best in you and push you to heights of achievement you've not reached before. But refuse to let it stress you.

If stress has become a major factor in your life, get help in dealing with it. Talk it through with family members or close friends. Consult your pastor or a Christian counsellor. Have a check-up from your doctor. Talk to an appropriate staff member at work.

TIME

We each have only one life to live; none of us knows how much of our life is left. As Christians, we're committed to living for the glory of God and to using our lives to fulfil his purposes in the world. This doesn't mean that we have to spend every moment in frenetic activity; God commanded his people to rest as well as to work. But it means that we shall choose to spend our time wisely, recognizing that both life and time are gifts from God; each morning we can exclaim, 'This is the day the LORD has made'

(Ps. 118:24); each year we can say, 'This is the year of the Lord [*anno Domini*].' We can choose to live as wise and responsible stewards of all the time he gives us.

No two of us are the same; there can be no blueprint for our use of time. Some have an incredible capacity for work, and seem to be able to keep going endlessly with little rest or relaxation. Others would collapse after a few days if they tried to keep up with them. Some have to struggle with physical or emotional weakness. We all need different amounts of sleep. We get things done at different speeds. And we each have a different calling.

Jesus had a strong sense of a task that he had to do, and a limited time in which to do it. As a result, his energies were focused: 'As the time approached for him to be taken up to heaven, Jesus resolutely set out for Jerusalem' (Luke 9:51). For the most part, we don't have as clear an understanding of the task we've got to do, or of the time left to do it, as Jesus had. Maybe we feel that this is a disadvantage: if we knew that we had just a few months left to live and a specific task to do in that time, we would find it much easier to be focused and to get on with it. But focusing is harder when we feel there's nothing specific to focus on.

For that reason, it's helpful periodically to make the effort to think through our goals, both short-term and longer-term, as far as we are able. The start of a new year might be an appropriate time, or our birthday. It's also valuable to look back and see what progress we've made, say, during the past year. Goals, of course, are always open to revision. They're not set in concrete. They're simply stating what we feel God is saying to us at the time. It's always possible that we haven't got the whole picture first time round, and that he'll clarify or change things as time goes by.

Some Bible teaching relevant to our use of time

'For six days, work is to be done, but the seventh day is a Sabbath of rest, holy to the LORD' (Exod. 31:15).

> I trust in you, O LORD;
>   I say, 'You are my God'.
> My times are in your hands (Ps. 31:14–15).

I went past the field of the sluggard,
    past the vineyard of the man who lacks judgment;
thorns had come up everywhere,
    the ground was covered with weeds,
    and the stone wall was in ruins.
I applied my heart to what I observed
    and learned a lesson from what I saw:
A little sleep, a little slumber,
    a little folding of the hands to rest –
and poverty will come on you like a bandit
    and scarcity like an armed man (Prov. 24:30–34).

... Keep watch, because you do not know on what day your Lord will come' (Matt. 24:42).

'Be on guard! Be alert! you do not know when that time will come' (Mark 13:33).

'I have come to bring fire upon the earth, and how I wish it were already kindled! But I have a baptism to undergo, and how distressed I am until it is completed!' (Luke 12:49–50).

'My food,' said Jesus, 'is to do the will of him who sent me and to finish his work' (John 4:34).

'I have brought you glory on earth by completing the work you gave me to do' (John 17:4).

Jesus said, 'It is finished' (John 19:30).

Never be lacking in zeal, but keep your spiritual fervour, serving the Lord (Rom. 12:11).

... do this, understanding the present time. The hour has come for you to wake up from your slumber, because our salvation is nearer now than when we first believed. The night is nearly over; the day is almost here. So let us put aside the deeds of darkness and put on the armour of light (Rom. 13:11–12).

... whatever you do, do it all for the glory of God (1 Cor. 10:31).

> 'Wake up, O sleeper,
>   rise from the dead,
> and Christ will shine on you.'

Be very careful, then, how you live – not as unwise but as wise, making the most of every opportunity, because the days are evil. Therefore do not be foolish, but understand what the Lord's will is (Eph. 5:14–17).

I consider everything a loss compared to the surpassing greatness of knowing Christ Jesus my Lord ... I want to know Christ and the power of his resurrection and the fellowship of sharing in his sufferings, becoming like him in his death, and so, somehow, to attain to the resurrection from the dead.

Not that I have already obtained all this, or have already been made perfect, but I press on to take hold of that for which Christ Jesus took hold of me ... one thing I do: Forgetting what is behind and straining towards what is ahead, I press on towards the goal to win the prize for which God has called me heavenwards in Christ Jesus (Phil. 3:8, 10–14).

... make the most of every opportunity (Col. 4:5).

... the day of the Lord will come like a thief in the night.

    ... you, brothers, are not in darkness so that this day should surprise you like a thief. You are all sons of the light and sons of the day. We do not belong to the night or to the darkness. So then, let us not be like others, who are asleep, but let us be alert and self-controlled (1 Thess. 5:2, 4–6).

'If a man will not work, he shall not eat.'

    We hear that some among you are idle. They are not busy; they are busybodies. Such people we command and urge in the Lord Jesus Christ to settle down and earn the bread they eat (2 Thess. 3:10–12).

Now listen, you who say, 'Today or tomorrow we will go to this or that city, spend a year there, carry on business and make money. Why, you do not even know what will happen tomorrow. What is your life? You are a mist that appears for a little while and then vanishes. Instead, you ought to say, 'If it is the Lord's will, we will live and do this or that.' As it is, you boast and brag. All such boasting is evil (Jas. 4:13–16).

What could I do?

Give your life and times back to God. He made them. He knows all about them. He has great purposes for them. He knows the best way of using your gifts and opportunities. He knows the setbacks and problems that are going to come your way, and how to use even them for good. So put it all back into his hands. Trust him. Let him be Lord. Say with the psalmist, 'As for God, his way is perfect ... It is God who ... makes my way perfect' (Ps. 18:30, 32).

Do an appraisal of your life and how you spend your time. Take a day out; wait upon the Lord. Listen to his voice. Get things in perspective. Commit yourself to his purposes. Respond to his call. You may find the following suggestions helpful.

- *Pray.* Ask God's guidance. Seek his presence. Ask the Holy Spirit to speak and lead.
- *Read what the Bible says about how we spend our time.* In addition to the passages above, you could study Matthew 24:36 – 25:46. The book of Proverbs has lots of homely advice, with countless warnings about wasting time through laziness. To balance those, you might like to look up the passages quoted in the section on **relaxing and holidays**. Write down what God says to you through these passages.
- *Write out all the major things that God has said to you or that you've said to God in the past about your life.* If you've already got them written out, refer back to them. Perhaps he said something specific to you on a particular occasion, or you told him that you'd be willing to go anywhere he calls you. Check that you're still living consistently with them.
- *List the main things that you've done so far with your life.* Give

thanks to God for all that has been achieved. If necessary, talk through with him any memories you're ashamed of, and seek his mercy and forgiveness.

- *List your long-term aims and goals.* These may be clearly formulated or still vague or conditional: 'If I get married I'd like to have a large family.' Be honest here. Don't just put down the hopes you think God will approve of; if one of your goals is to get rich, or to enjoy yourself, write it down!

- *Talk through your long-term goals with God.* Listen to discover if he's got anything to say about them. Ask him if there are any he wants to add or remove. Pray over them; ask for his blessing on them.

- *For each long-term goal, list your aims and intentions for the immediate future or for the coming year.* Again, these may be specific or vague. If one of your long-term goals is to be the best parent you can be to your three children, you might list the specific decision to spend twenty minutes reading to them before bedtime each evening. Less specific (but still important) would be the resolve to deal constructively with Michael's outbursts of temper. Pray over these; ask the Holy Spirit to enable and direct.

- *Review how you spend your time.* Do this in the light of what God has been saying to you about his purposes for you. As far as you can, list how many of the 168 hours in each week you spend on various activities: sleeping, working, being with the family, exercise, shopping, church, time with the Lord, travel, relaxing, hobbies, serving others, watching TV, and so on. Again, talk the result over with the Lord. Have you got the balance right? Have you got your priorities right? Are you too busy? Are you wasting time? Listen to anything he has to say about changes and modifications. Write down any specific decisions.

- *Talk to God about the time you have left.* You don't know how much of your life remains; it could be a lot or a little. But Jesus is the one who holds the keys of death (Rev. 1:18). He will make sure that your life isn't cut short before you've had time to do everything he wants you to do. Again, put your trust in him and in his wisdom. Remember his words: 'Who of you by worrying can add a single hour to his life? ... seek first his kingdom and his righteousness, and all these things will be given to you as well' (Matt. 6:27, 33).

Start and finish each day by putting your times into God's hands (Ps. 31:15). It doesn't need a long prayer; a few seconds will do, as long as you mean it. First thing in the morning give him all the day, what you'll be doing, how you'll spend your time. Then in the evening look back. Thank him for the day. Put its various events into his hands. Leave anything that concerns you in his keeping. Seek his forgiveness for anything that has gone wrong. It's the day he made; leave it with him.

Remember, Jesus is coming again. Christian fashions come and go. Sometimes the second coming rates highly in the top ten doctrines. At other times we seem to forget all about it. Never mind the fashions; do what Jesus commanded, and live each day aware that he could return at any time. Don't concern yourself particularly with how he's going to return and precisely what will happen. Just make sure that, however he does come, you'll be ready. You'll be glad to see him. You'll have nothing for which you'll feel ashamed.

TRUTH: TELLING THE TRUTH

The Bible is a very realistic book. It accepts truth as a foundational aspect of the nature of God, and telling the truth as a principle by which we should live. But life is complex. We all know of situations where a naïve application of the principle 'Always tell the truth' would be inappropriate. So the Bible tells us stories where the principle was not followed, and rightly so. The Hebrew midwives were economical with the truth to save the lives of the baby boys (Exod. 1:19). Rahab lied to save the Israelite spies (Josh. 2:4–6; Heb. 11:31). Samuel pretended, out of fear of Saul, to be going to Bethlehem in order to make a sacrifice (1 Sam. 16:2). Elisha deliberately deceived the enemy (2 Kgs. 6:19). Jesus told his disciples to make it look as though they were not fasting when they were (Matt. 6:17–18), and acted as though he was going further than Emmaus (Luke 24:28).

Paul's great principle of 'speaking the truth in love' (Eph. 4:15) gives us the key to the issue here. Speaking the truth is a Christian principle that we should seek to follow as far as possible, since we are followers of the God of truth, and of Jesus, who said, 'I am the truth.' But truth-speaking is not the only principle we are called to follow. We are also called to love, to express the love of God in all our dealings with others. And sometimes telling the straight truth is not the most loving thing to do.

Our friend may have a face like the back of a bus, but it would hardly be loving to tell her so. Telling the whole truth to a seriously ill person may not be the most loving thing to do. And it was surely right for those trying to save the lives of Jews in the Second World War to lie to the Gestapo about their whereabouts.

Of course, there are more trivial ways in which failure to be strict over truth-telling is perfectly acceptable, such as when we're telling a story or a joke, or teasing a friend, or using a readily understood element of exaggeration, as, say, Paul did when he said that for three years he never ceased night and day warning the Ephesian church leaders with tears (Acts 20:31). There is no intention here to deceive our hearers; if we were to discover that our words were misleading them, we'd be quick to say, 'I was only teasing,' or, 'I didn't mean that literally.'

Inevitably, there are many borderline issues. Since, for example, most firms have long since abandoned Christian principles as the basis on which they work, Christian employees are often under pressure to be less than totally honest. Since it is important to make a stand for Christian principles, it would be wrong simply to ignore the issues involved here, but sometimes it takes considerable wisdom and grace to know how to deal with them. Sometimes we may be feel that a subtle use of words will do the trick. Told to lie that the boss is out, we can say that Mr Smith is unavailable. Told to make claims for a product that we know are untrue, we can say, 'Our publicity brochure says that this product is the best value for money in Europe.'

But this won't always do. There will be occasions when we will feel this kind of procedure is unacceptable, and the only way forward is to refuse to practise any form of deceit, even if that costs us our job.

Members of the armed forces, the police, politicians and others will from time to time be placed in the position in which the midwives and Rahab found themselves, where telling the truth will be dangerous or disastrous for others. Clearly, it would be tragic if no Christians could follow these professions because of a desire for strict adherence to truth; the inclusion of the biblical examples shows that in these special circumstances being economical with the truth or, in extreme cases, even lying for the good of others may have to be accepted.

So there's a range of possible situations. Most of the time there will be no conflict between truth and love: we lovingly speak the truth. Sometimes love will dictate that we withhold the truth, are very careful about what we say, or even say something that is strictly untrue. In other situations love will dictate that we refuse to manipulate the truth or tell lies, even though we are under considerable pressure to do so.

Nevertheless, truth is never something we can treat lightly. Truth is firmly rooted in the nature of God. He *is* truth. Jesus is 'the truth'. The Holy Spirit is 'the Spirit of truth'. So, since we belong to him, our lives must be characterized by transparent truthfulness. God detests falsehood; specially severe judgment was pronounced both on the deceit of Achan at the start of the possession of the Promised Land (Josh. 7) and on that of Ananias and Sapphira at the beginning of the Christian church (Acts 5:1–11). God is concerned that we should be a people of truth.

Bible passages on speaking the truth

'You shall not give false testimony against your neighbour' ...
 'Do not spread false reports' (Exod. 20:16; 23:1).

> Whoever invokes a blessing on the land
> will do so by the God of truth;
> he who takes an oath in the land
> will swear by the God of truth (Is. 65:16).

'These are the things you are to do: Speak the truth to each other ... do not plot evil against your neighbour, and do not love to swear falsely. I hate all this,' declares the LORD (Zech. 8:16–17).

The Word became flesh and made his dwelling among us. We have seen his glory, the glory of the One and Only, who came from the Father, full of grace and truth (John 1:14).

Jesus answered, 'I am the way and the truth and the life' (John 14:6).

'The Counsellor ... the Spirit of truth' (John 15:26).

Jesus answered, '... for this reason I was born, and for this I came into the world, to testify to the truth. Everyone on the side of truth listens to me' (John 18:37).

We put no stumbling block in anyone's path, so that our ministry will not be discredited. Rather, as servants of God we commend ourselves in every way ... in purity, understanding, patience and kindness; in the Holy Spirit and in sincere love; in truthful speech and in the power of God (2 Cor. 6:3–4, 6–7).

... speaking the truth in love, we will in all things grow up into him who is the Head, that is, Christ ...
    Therefore each of you must put off falsehood and speak truthfully to his neighbour, for we are all members of one body (Eph. 4:15, 25).

My dear brothers, take note of this: Everyone should be quick to listen, slow to speak and slow to become angry (Jas. 1:19).

What could I do?

Test your life for truth. God is truth, and we must reflect his nature. Check whether your standards of telling the truth have slipped.

Have you got into the habit of unjustifiable exaggeration? Do you manipulate the truth to suit your own ends? Has it become relatively easy to tell a lie? The (very few) special occasions in the Bible where telling a lie is sanctioned definitely do not give you permission to claim more than you're due in your expenses account, or to make up some excuse when you're late for work. Commit yourself to transparent truthfulness, even if it is costly. Let the people around you see that being a Christian makes a significant difference.

Ask the Holy Spirit to make you, like Jesus, 'full of truth'. The promise that the Spirit of truth 'will guide you into all truth' (John 16:13) has a number of applications, but it includes the promise that he will make truth a characteristic of our lives if we let him do so.

Think before you speak. James is right; as a rule we rush in too fast with words. Take your time. And use that time to put God in charge of your words, and to consider, 'Am I speaking the truth in love?'

Stay faithful to God when the pressure from the world around is high. If you're in a job situation where you are required to manipulate the truth or to lie, be determined that, however you handle it, you will not act simply out of self-interest or fear. Rather, when there's no easy way out, pray that God will show you a way through that does not dishonour him. Be encouraged by Paul's words in 1 Corinthians 10:13, where he accepts that we all face these pressures (the New International Version calls them 'temptations', but the word also means 'trials' or 'times of testing'). But, he says, God is faithful; he'll give you what it takes to get you through; what's more, he'll provide a 'way out', an answer even in the most difficult circumstances.

Here are a few suggestions you might try when faced with this kind of issue:

- *See if you can handle it yourself.* You may be able to find ways, like those suggested above, that enable you to live with the situation.
- *Talk the matter through with the boss.* In many circumstances the best approach is to talk directly with the person who is asking you to practise dishonesty. In doing so, avoid a confrontational

approach, such as, 'You are wrong to make me tell lies.' Rather, explain that you are a Christian and are committed to high standards of honesty, and that you therefore have a problem with the firm's policy in certain respects. Such an approach will not always work, but it may well elicit a sympathetic response. After all, at the very least, most employers are wary of being seen to be discriminating against someone's religious beliefs.

• *Talk to some other suitable person.* Where appropriate, talk the issue through with a suitable person in the firm or organization who is concerned with personnel or human-resources issues. They have a responsibility to ensure that your rights as an employee are respected. If there's no such person, or if talking with the person proves unhelpful, consider appealing to an outside body, such as a trade union or a tribunal. Taking such a step may bring you into conflict with your employer, and shouldn't be taken without trying to resolve the problem internally first. But in normal circumstances an employer has no right to force an employee to be dishonest, and an outside union or tribunal is in a strong position to make this clear.

• *As a last resort, change your job.* In some circumstances it may be possible to ask for a transfer within the same firm or organization; otherwise you will have to find a new job.

WAR AND PEACE

Christians have always struggled over the issues raised by war and pacifism. Though some parts of the Old Testament can be used to sanction war, there is a strong element of pacifism in the New Testament. It was pacifism, in fact, that predominated in Christian teaching for the first few centuries; it gave way to a view that it is right for Christians to fight in certain circumstances, a change that may have been influenced to some extent by the alliance between church and state.

Probably almost all Christians today would regard war as an

abomination, to be avoided if at all possible. A substantial number of Christians would probably think seriously about being conscientious objectors should they ever be called up to fight. But, given the threat of terrorism and the horrific results that would come about if all 'good' people simply did nothing to resist those with access to weapons of mass destruction, many Christians would grudgingly concede that it is sometimes acceptable for the legitimate authority (ideally an international alliance such as the United Nations) to use force in order to save life and protect the innocent.

Even apart from terrorism and weapons of mass destruction, conventional wars are still killing about a million people (mostly innocent civilians) every year. Though 'peacekeeping' operations by the United Nations and other bodies are fraught with difficulties, such action often seems to be the only way we can seek to prevent such terrible slaughter.

Christians who feel that military action is sometimes justified are not suggesting that war is good. It remains evil, but it is the lesser of two evils. To kill one person is always evil. But if, by doing so, many people are saved from suffering and slaughter, it can be accepted.

Pacifists would respond that this approach disobeys Jesus' teaching about loving our enemies and not resisting an evil person. Obedience should be our priority, and we should trust God and not feel that we have to take on the responsibility of defending those who are vulnerable.

Some New Testament passages relevant to war and pacifism

> 'Blessed are the peacemakers,
>   for they will be called sons of God' (Matt. 5:9).

'You have heard that it was said, "Eye for eye, and tooth for tooth." But I tell you, Do not resist an evil person. If someone strikes you on the right cheek, turn to him the other also. And if someone wants to sue you and take your tunic, let him have your cloak as well. If someone forces you to go one mile, go

with him two miles. Give to the one who asks you, and do not
turn away from the one who wants to borrow from you.

'You have heard that it was said, "Love your neighbour and
hate your enemy." But I tell you: Love your enemies and pray
for those who persecute you, that you may be sons of your
Father in heaven. He causes his sun to rise on the evil and the
good, and sends rain on the righteous and the unrighteous. If
you love those who love you, what reward will you get? Are not
even the tax collectors doing that? And if you greet only your
brothers, what are you doing more than others? Do not even
pagans do that? Be perfect, therefore, as your heavenly Father is
perfect' (Matt. 5:38–48).

Then the men ... seized Jesus and arrested him. With that, one
of Jesus' companions reached for his sword, drew it out and
struck the servant of the high priest, cutting off his ear.

'Put your sword back in its place,' Jesus said to him, 'for all
who draw the sword will die by the sword' (Matt. 26:50–52).

'When you hear of wars and rumours of wars, do not be
alarmed. Such things must happen, but the end is still to come.
Nation will rise against nation, and kingdom against kingdom'
(Mark 13:7–8).

Jesus went up to Jerusalem. In the temple courts he found men
selling cattle, sheep and doves, and others sitting at tables
exchanging money. So he made a whip out of cords, and drove
all from the temple area, both sheep and cattle; he scattered the
coins of the money-changers and overturned their tables. To
those who sold doves he said, 'Get these out of here! How dare
you turn my Father's house into a market!' (John 2:13–16).

Bless those who persecute you; bless and do not curse ...

Do not repay anyone evil for evil. Be careful to do what is
right in the eyes of everybody. If it is possible, as far as it depends
on you, live at peace with everyone. Do not take revenge, my
friends, but leave room for God's wrath, for it is written: 'It is
mine to avenge; I will repay,' says the Lord. On the contrary:

'If your enemy is hungry, feed him;
   if he is thirsty, give him something to drink.
In doing this you will heap burning coals on his head.'

Do not be overcome by evil, but overcome evil with good (Rom. 12:14, 17–21).

Everyone must submit himself to the governing authorities, for there is no authority except that which God has established ... the one in authority ... is God's servant to do you good. But if you do wrong, be afraid, for he does not bear the sword for nothing. He is God's servant, an agent of wrath to bring punishment on the wrongdoer (Rom. 13:1, 3–4).

I urge, then, first of all, that requests, prayers, intercession and thanksgiving be made for everyone – for kings and all those in authority, that we may live peaceful and quiet lives in all godliness and holiness. This is good, and pleases God our Saviour, who wants all men to be saved and to come to a knowledge of the truth (1 Tim. 2:1–3).

What could I do?

Think. Don't adopt a position just because others hold it or because you like the feel of it. Recognize the complexity of the issues. Try to find a way of viewing things that does justice to all the relevant biblical teaching as well as to the contemporary situation.

Respect the right of other Christians to hold views different from yours. The issues involved in war have always been complex, with no simple answers. Our contemporary weapon capabilities and the existence of terrorism make them even more complex. Christians will inevitably adopt different stances, and, though we may fruitfully engage in debate, nothing is to be gained by simplistic criticism or out-of-hand rejection of the views of the other side.

Pray. Pray against evil powers (Eph. 6:12). Pray for national and international leaders and organizations. The decisions they have to make can affect the lives of millions. Paul urges prayer for 'all those in authority' as a priority, and adds 'that we may live peaceful and quiet lives in all godliness and holiness' (1 Tim. 2:1–2). Were it not for the prayers of God's people, the human race may already have destroyed itself through war. Whatever your views about war and pacifism, keep praying!

Do what you can to alleviate the suffering caused by war. Choose a specific project that you can support, such as removing land-mines, or helping asylum seekers. Pray, give and be involved in practical ways.

Be careful to apply Jesus' teaching on a personal level. Even if you feel there are some circumstances where the state or the United Nations should resist an evil person, still 'turn the other cheek' and do good to your enemies in your personal relationships.

Work for the coming of Christ's kingdom. Do everything you can to enable as many people as possible to find Jesus as their Lord and Saviour. The only hope for 'peace on earth' is that the whole world should 'be saved and ... come to a knowledge of the truth' (1 Tim. 2:4).

WORDS

Jesus put a great deal of emphasis on the importance of what we say. 'By your words you will be acquitted', he said, 'and by your words you will be condemned' (Matt. 12:37). This isn't offering an alternative to Paul's great doctrine of justification through faith; Jesus wasn't teaching that we earn our salvation by what we say. But he was underlining that our words truly indicate what's inside us. If we're true children of God, filled with his love and goodness, our words will demonstrate this. If what we say is contrary to the heart and mind of God, we demonstrate that he's not living in us.

The Bible, especially Proverbs in the Old Testament and the letter of James in the New, gives us plenty of practical advice on what we should or should not be saying. Foundational to all our words are the presence and lordship of God in our lives through the Holy Spirit. Don't try to sort out the outside, Jesus would say, before dealing with the inside. Get that right first, and then the rest can follow (Matt. 23:25–26).

Some of the Bible's teaching about our words

Set a guard over my mouth, O LORD;
   keep watch over the door of my lips (Ps. 141:3).

The mouth of the righteous is a fountain of life,
   but violence overwhelms the mouth of the wicked ...
Wisdom is found on the lips of the discerning ...
   but the mouth of a fool invites ruin ...
When words are many, sin is not absent,
   but he who holds his tongue is wise.
The tongue of the righteous is choice silver ...
The lips of the righteous nourish many ...
The lips of the righteous know what is fitting,
   but the mouth of the wicked only what is perverse
   (Prov. 10:11, 13–14, 19–20, 32).

Like a madman shooting
   firebrands or deadly arrows
is a man who deceives his neighbour
   and says, 'I was only joking!'
Without wood a fire goes out;
   without gossip a quarrel dies down (Prov. 26:18–20).

The Sovereign LORD has given me an instructed tongue,
   to know the word that sustains the weary.
He wakens me morning by morning,
   wakens my ear to listen like one being taught.
The Sovereign LORD has opened my ears,
   and I have not been rebellious;
   I have not drawn back (Is. 50:4–5).

'... let your "Yes" be "Yes", and your "No", "No"' (Matt. 5:37).

'Make a tree good and its fruit will be good, or make a tree bad and its fruit will be bad, for a tree is recognised by its fruit ... out of the overflow of the heart the mouth speaks. The good man brings good things out of the good stored up in him, and the evil man brings evil things out of the evil stored up in him. But I tell you that men will have to give account on the day of judgment for every careless word they have spoken. For by your words you will be acquitted, and by your words you will be condemned' (Matt. 12:33, 34–37).

Bless those who persecute you; bless and do not curse. Rejoice with those who rejoice; mourn with those who mourn (Rom. 12:14–15).

... speaking the truth in love ... (Eph. 4:15).

Do not let any unwholesome talk come out of your mouths, but only what is helpful for building others up according to their needs, that it may benefit those who listen. And do not grieve the Holy Spirit of God, with whom you were sealed for the day of redemption. Get rid of all bitterness, rage and anger, brawling and slander, along with every form of malice.
　　... among you there must not be even a hint of sexual immorality ... Nor should there be obscenity, foolish talk or coarse joking, which are out of place, but rather thanksgiving (Eph. 4:29–31; 5:3–4).

Let your conversation be always full of grace, seasoned with salt, so that you may know how to answer everyone (Col. 4:6).

My dear brothers, take note of this: Everyone should be quick to listen, slow to speak and slow to become angry ... If anyone considers himself religious and yet does not keep a tight rein on his tongue, he deceives himself and his religion is worthless (Jas. 1:19, 26).

Not many of you should presume to be teachers, my brothers, because you know that we who teach will be judged more strictly.

We all stumble in many ways. If anyone is never at fault in what he says, he is a perfect man, able to keep his whole body in check ...

Consider what a great forest is set on fire by a small spark. The tongue also is a fire, a world of evil among the parts of the body. It corrupts the whole person ...

... no man can tame the tongue ...

With the tongue we praise our Lord and Father, and with it we curse men, who have been made in God's likeness. Out of the same mouth come praise and cursing. My brothers, this should not be. Can both fresh water and salt water flow from the same spring? (Jas. 3:1–2, 5–6, 8–11).

Brothers, do not slander one another. Anyone who speaks against his brother or judges him speaks against the law and judges it (Jas. 4:11).

Christ suffered for you, leaving you an example, that you should follow in his steps.

> 'He committed no sin,
>   and no deceit was found in his mouth.'

When they hurled their insults at him, he did not retaliate; when he suffered, he made no threats (1 Pet. 2:21–23).

Do not repay evil with evil or insult with insult, but with blessing, because to this you were called so that you may inherit a blessing. For,

> 'Whoever would love life
>   and see good days
> must keep his tongue from evil
>   and his lips from deceitful speech' ...

Always be prepared to give an answer to everyone who asks you to give the reason for the hope that you have. But do this with gentleness and respect (1 Pet. 3:9–10, 15).

What could I do?

Start with the inside. We'll never get our words right if our thoughts and heart are wrong. Ask God to deal with any of your attitudes and feelings that are sinful; declare his lordship over every part of your being; ask the Holy Spirit to fill you.

Stop and think. James says we should be 'slow to speak' (Jas. 1:19); most of us are far too quick with our comments or remarks. Before opening your mouth, give yourself a moment to check that what you're going to say is the kind of thing Jesus would say in that situation.

Build, don't demolish. The world already has too much negative and destructive talk. Leave it to others to make the cutting remark, to show how clever they are and how stupid the other person is, to put others in their place or to cut them down to size. Let others grumble, moan, criticize and be negative. As a Christian, your calling is to be constructive and creative, building people up by what you say. When Jesus commanded us not to judge (Matt. 7:1), he wasn't telling us we shouldn't be discerning; he was saying that we must not make negative or critical remarks about other people, even if we're sure they're justified.

In particular, be a great encourager. Many people are struggling or hurt, or feel rejected or a failure. Even those who normally cope well with life get weary and down at times. So there's a great need for encouragement. A hallmark of Jesus' ministry as the Suffering Servant was that he didn't break the bruised reed or snuff out the smouldering wick (Matt. 12:20; Is. 42:3); instead, he had 'an instructed tongue, to know the word that sustains the weary' (Is. 50:4). Make a point of following his example.

Say thank you often. There isn't enough gratefulness around, so do your best to make up for the shortage. It's a great way of encouraging people, and showing that we value them.

Be cheerful. Even if you don't feel cheerful and it costs you to do it, say something pleasant to the miserable check-out assistant. You've got the joy of the Lord; spread it around. If the atmosphere at work is gloomy, God calls you to be the one who brings the light.

Tell people about Jesus. They may not be interested in church or in religion, but the living God coming to us in love and goodness is something they need to hear about. Do it naturally, 'with gentleness and respect' (1 Pet. 3:15); don't force it upon people. Ask God to give you opportunities and the wisdom to know what to say, and he'll open up the conversation.

Be truthful. We serve a God who is utterly trustworthy; we should be like him. See **truth: telling the truth**.

Be transparent. Don't say one thing and mean another.

Tell lots of jokes (clean ones), but avoid anything personal. Don't make digs at people under the pretext 'I was only joking'. A lot of hurt is caused that way; we may feel that people are being too sensitive, but Christlike love takes people's oversensitivity into consideration.

'Bless' people. The Old Testament priests were commanded to speak words of blessing to the people:

> 'The LORD bless you
>   and keep you;
> the LORD make his face shine upon you
>   and be gracious to you;
> The LORD turn his face towards you
>   and give you peace' (Num. 6:24–26).

When they did that, said God, they put his name on the people, and he blessed them. Similarly, in the New Testament, Jesus told his followers that when they entered a home they should say, 'Peace to this house'; those in the house had the option of receiving or rejecting the peace they brought (Luke 10:5–6).

Avoid gossip. Be careful not to gossip yourself, and graciously refuse to listen if it comes your way. In churches and Christian groups, because we're in close relationships and are often very open with each other, it's all to easy to slip into gossip, with or without the fatal phrase 'I'm only telling you this so you can pray about it.' So be particularly careful; better to delay passing on the news than to run the risk of causing hurt or trouble.

Keep confidences. People should be able to take you into their confidence knowing that it won't go any further. Assume that what you've been told is for you alone, unless it's certain that the person wants you to pass it on. If necessary, check this out. On the rare occasions when you feel it is necessary to break a confidence for the good of someone else, if at all possible explain the reason to the person who has given you the information, and get his or her permission to break it. Very occasionally you will be justified in breaking a confidence without permission; when something criminal is involved, the law of the land requires you to do so. When necessary, take precautions beforehand; if someone comes to you and tries to make you promise that you won't pass on what they are about to tell you, give yourself an escape clause, such as 'I won't say a word to anybody, unless of course it would be illegal or disastrous to keep quiet.'

Use words to express respect for others. They are made in the image of God, and loved by him. Respect is a mark of our love for them. 'Full of grace, seasoned with salt' is Paul's way of putting it (Col. 4:6). Politeness, acceptance, kindness, graciousness and affirmation are all ways of showing that we value others highly, as God does.

See also **truth: telling the truth**.

WORK

For many people their job takes up nearly a quarter of their time, or a third of their waking hours. It's their source of income, of status, and of their sense of achievement and fulfilment. It may also be the basis of their social life.

Few jobs today are unaffected by the pressures and changes of society. Technological development, market-place competition, mergers and takeovers, and the demands of productivity, all add to work pressures and threaten the stability of jobs and careers. Adaptability, retraining, keeping ahead of the game, and the ability to cope with high demands and pressures and to stay on top have all become essential.

The Bible doesn't set 'secular' work over against Christian service. All work is Christian service (Col. 3:17, 23–24), done specifically for the Lord, as an act of worship. It is also to be seen as service for others, an expression of our love and self-giving. The principles of paid work (1 Tim. 5:18) and unpaid 'voluntary' work (Acts 20:33–35) are both present in the New Testament.

There's a tendency in our society to see our work as our source of significance. It's our job that gives life meaning. It's the basis of our sense of self-worth. We're defined by the job we do. This can lead to a discriminatory attitude: a bank manager is thought to be more important than an unskilled manual labourer.

The Bible rejects this attitude. Work isn't the basis for our value or worth. These arise from our relationship to God, not from what we do. This isn't to say there's no source of value in work. Like everything we do, it does give us a sense of self-worth. It's right to feel a sense of achievement and fulfilment in what we are able to do; we're sharing God's pleasure at seeing what he had made and recognizing that it was very good. But this is not the primary source of our value. Someone who, perhaps through disability, is never able to do what our society calls 'work', can still have an awareness of true worth in the family of God.

Some of the Bible's teaching on work

The LORD God took the man and put him in the Garden of Eden to work it and take care of it (Gen. 2:15).

'Because you ... ate from the tree ...

> 'Cursed is the ground because of you;
> through painful toil you will eat of it ...'

So the LORD God banished him from the Garden of Eden to work the ground from which he had been taken (Gen. 3:17, 23).

'Remember the Sabbath day by keeping it holy. Six days you shall labour and do all your work, but the seventh day is a Sabbath to the LORD your God. On it you shall not do any work ... For in six days the LORD made the heavens and the earth, the sea, and all that is in them, but he rested on the seventh day. Therefore the LORD blessed the Sabbath day and made it holy' (Exod. 20:8–11).

'Do not hold back the wages of a hired man overnight ...

'Do not use dishonest standards when measuring length, weight or quantity. Use honest scales and honest weights ... I am the LORD your God' (Lev. 19:13, 35–36).

'... the worker deserves his wages' (Luke 10:7).

'I have brought you glory on earth by completing the work you gave me to do' (John 17:4).

'You yourselves know that these hands of mine have supplied my own needs and the needs of my companions. In everything I did, I showed you that by this kind of hard work we must help the weak, remembering the words the Lord Jesus himself said: "It is more blessed to give than to receive"' (Acts 20:34–35).

He who has been stealing must steal no longer, but must work, doing something useful with his own hands, that he may have something to share with those in need (Eph. 4:28).

... whatever you do, whether in word or deed, do it all in the name of the Lord Jesus, giving thanks to God the Father through him ...

Slaves, obey your earthly masters in everything; and do it, not only when their eye is on you and to win their favour, but with sincerity of heart and reverence for the Lord. Whatever you do, work at it with all your heart, as working for the Lord, not for men, since you know that you will receive an inheritance from the Lord as a reward. It is the Lord Christ you are serving. Anyone who does wrong will be repaid for his wrong, and there is no favouritism.

Masters, provide your slaves with what is right and fair, because you know that you also have a Master in heaven (Col. 3:17, 22 – 4:1).

Make it your ambition to lead a quiet life, to mind your own business and to work with your hands, just as we told you, so that your daily life may win the respect of outsiders and so that you will not be dependent on anybody (1 Thess. 4:11–12).

... you yourselves know how you ought to follow our example. We were not idle when we were with you, nor did we eat anyone's food without paying for it. On the contrary, we worked night and day, labouring and toiling so that we would not be a burden to any of you. We did this, not because we do not have the right to such help, but in order to make ourselves a model for you to follow. For even when we were with you, we gave you this rule: 'If a man will not work, he shall not eat' (2 Thess. 3:7–10).

Submit yourselves for the Lord's sake to every authority instituted among men ...

Slaves, submit yourselves to your masters with all respect, not only to those who are good and considerate, but also to those who are harsh (1 Pet. 2:13, 18).

What could I do?

Whatever you do, work for the Lord (Col. 3:23). Break down any barrier that may exist in your mind between your 'secular' work and your 'Christian' life and service. Do everything, including your job, in the name of Jesus Christ, and for him as Lord.

Give God your job. Specifically give your job, your work situation, your career and your relationship with your work colleagues over to God. Recognize it as a task he has given. Tell him that from now on you will do it for him, not for the boss or for money. You might choose to make this act of dedication of your work to God public, in the presence of other Christians, and with their prayer support.

Think through your work and try to view it as Jesus would if he were here today. In particular, try to see it as a means of service, and so of expressing love, to others. Clearly, this will be easier in some jobs than in others. But even if your work is not directly related

to helping people, it should be possible to think of ways it ultimately benefits others.

Try to do your job as Jesus would do it. Don't take your standards
and principles from others; take them from him.

Make your job a matter of regular prayer. Get others to pray for
you and with you about it and about issues that arise. Pray while
at your job; get into the habit of sending up quick prayers each
time you start a new piece of work, or begin a new conversation
with a colleague or client. Pray for your boss, the company and
those you work with. In particular, bring to God the problem
areas, the stresses and the immoral practices.

Share the load with other Christians. When possible, get together
with your fellow Christians in your place of work to encourage
and support each other and to pray together for the workplace.
Without breaking confidences, share your work concerns with
those in your house group or church fellowship so that they can
share in praying for you and supporting you.

Be balanced. Don't let your job dominate your life or your
family. Guard against the temptation to allow earning money to
become the controlling feature of your life. Work out a healthy
balance between time spent at work and that spent with family
and friends, leisure pursuits and church activities.

Remember the Sabbath principle. Give yourself breaks from
work. Make sure holidays are holidays; leave the mobile phone
and email behind.

Trust God for your career. Give it over to him, whether it's to be
a climb to the top of the tree, or one redundancy after another.
Put your faith in God and his faithfulness, not in your job and
career development. If you do face job insecurity or redundancy,
remember Abraham in Hebrews 11:8 and follow his example.

*Be prepared to stand by your Christian principles when ethical
issues arise.* Many business practices are contrary to Christian principles of honesty and fairness. But make your stand with grace and
gentleness. It's not likely to help if, say, you accuse your boss of
making you tell lies. It's better to explain to him or her that
because you're a Christian you choose to speak the truth whenever
possible, and look for some way of working within the system
without letting go your Christian principles. It may be of value to

talk to other Christians who have faced similar difficulties in their workplace. (See also **truth: telling the truth** and **injustice**.)

Remember you're a missionary. God wants the people you work with to see his love and goodness expressed through your life, and to hear his truth from your lips. That's why he put you there. Your missionary work in your workplace is just as significant as being called to some distant country.

What could I do if I lose my job?

Don't try to cope on your own. Use all the help you can get. Redundancy and unemployment are hard to face alone. For many, they raise significant personal and emotional problems, as well as practical issues such as loss of income. Allow family and friends to help and support you. Get others to pray for you. Find a counsellor or understanding friend with whom you can talk about your reactions and feelings. Join a local support group for the unemployed.

Watch out for negative reactions like anger and depression. They may not come at once, but most unemployed people experience them sooner or later. Do what you can to deal with them as soon as they begin to appear. Be aware that there will be an extra strain on your family; watch for signs of tension and sort out difficulties before they get too serious.

Pace yourself. Combine a hope that the period of unemployment will be short with a realism that accepts that it may not be.

Keep yourself occupied. Don't sit around doing nothing. Here's your chance at last to get on top of those jobs around the house. Give a couple of mornings a week to the church office or a local charity. Join an amateur dramatic group. Do voluntary work in your local school. Look after the garden of the elderly lady down the road. Take on a new ministry in the church. Try a new sport or a new hobby. Grow flowers. Join a local walking club. Develop new domestic skills. Do a project on local history, or wildlife in your local park. Run, swim, keep fit. Offer your skills to your neighbours. Work out your family tree. Write your autobiography. Every week, plan and do something you've never done before.

Structure your day and your week. Don't be aimless. Lack of structure will lead to boredom. Follow as clear a structure as you had when you were working.

Use the opportunity to learn new skills. Take advantage of retraining schemes. Do a course in your local college.

Take it that God is allowing you to have a 'sabbatical' from work so that you can do something special for him. It may be some special service, or it may be giving a lot of time to prayer or to study of the Bible.

Use the opportunity to reflect. Give yourself time to do some serious thinking about your career, your values, your goals, your family, your priorities, the principles that are controlling your life, and your relationship to God. Work out and put into practice any necessary adjustments.

Try developing a simpler lifestyle. Learn to live on less. Gain in your understanding of the less fortunate in the world.

Maintain and develop your relationships with friends and family. Beware of the tendency to withdraw. Make the most of the opportunity of spending more time with your children and close members of your family. Get in touch with all those friends you've been too busy to contact. If you've lost touch with friends at work, make every effort to develop new friendships to replace them. Get alongside lonely people. Widen your circle of friends at church and in the community.

Get help over any financial problems you may have. Replan your budget. Explain your situation to your mortgage company. Talk to the Citizens' Advice Bureau. Make sure you are getting any state benefits available.

Make full use of schemes and centres for the unemployed run by the government and churches and voluntary organizations. Such centres are a valuable source of support and ideas, and of practical help with such things as letter-writing skills, composing a CV, filling out job applications, and interview techniques.

Look to God to use even unemployment for his glory. A God of grace is able to change even losing a job from a disaster into something through which you can grow as a person and as a Christian.

What could I do if I'm thinking of changing my job?

Pray. Put the whole matter in God's hands and ask him to guide you. Tell him you're willing to take any job he leads you to.

Take the opportunity prayerfully to assess where you're at. Is your job in the right place in your life? Or has it taken over some of the time and energy which ought to be given to your family, to God or to relaxation and leisure? Are you succumbing to the pressures of our culture with its lies that to be a success you must keep climbing higher up the tree? Are you being motivated by the desire for more money, more possessions or a bigger house? A better job and more money aren't necessarily wrong, but make sure your motives in going for them are right. Remember Paul's words: 'godliness with contentment is great gain ... if we have food and clothing, we will be content with that. People who want to get rich fall into temptation and a trap and into many foolish and harmful desires that plunge men into ruin and destruction. For the love of money is a root of all kinds of evil' (1 Tim. 6:6–10).

Talk with your family and close friends. Encourage them to be honest with you, and not just tell you what you want to hear. Listen carefully to their point of view.

Get your new job before you resign from your old one. You can never be sure how long it will take to find a new job. And prospective employers are likely to be suspicious if you've just walked out of a job.

If you're considering a major change, get all the information you can. The grass may look greener, but do all you can to make sure it will suit your digestion.

APPENDIXES

1. TWELVE STEPS TO CONQUERING LONELINESS

1. Accept that the basic source of your loneliness is not in others but in you.

2. Accept that loneliness as you are now experiencing it is not God's will for your life. He wants you to have rich and meaningful relationships with a whole range of people. Accept that it is possible for you, with God's help, to deal with the source of your loneliness. You do not have to stay as you are. Rightly faced and dealt with, even your loneliness can become a stepping stone to a richer life.

3. Make a clear and definite choice that with God's help you will fight loneliness and win, even if you get hurt on the way. Specifically reject ideas like 'I will hang on to loneliness because it is safe,' 'Things will never change,' or 'It isn't worth the effort.'

4. Start keeping a daily journal. Observe and record your thoughts and behaviour over a period of time. Think through and analyse the factors in you (not in others) which prevent you having friends. For example, are you shy or tongue tied? Are you afraid of people? Do you find it difficult to trust people? Do you simply dislike them? Are you fearful they might get to know the real you? Do you feel you have nothing to contribute to a relationship? Are you afraid that any friendship will not last?

5. When you have made a list of these factors, try to discover the underlying causes that give rise to them. There are all sorts of possible causes. Here are a few examples:
• As a child, you were constantly told that no-one would want

you as a friend. You believed it and it has become a self-fulfilling prophecy.

- Someone you loved and trusted, for example a parent, let you down badly, hurting you so much that you can't trust anyone any more.
- You don't like yourself, and are unwilling to let others get to know the real you.
- You feel inferior to all the people you meet.

6. When you have decided the underlying cause or causes, imagine that someone comes to you for help with that particular problem. Use all your ingenuity to think of good advice and positive encouragement. Look up relevant Bible teaching. Think through what Jesus would say about it. Give the person hope and lots of good ideas. Write all these things down.

7. Use the suggestions you have written to work out a self-help programme for yourself. Pray over all the details. Write in your journal the basic principles you will follow, specific falsehoods you will need to reject, and truths you are determined to get hold of. Work out specific actions you will take.

8. Take the whole programme to God. Ask for his strength and wisdom as you prepare to follow it. Accept that without his help you will fail, but that it is his will you should not do so. Throw yourself on his grace, and expect him to act.

9. Implement your programme. Give yourself time. You may not make a lot of progress at first, and you may often fail. Keep a daily record, highlighting progress, and using failures to learn how to do it better next time.

10. Run some risks (small ones to start with!). Pray that God will lead you to one or two people who need your help; locate such people and get stuck into helping them for their sake, not yours.

11. Fight self-pity, apathy, defeatism, false indoctrinated beliefs and self-centredness.

12. Make sure you continue to operate at the two levels of changing inner beliefs and ideas, and of practical outward action. Don't give up on either front. Above all, keep looking to God to enable you to defeat loneliness in your life, and become the means through which his love is able to flow into the lives of others.

2. SUGGESTIONS ABOUT SINGLENESS

Four Bible truths to build your life on

1. As a Christian you are an individual person who has been specifically designed and shaped by the love and power of God. You are not an accident or a freak. All the events of your life leading up to this day and every aspect of your developing personality have been in the hand of God; you are who you are because he has planned and made you. Even the things that you see as disasters he can transform into something beautiful and creative.

2. Jesus was perfect, whole and complete. He lived a perfect life, fulfilled and full of God's grace to others. And he was single. He sets the pattern for our lives. He lives in us and gives us his completeness and fullness (Col. 2:10).

3. In Christ God has brought into being a new type of community, something richer and more lasting than the natural human family. Natural families are good, and one of his gracious gifts to the human race. But they are not permanent, they may break down, and they may clash with our loyalty to Christ (Luke 14:26). So, alongside and in some ways replacing the natural family, God has given us a new family, the community of his people in the local church or small group, with Jesus at the centre (Mark 3:34–35).

4. There is a cost to following Jesus and allowing God to work out his purposes in our lives. But Jesus promises that each sacrifice and every price paid will, in his time, be rewarded a hundred times over (Mark 10:28–31).

Four things to resist

1. Resist the tendency to turn in on yourself and feel sorry for yourself. You may find you are alone a lot; but that doesn't have to make you lonely. You will probably need to make a special effort to build friendships and maintain an active social life. Self-pity is a killer; fight the insidiousness of 'if only'. Work at being thankful and rejoicing in the Lord always (Eph. 5:20; Phil. 4:4).

2. Resist the feelings of envy and bitterness. Remember that what God has given you is his best for you, and that, in his way of seeing things, it is far better than those things you envy in others or feel bitter about.

3. Resist the pressure to adopt the attitudes of those around you. Plenty of people, including parents and well-meaning friends, will try to impose their way of seeing things on you. 'There must be something wrong with you if you're not married.' 'Are you still single? What a pity!' 'It must be awful being alone.' If they think that way, that is their problem; but don't let them make it your problem. Shape your thinking and attitudes according to the way God sees you, not according to their prejudices and stereotyping.

4. Resist the tendency to drift. Don't spend your life hanging around and waiting for someone to turn up. True, you don't have the predetermined structure to follow that many marrieds have: courting, wedding, mortgage, new home, jobs, first baby, second baby, larger home, and so on. But in many ways that's an advantage. As Paul found, it opens up the possibility of doing some really effective things with your life (1 Cor. 7:32–35). After all, you are you; you don't have to wait until you've got a partner to live for God's glory.

Six steps to take

1. Deliberately and decisively give yourself to God. Give him your concerns, your fears, your body and sexuality, your future, your relationships – everything you can think of. When you find yourself taking these things back, give them over to him again. Tell him that by his grace you choose to accept his purpose for your life.

2. Where you are aware of particular areas of pressure like the pain of seeing all your friends getting married and having children, or loneliness, self-pity or sexual issues, ask for an extra gift of his special grace (Jas. 4:6; 2 Cor. 12:9). Accept this gift, and let it shape your reaction.

3. Be thankful (Eph 5:20). Cultivate an attitude of thanksgiving. Focus on the good things in your life. Thank him for the special freedoms and opportunities singleness brings. Thank him for trusting you with something that many others can't cope with. Thank him for his grace.

4. Build, cultivate and grow. Build deep friendships; cultivate interests; grow as a person; become more like Jesus. Have a wide circle of friends; develop your career; seize opportunities; be adventurous; exploit the benefits of singleness. Show the world how wrong they are if they suggest you're a might-have-been or a reject.

5. Learn how to be a healthy sexual person without having to have intercourse. Allow God to channel your love and relationships and creative powers in ways that are wholesome and pleasing to him. God's gift of loving does not have to be repressed; express it as fully and as richly as Jesus did.

6. If you find specific issues like bitterness or self-pity hard to deal with, get help. Find a wise Christian friend or a counsellor and talk things through together. Where appropriate ask others to pray for you, maybe in a time of specific prayer ministry.

3. A MARRIAGE CHECK-UP

This is something for wife and husband to do together, perhaps once a year. You could make it a regular fixture in your diary, say round about your wedding anniversary.

Take time over it, and, while taking it seriously, let it be something you enjoy rather than find threatening. It would probably be best to write out together your answers to the questions.

Where you do list specific issues, always go on to decide what you are going to do about them. Keep a record of these decisions.

Where you don't agree over your analysis or theory, don't worry; simply write down both views. But try hard to agree when it comes to deciding on courses of action.

1. In what areas has our marriage become richer since we last had a check-up? What problems have we faced and overcome?

2. Are there any areas, such as communication, love-making, or the sense of excitement, where our marriage could be improved?

3. Are there any issues, personal or marital, over which we should get counselling help?

4. Do we spend enough relaxed time together and for each other? Are there ways, apart from sexual, in which we could show our love for each other more clearly?

5. What are the external pressures or stresses on our marriage at present and how are we coping?

6. Where is God in our marriage? Is Christ at the centre? Are we as in love with God as we were? Are we doing all we can to encourage each other to go forward as Christians? How could we strengthen the spiritual basis of our marriage? Do we pray enough together?

7. Have we got our priorities right?

8. Are we happy with the way we are working out our respective roles?

9. Are there any ways we could improve our parenting, or our relationship with others?

10. Are we managing our finances satisfactorily? Are there ways we could be managing them better?

11. Are there any specific issues we need to be facing and dealing with in the next few months?

12. What areas do we want to be concentrating on for growth and enrichment in the coming year?

4. TEN STEPS TO CHANGING THOUGHT PATTERNS

1. Accept that you are not going to stay as you are. You are determined to change. Even more importantly, God wants you to change and has promised he will give you what you need to change. Changes in feelings and actions start with change in the thought patterns that express our basic attitudes and beliefs. See the words of Jesus in Mark 7:21–23 and Matthew 12:35. Commit yourself before God to change at every level.

2. Write down, preferably with the help of a friend or a counsellor, the attitudes and beliefs that underlie the thought patterns that influence the area of your life you are concerned about. For example, if you cannot take criticism, you might write down, 'Criticism is rejection,' 'People criticize me because they don't like me,' or 'I need to be accepted fully by everyone.'

3. Look at what you have written as objectively as possible, or, better still, ask a friend to comment on it. Are your statements true? Are they partially true? Can they be rewritten or rephrased to make them nearer the truth? Most importantly, what would God say about them? How do they tally with the teaching of Jesus and the rest of the Scriptures? Can you find any Scripture passages that comment on them or correct them?

4. Write down alternative or revised statements. In our example you might write, 'Criticism is not necessarily rejection,' 'Sometimes people criticize me in order to help me,' 'I don't have to believe everything everyone says,' 'Jesus lived a great life without being accepted by everyone.' Try to make this second list as positive as possible, but don't put on to it anything that is impossible for you to believe. For example, you might feel it impossible to write, 'I don't care what anyone says about me'; but you could write, 'I need to take more notice of the positive things people say about me than of the critical things.' Add to the list any relevant Bible teaching.

5. Now the real work begins! Your task is to reprogramme your thinking by continually feeding in the second list of attitudes and beliefs, such that your old beliefs get pushed out. Remember, this will take time, since your old beliefs and attitudes are so well entrenched in your mind. Start by clearly and decisively rejecting the first list. Ask the Holy Spirit to purge them from your mind and life. Then, equally decisively, commit yourself to the second list. 'From now on, with the help of the Holy Spirit, these are going to be the things that form my thought patterns.' Aim for

nothing less than that great statement at the end of 1 Corinthians 2: 'we have the mind of Christ'.

6. Enlist the help of a friend who will pick you up when you revert to the old pattern and encourage you to keep going when you feel like giving up.

7. Find ways of continually reminding yourself of the points on the second list. Write them on bits of card and put them where you can see them often. Learn the relevant Bible passages by heart and keep reciting them to yourself.

8. Keep a journal, and record progress or otherwise in it each day. This will be a stimulus to you to keep the process going. Pray over the ups and downs of the process. Don't be too discouraged if the progress is slow. Any progress at all towards the renewing of our mind is worth it.

9. The hardest time to apply the second list is when you have to respond or act in the heat of the moment. Someone criticizes you, and, without thinking, you respond as you always have, completely forgetting your new set of beliefs. So train yourself not to make instant responses. Stop. Wait. Think before you respond. Respond on the basis of your new beliefs.

10. Keep reinforcing your new beliefs and thought patterns. Remind yourself of their importance. Watch out for additional ways of confirming their truth. After a time, you may even be able to build further on them and reshape them into even better forms. Above all, keep praying for the ongoing renewing of your mind.

5. Twelve steps to break free from sexual sin

Not all these suggestions will be relevant in every situation. Take the ones that are helpful for you, and adapt them if necessary.

1. Admit once and for all to God, yourself, and to someone you can trust that what you are doing is sinful.

2. Make a clear decision, suitably recorded and shared with someone else, that you are committed to a process in God's strength of ridding your life of this sin.

3. Pray. Not just 'God, solve this problem for me', but a good long conversation with God over the issue, in which you are honest with him, and you allow him to be straight with you.

4. Pray again. And again. Pray each morning for sexual purity through the day. Pray when you are feeling particularly vulnerable. Keep open a hotline to God.

5. Give yourself totally to God, specifically including your mind, your eyes, your maleness or femaleness, and your sex organs. Ask the Holy Spirit to fill every part of your body and your being. Ask him to make you as holy as he is. Do this daily, and repeat it when the pressure is on.

6. Become accountable to a Christian friend/counsellor with whom you have to be totally honest and who will hold you to your commitment. Talk through the suggestions in this list.

7. Take specific steps to avoid situations, places, people and so on that push you towards sexual sin. If necessary, be drastic (Matt. 5:30). In particular, guard your eyes (Matt. 6:22–23). Be drastic over what you look at. You will not be able to avoid *seeing* sexually titillating things, but you can avoid *looking at* them. Turn off the TV; look the other way. 'If your eye causes you to sin, gouge it out and throw it away' (Matt. 5:29).

8. Be aware of your especially vulnerable times or feelings, such as when you are lonely or down. Work out ways of dealing with these things other than by resorting to sex.

9. Train yourself to take immediate action as soon as the first thought of sexual sin comes into your mind. Don't play around with the serpent – kill it! Have escape routes: things to which you can switch your thoughts. Wear a WWJD (What would Jesus do?) bracelet or use some other helpful device.

10. Study the New Testament teaching on holiness. Model your living and thinking on those of Jesus.

11. When you fail, quickly ask for cleansing and forgiveness.

12. Work continuously at getting your mind and life so filled with good, wholesome and Christ-centred things that there is no space left for sexual sin to get in.

INDEX